W9-BLP-594

WITHDRAWN

WITHDRAWN

Effective Teaching and Mentoring

Realizing the Transformational Power of Adult Learning Experiences

Laurent A. Daloz

Foreword by K. Patricia Cross

Effective Teaching and Mentoring

Jossey-Bass Publishers

San Francisco • London • 1986

EFFECTIVE TEACHING AND MENTORING
Realizing the Transformational Power of Adult Learning Experiences
by Laurent A. Daloz

Copyright © 1986 by: Jossey-Bass Inc., Publishers
433 California Street
San Francisco, California 94104
&
Jossey-Bass Limited
28 Banner Street
London EC1Y 8QE

Library of Congress Cataloging-in-Publication Data

Daloz, Laurent A.
    Effective teaching and mentoring.

    (The Jossey-Bass higher education series)
    Bibliography: p. 245
    Includes index.
    1. Mentors in education—United States. 2. Adult
education—United States. 3. Motivation in adult
education—United States. I. Title. II. Series.
LC5225.M45D35   1986   374′.973   86-10317
ISBN 1-55542-001-X (alk. paper)

Manufactured in the United States of America

The paper in this book meets the guidelines for
permanence and durability of the Committee on
Production Guidelines for Book Longevity of the
Council on Library Resources.

JACKET DESIGN BY WILLI BAUM

FIRST EDITION

Code 8635

৯১ ৯১ ৯১

The Jossey-Bass
Higher Education Series

Consulting Editor
Adult and Continuing Education

Alan B. Knox
University of Wisconsin at Madison

Foreword

Mentoring is a slippery concept. Most people think of a mentor as a person, usually older and more experienced, who is able and willing to help a protégé get where he or she wants to go. Perhaps the best known kind of mentoring takes place in the presumably tough world of business, where a mentor who knows the people and the pathways takes a special interest in helping the protégé move up the corporate ladder. There is not much question about the goal, and the mentor clears the way, gives some travel tips, and smooths the bumps. Occasionally the mentor helps the protégé develop the necessary skills to navigate an especially difficult turn in the road, but by and large, the mentor concentrates on providing a map and fixing the road rather than on developing the traveler.

In this book, Larry Daloz is not talking about the mentor of the business world. He is talking about a teaching mentor, for whom the goal is less clearly defined. Although a typical adult enters an educational program with the desire to "get a degree" or learn job skills, on the way to the degree, many adults discover that the journey upon which they have embarked is full of surprises. In exploring previously unknown byways that are revealed to them as they travel, they discover goals never before considered and satisfactions not previously experienced. The mentor of adult learners is not so much interested in fixing the road as in helping the protégé to become a competent traveler.

Daloz uses the metaphor of a journey throughout the book. Consistent with his conviction that the mentor is a trusted guide rather than a tour director, Daloz leads the reader to an understanding of adult development that is comprehen-

sible at many different levels of sophistication. Readers who
have studied the numerous charts and theories of adult development in the literature today will find their understanding of
these theoretical models deeply enriched by the sensitive insights of the author. At the same time, readers who know little
about the various theories will read this book the first time
through as a series of fascinating vignettes about the encounters
of adult learners with liberal learning. But it is probably not
possible to leave it there. A second reading will reveal the story
of the developmental process. This is a book to own, to re-
read, and to mark for continuing reference.

For myself, I found that some pages brought to life fascinating stories of people searching for meaning. In other pages, I
found new relationships to academic knowledge about human
development, not only as it is revealed in modern psychological
study but also—because of Daloz's background in literature—as
it has been revealed by the world's great writers. And in still
other pages, I found new insights, new ideas, new interpretations that made me think hard about what we mean by "excellence" in education.

Clearly, Daloz is talking about excellence in education,
yet he is not discussing standards or tests or "value added." He
is not talking about *how much* is learned or even how well a
subject is understood. He is talking about how learning changes
the learner. To Daloz, it is inconceivable that an excellent education would not make a profound difference in a person. He is
less interested in the concept of education as knowledge "out
there" to be learned than in the impact of knowledge once it
gets under the skin of the learner.

This book should make a difference in the way people
work with students, whether as mentors, classroom teachers,
advisers, or counselors. Adult educators have assumed that
teachers and advisers should know something about adult development. The contribution this book makes is to show us why.
And it shows us how important skillful mentoring and caring
teaching can be.

Cambridge, Massachusetts   K. Patricia Cross
January 1986

Preface

Happily, it is no longer necessary to argue that colleges must pay special attention to adult learners. Plummeting enrollments of traditional-age students have made the case far more effectively than could those of us who have been in the trenches these long years. College after college has faced the choice: either reach out for these "new learners," as K. Patricia Cross called them over a dozen years ago, or hire an auctioneer. Partly as a consequence of this and partly because of broader technological, demographic, and social changes, the proportion of students above the age of twenty-five has billowed from barely a quarter to over 43 percent in the past decade alone. By the turn of the century, fully half of all students in higher education will be adult learners.

Although for younger students the campus is often the central focus of social and intellectual life, this is rarely the case with older learners who often return to school complete with jobs, spouses, children, well-developed roles in their communities, and extensive experience in both love and work. To adapt appropriately to this group, colleges have learned to offer classes in the evenings, to make degree requirements more flexible, and in some cases, to accredit off-campus courses and less formal learning experiences. Such modifications have been important, the changes necessary.

But one program's flexibility has become another's slovenliness. Along with these developments, though by no means solely because of them, have come charges of a decrease in quality, a diploma-mill mentality, grade inflation, and a general failure to achieve a definition of excellence derived from an earlier era. A fresh "educational crisis" is upon us, and words like

Quality and *Excellence* buzz through media reports like flies after carrion. Something must be done; everyone agrees about that. Critics differ only in the direction of their gaze.

For some, the Quality that has fled and the Excellence that is our proper legacy will be regained only when the liberal studies are returned to pride of place in the curriculum—and all those "merely applied" vocational subjects and technical studies are consigned to the shop whence they came before those meddling Progressives muddied the clarity of our Platonic vision. If only we could fill again our classrooms with ears eager to quiver at Shakespearean iambs or minds anxious to dance between Hegelian dilemmas, then we could truly call ourselves educated.

For others, education must have immediate utility. If college simply turns out graduates without salable skills, the taxpayer has no business supporting it, and the number of consumers who will squander on so impractical a dalliance the small fortune it takes nowadays is miniscule. Said my farmer neighbor recently, "Anyone dumb enough to want a Ph.D. these days ain't smart enough to get one."

Yet however venerable the argument between purist and pragmatist, it springs from a spurious dilemma. For quality and excellence are to be found neither in some mystical characteristic of the subject matter alone nor in the raw demands of the market but in the behavior and attitudes of the human beings who embody that tension—in the teacher and in the student. We know that the quality of learning is high when students show intellectual, emotional, and ethical growth; we know that teaching is excellent when it fosters such growth, when we have teachers who are willing to care—both *about* their subjects and *for* their students.

But it is one thing to say these things, another to do them. What do those fuzzy words *growth* and *care* really mean? How do we know them when we see them? What principles underlie excellence in advising and teaching? And how do we incorporate the elements of care into the design of our programs, the practice of our teaching, the everyday work of advising our students? The book in your hands is an effort to provide an answer to those questions in an engaging yet practical way. Using the central metaphor of a transformational journey, it combines a fresh look at the intuitive wisdom of the mentor with an informative introduction to current adult development theory. Lacing these with a series of vignettes and conversations with adult students, the book goes on to derive a number of principles for enriching instruction and revitalizing the advising process so that regardless of their age, the growth and development of students can take its place as the proper aim of education.

When I began teaching over twenty years ago, I quickly came to see that teaching was a good deal more than simply asking my students questions, telling them the answers, and asking the questions again. True, they had to acquire certain content, but over the years I felt with increasing urgency that if education were to make any real difference in their lives, my students had to learn how to think for themselves as well. That ability, it was obvious, did not necessarily come with the territory. But it was not until I became familiar with the idea of intellectual development—and later with the whole field of adult development theory—that I began to understand in specific and concrete ways the meaning of the word *growth.*

I first began to splice the principles I was learning into the design of a "process curriculum" for community college students. Later, as participant in a national project to apply current developmental findings to adult programs, I was able to carry out further research with a number of nontraditional students. This work convinced me of the potential that developmental theory holds for adult and continuing education. Shortly thereafter, I directed a project examining the impact of the liberal studies on the intellectual and ethical development of rural, adult learners. The results made it abundantly clear that higher education can bring about substantial changes in the lives of adults. But one finding stood out with particular clarity. Almost without exception, the students cited certain teachers or mentors as having been of particular importance in the changes they had made. A mentor myself in two different external degree programs, I resolved to look more closely at what good teachers and mentors actually do as they guide their charges along on their transformational journeys. With the help of a Mina Shaughnessy grant from the Fund for the Improvement of Postsecondary Education, I conducted a close look at a variety of mentor-protégé relationships over the course of several years. Out of that study, augmented by some ten years of direct experience in teaching and advising adult students, have emerged the principles and materials on which this work is based. The story of that study appears in the appendix. I should note, however, that this book is primarily the story of one person's effort to see his students in a fresher, more promising way. I have tried to share with the reader what I have seen through those theoretical lenses that proved most helpful in my search, but I make no pretense of offering a comprehensive survey of current research. This is neither a textbook nor a technical manual. At the same time, it is my hope that in the pages that follow the reader will hear something familiar, something universal in the words of this tiny sample of the human family.

This book is directed to all those who seek a fuller understanding of the life changes accompanying adult learners as they go on to postsecondary education. But it does more than simply describe or dramatize those changes. It goes on to suggest how we can work more effectively with the new learners to enrich their educational experience and decrease the likelihood that they will drop out. Thus it has special value for student affairs practitioners trying to understand this new population, counselors and advisers helping adults returning to college, faculty facing the mature students in classes, academic administrators seeking a fresh view of their changing student body, adult and continuing educators working in all settings, and finally, that small but growing band of practitioners who actually call themselves mentors and who are by definition committed to making an "education of care" really happen.

The primary purpose of this book is to offer new perspectives for understanding adult learners and to suggest in concrete and practical ways based on current developmental theory how we can work more effectively to improve the quality of their educational experience. At the heart of the work are the interviews and personal descriptions, which are needed to ground the principles, concepts, and theories. For it is in the living tissue of conversations between real students and real teachers that we can best apprehend the meaning of developmental advising and instruction.

But while the perspectives may be new, teachers and learners have been going about their business in some form for nearly as long as they have been walking upright. Mentor figures appear prominently among the earliest written epics, *Gilgamesh* and *The Odyssey*. Not surprisingly, mentors abound in children's stories as well. For that reason, I have included material from the great myths as well as from children's literature. For each of us writes with his or her life the story of our species, and in those tales of transformation can be found the maps by which we guide our own lives—and the lives of those for whom we care.

Thus, while I have tried to include ample practical ideas and illustrations, the book is more than simply a how-to manual. It is an effort to encourage all of us in postsecondary education to assess our stance toward our students, to think afresh about the meaning of teaching. Education, it asserts, is not a bunch of tricks or even a bundle of knowledge. Education is something we neither "give" nor "do" to our students. Rather, *it is a way we stand in relation to them.* The nature of that relationship is best grasped through the metaphor of a journey in which the teacher serves as guide. For that reason, the book itself is constructed as a voyage of discovery, beginning with the appearance of a few shards, questions about our mutual goals on this educational quest.

Arguing that development continues throughout the life span and that education plays a central part in that process, the first chapter presents a vignette of a meeting between a student and myself at a roadhouse in midwinter Vermont. The conversation is about what is worth learning in our lives, and it sets the questions for the remainder of the book—questions about education and personal growth, effective teaching, and the teacher-student relationship.

Chapter 2 introduces the idea of the mythic journey as a way of making sense of life's changes. Through legends and lit-

erature, it illustrates how humankind has used tales of transformational journeys to address the problem of growing both older
and wiser. As master teachers, mentors are guides on such journeys, appearing in a variety of forms. Here, *The Divine Comedy*
provides a model of the mentor-protégé relationship as it
evolves during Dante's epic journey. The chapter includes a discussion of some principles of teaching embodied in the story
and ends with a real-life journey tale.

Three detailed vignettes of conversations with adult students form the basis for Chapter 3. Each highlights a major current theory of adult development that is then described and
serves as an overlay for analysis of the vignette. These theories
are then used extensively throughout the remainder of the book
as "maps" with which to understand the educational journey.

Chapter 4 follows several teachers and their adult students on their respective journeys. As before, vignettes of actual conversations with students are interspersed with discussion of the significance of each particular experience. Initially,
the journey involves a downward movement from simple "rights
and wrongs" into the confusion of a multifaceted world in
which authority no longer has the answers. It parallels the
descent into Hell, the "deep and savage way."

It is in the "winter of our discontent" that transformation can most readily take place. Chapter 5, the central chapter, at the heart of both the journey and the book, discusses the
meaning of the word *transformation* in light of developmental
theory and shows how such change occurs through the confron-
tation of opposites, a dialectical resolution of tensions arising
from the search for "the truth."

With the dissolution of former, simpler perspectives
comes a need to reconstruct meaning in more complex and inclusive ways. In Chapter 6, the reader accompanies teachers and
students as they grapple with new forms of "truth" and reconstruct "reality" in new, more contextual and socially responsive
ways. With this evolution, the mentor-student relationship also
undergoes a change from the earlier hierarchical form to a more
equal one—from "god" to "friend."

In Chapter 7, we pull back again and look at what it is that helps or hinders personal growth. Using a lengthy case study, the chapter argues that people live in environments that alternately support and challenge development. To understand who changes and how, we must shift our focus to the *whole systems* in which people live.

How do teachers and advisers fit into all of this? Arguing that growth is best understood in the context of human relationships, Chapter 8 shows how mentors provide support, challenge, and vision for their protégés, suggesting numerous concrete ways in which teachers and advisers can strengthen their work with students. It includes a discussion of some of the pitfalls in mentoring relationships and concludes with a summary of the teacher's functions as catalyst for development.

The final chapter, Chapter 9, presents a summary of the major themes of the book and suggests a number of next steps toward fostering an education of care and a respect for the development journeys undertaken by both mentors and students in postsecondary institutions.

Although the book has emerged from the study of one-to-one relationships, it is ultimately about teaching and learning in any setting. For when the aim of education is understood to be the *development* of the whole person—rather than knowledge acquisition, for instance—the central element of good teaching becomes the provision of *care* rather than use of teaching skills or transmission of knowledge. And because care is so profoundly human an activity, it is fully within the reach of all of us. Do not be deceived that the setting and some of the episodes described in the book may appear at first to be impossibly distant from the everyday press of your own life and work. Whether you teach accounting to classes of three hundred or psychological anthropology to a seminar of six, whether you are semesterly swamped with a river of advisees or meet individually as tutor for a dozen, the material here is pertinent. For although students do indeed learn differently in groups than alone, and although it may seem that when we enter the lecture hall we are "teaching a class," always it is individuals who are learning. Each is bound to learn in a unique way. Recognizing this,

- We can listen to our students' stories, seeking to understand how their quest for education fits into the larger questions and movement of their lives;
- We can view ourselves as guides on our students' journeys, challenging them to their best, supporting them when they falter, casting light on the territory ahead;   .
- We can sense the whole lives of our students, recognizing how the aspirations, relationships, and values of their lives hold them in a web of forces enhancing or inhibiting their movement; and
- We can recognize the place our students have in our own lives, in our own attempts to care for ourselves as we care for others.

Developmental theory can help us to do these things. It can teach us to respect each student's uniqueness while we illuminate common questions about meaning in their lives—questions to which, regardless of subject matter, we all hold relevant answers. For the principles of an education of care are no more limited to a lone itinerant teacher in northern Vermont than are the questions that give rise to them. If we are willing to listen afresh to the words of our students, we can help them to make of their education an experience that will meet more than simply their needs to be either knowledgeable or rich. We can help them grow wiser. This book offers a way that we can begin to do that.

One of the problems with acknowledgments is that no one ever reads them except the people one inadvertently left out. Still, I think I finally understand why authors almost always write them. For the process of reaching back through the years that grew this book has been an unanticipated delight. I had forgotten how much I owe to so many. What a pleasure to remember!

To the students, of course, goes my deepest gratitude. Yours is the earth from which everything sprang, without which nothing could have grown. There is no naming all of you, but I want you to know that this book came from you, and for that I am grateful. May we never cease to hear one another.

To my fellow teachers and mentors who have so freely offered your words, experience, and wisdom and yet who go nameless, my thanks too. We are brothers and sisters in our work. I only hope this book can begin to repay the gift.

For the planting and care of the seeds, to my own teachers and mentors I also offer thanks. To Jill Mattuck Tarule, Rita Weathersby, John Griffith, Mary Belenky, Bob Kegan, and Zee Gamson, all of whom helped me not only to understand developmental theory but also to respect its place in the lives of real people, thanks. And thanks, too, to Alan Knox, who saw something in there moving and snatched a dying manuscript from the Jossey-Bassian flames, to Ron Gross, whose outrageous enthusiasm kept me alive in the dark, and to the staff and outside readers at Jossey-Bass who spent so many hours pouring over draft after draft of the manuscript, helping to produce a work that I have grudgingly come to acknowledge is notably improved. Pat Cross, who has encouraged me for years, has been more than gracious in her contributions. Fred Rudolph, recipient of the first tercentenary Yoda Award, has truly been a mentor's mentor. And finally I owe a special debt of gratitude to Bill Perry, who first suggested that I tape-record my meetings with students and whose work in its simplicity is so profound.

I'm not sure how one thanks the sunlight. I've a hunch that gratitude is not what it's about at all. But, my friends—Kate, Todd, and Judy Daloz, Cyrie Barnes, Bob Duggan, Alice Eichholz, Ella Farrow, Len Foote, Bill Mitchell, Joanna Noel, Sharon Parks, Lyn Sprogell—you read and listened, prodded, suffered, cajoled, and loved me long before dawn. I know that and I'm glad.

Finally, there are the gardeners, those who provided the setting and the concrete help to make it possible: Peter Smith and Myrna Miller, whose vision transformed higher education in Vermont (though it may not know it yet), Carol Stoel, Richard Hendrix, Alison Bernstein, and Leslie Hornig of FIPSE, who

leave candles burning in the most unlikely places, and finally
(especially!) to Louise Eldred, who listened to weeks of tapes,
turning them one after another, painstakingly and brilliantly,
into the printed word.

Glover, Vermont   Laurent A. Daloz
July 1986

Contents

≈ ≈ ≈

The Author

Kate and Todd's father, Laurent A. Daloz, is currently an adjunct faculty member with the Norwich University Adult Degree Program and the Johnson College External Degree Program, where he formerly served as mentor. He received his A.B. degree in American history and literature (1962) from Williams College, his M.A.T. in English (1963), and his Ed.D. in educational planning (1972) from Harvard University. He was a Peace Corps volunteer in Nepal, a curriculum consultant in West Virginia, a teacher in Hawaii, and an educational planner in New Guinea before settling in Vermont, where he helped to found the nontraditional community college system. Thereafter, he served for ten years as teacher and adviser to adult learners. In 1982, he received a Mina Shaughnessy fellowship enabling him to reflect on the implications of his experience.

In recent years, Daloz has become interested in the human contexts of development, directing research on the interplay of education with adult development. He notes with mixed feelings the coming of his generative years and feels the tug of his earlier dreams once again. The apparent self-centeredness of many young people today concerns him, and increasingly he wonders how he can work more effectively as a part of the mentorship of the whole culture to bring our next generation into a fuller sense of commitment to and caring for the health of the whole planet.

He is the author of numerous articles and reports, some of which have appeared in *Change Magazine, Chronicle of High-Education, Educational Technology, Community and Junior College Journal,* and various international journals.

To my father, Al Daloz, with love

Effective Teaching and Mentoring

Realizing the Transformational Power of Adult Learning Experiences

Chapter One 🌢

The Adult's Search
for Meaning as a Motive
for Learning

> What is education? I should suppose that education
> was the curriculum one had to run through in or-
> der to catch up with oneself.
>   *—Kierkegaard,* Fear and Trembling

We are all adult learners. Most of us have learned a good deal
more out of school than in it. We have learned from our families, our work, our friends. We have learned from problems resolved and tasks achieved but also from mistakes confronted
and illusions unmasked. Intentionally or not, we have learned
from the dilemmas our lives hand us daily.

  Some of what we have learned is trivial; some has changed
our lives forever. Much of the time, learning is a joy, especially
when it meets a clearly felt need, takes us toward some destination, or helps us make sense of something formerly obscure. But
sometimes it brings pain, and we struggle mightily not to see the
obvious. There are few among us who have not wondered at
such times whether it was all worth it, why it was that the more
we learned the less we knew, and where our lives were taking us.

  Our students are no different. Most have sacrificed a good
deal to return to school. Education is important for them, not
simply because they see it as a ticket to a better life but because
in some more profound sense, they hope it will help them make
sense of lives whose fabric of meaning has grown frayed. For a
multitude of reasons, they will seldom lead with this revelation;

some have yet to realize it. Fewer still see the erosion of meaning in their lives as a normal process, part of a lifetime of growing up. Yet both recent research and timeless insight have made it clear that our lives do not simply level off after the age of eighteen (Knox, 1977). We continue to grow and change. What was once trivial can turn suddenly monumental, and what earlier appeared essential now seems unimportant. Women who for years sacrificed themselves for their families suddenly declare, "It's Mom's turn," replacing a kitchen tableful of cookware with textbooks; and men who were locked into the upward struggle for money and prestige may all at once turn inward, wondering what it all means.

A good education can help people understand these changes; indeed, it may play a part in bringing them about. For a good education tends to our deepest parts, enriches them, nourishes the questions from which grow the tentative answers that, in turn, sow fresh questions about what is important. As teachers, we do vital work in the lives of our growing students. This book is an attempt to portray students and teachers at work, to demonstrate how we can discuss important matters together so that our students can regain the courage, insight, and passion they will need to move ahead in their lives more fully, to weave and reweave the fabric of meaning more richly and strongly.

As I began writing this book, I struggled with the tension between writing a "scholarly" work on the one hand and something with a broader appeal on the other. Gradually I came to see that what I wanted most was to tell a good story, to engender good conversation. I have tried to do that, and because I am writing about what I do, I have attempted to remain a visible storyteller. For me, being a teacher is more art than science. I am uneasy with claims to an "objectivity" that I doubt exists. Perhaps that is why I have found the metaphor of a journey to be a particularly useful way of understanding what my students and I are going through. For although journeys differ for each of us, like education, they do have direction, they have a common syntax, and we can mark our progress by the passing signposts. In their form itself lies their meaning. Thus, although some of what happens between teacher and student has about it the quality of magic, by casting our two protagonists as pilgrim and guide, we can learn much about that dark and fertile art. The question for us as teachers is *how* we influence our students, not whether. It is a question about a relationship: *Where are our students going, and who are we for them in their journey?*

That question underlies most of this book. In this chapter, I will try to illustrate why it became so important for me and why I believe it to be central for all of us who are struggling to construct an education of care. So let me invite you along on a short journey to eavesdrop on a conversation between Emerald and me.

Emerald was one of twenty returning adult students I was working with as mentor for an external degree program several years back. My job was to guide them along the misty and often confusing pathways through higher education. I would help people to decide what they wanted to learn, explain the program requirements, and work with them to select courses or design independent studies that would take them to their goal. Once under way, it was my job to provide moral and academic support. Often that would involve conversations like this.

When the Thunder Comes

The ski trails on the side of Mt. Mansfield were etched white against the blue of the horizon as the car glided around the corner, a bit fast for the icy conditions. It was one of those perfect winter days, utterly clear, but still below zero in midmorning. Glittering flakes of frozen air drifted in the sunlight as a carful of skiers headed for the mountain passed me in the opposite direction, eager no doubt, to play in the fresh powder of yesterday's storm. Days like today are the stuff of postcards, I thought to myself, everything in its Sunday best. Yet there's something glossy and unreal about the countryside in winter. People who live here know what's under the snow, and one needn't drive far off the main roads to see the trailers and the shacks, the shattered doors and the torn, polyethylene-covered windows to know that *Vermont Life* is a magazine intended mostly for export.

I turned north outside of Hardwick and headed into the

heart of the Northeast Kingdom where I live and work. So named some years ago by Senator George Aiken in recognition of the northeastern three counties' determined insularity, the region is Vermont's poorest and probably harbors most of what's left of a way of life earlier called Yankee, now outdated and overromanticized. The barn, once our predominant architecture, has been largely replaced by the trailer, topped as soon as the owner can afford it, by a pitched roof against the cold.

The road and the frozen river danced together as I glided past overgrown pastures scored from time to time with the tracks of snowmobiles. Just beyond a half-buried "garage sale" sign—the tip of our underground economy's iceberg—the Come & Eat roadhouse peered over the stacks of snow. I slowed down and pulled into the newly scraped lot beside a huge semi loaded with pulp.

The steam swirled around me as I swung through the door, struck by the blast of warm air redolent of coffee and bacon fat, gravy and canned string beans. The place was nearly empty save for a couple of men layered in chocolate rags huddled over coffee cups and cigarettes. They must belong to the truck, I thought, as I looked for Emerald. I spotted her nestled in the next-to-last booth, nodded, and peeled off my parka as I made my way to join her.

Widowed after a brief marriage some years ago, Emerald returned here to her hometown, where she has worked since as a bookkeeper in her brother's small sawmill. Now in her mid thirties, she dresses softly and with incongruous class, bats her eyelids with accomplishment. Seemingly shy, she scarcely opens her mouth in group meetings; even outside, she volunteers little. Yet when she does speak, she does so with near perfect certainty, ending her sentences in the air as if to say, "Isn't it obvious?"

A year ago she graduated from the local community college and entered the external degree program to study for a degree in business management. The program requirements were broad and flexible, allowing her to take courses at a number of different institutions but specifying a certain number of liberal studies as well. The task of the mentor was to help her design a program that met both her needs and the program's expectations. Like many adults, Emerald began her studies with courses directly relevant to her work: accounting, office management, computers. As her adviser, I chose not to resist that, for older students are generally much clearer about what they're doing in college than their younger counterparts, and it doesn't do to thwart their firm intentions—at least not at first. But the time had come for Emerald to plan her program more comprehensively. We had arranged this meeting to discuss it.

Emerald reached into a folder on the seat beside her, removed a neatly typed sheet of paper, and slid it across the table toward me. The brief narrative noted that her objective was to attain a degree in business management; her long-term goal was to become a CPA. Beneath the narrative was written,

> Liberal arts will be useful to offset patterns of rigidness prevalent in my main objective, achieving a balance in education. I realize that all numbers and heavy concentration in one single area with no balancing influence is apt to lead to undesirable personality maladjustments and mental introversion. Liberal arts is and has been my mode of relaxation.

Then she had listed the studies she planned to undertake during the next six semesters. Her intention was to study two at a time—a full load when combined with a normal workday. The list was fascinating. Next term she planned to combine budgeting with the Old Testament, then data processing and archeology, business law and poetry, insurance and dance. Balance, indeed, I thought to myself as I scanned the list. The dichotomy was relentless, but I could discern no pattern beyond that. Why those subjects? Why that order? It baffled and fascinated me at once. What did this woman want for herself? Or, I wondered, isn't this for herself at all? Then I noticed her one liberal study course thus far—a death and dying course she took last term. How could I have forgotten? Something about her mouth as she had described her widowhood during an earlier meeting had prompted me to suggest that she take it. I decided to begin there.

"So. How was that death and dying course?"

"Oh, fine," she replied, sealing the statement with a tight smile, inviting more but offering nothing. She's going to make me work, I thought. Off balance already, but the game begun, I played another card.

"Fine? How do you mean that? What was good about it?"

"Oh," she replied, "we learned a lot of useful stuff." Silent again, but there was an opening.

"Like?"

"Oh, you know. If somebody dies on the job, what you have to do. How morgues work, you know. We had an interesting trip to the morgue."

How morgues work? That escaped me. This fragile, tough widow whose lip trembles at a seven-year-old memory, takes a death and dying course and learns nothing but how morgues work? I tried to mask my disbelief and moved to check out what seemed obvious.

"Besides that—besides the trip and the practical stuff—did you get anything out of the course of *value* to you?" Palms toward her, I underlined "value" with empty hands. I wanted her to know that I knew without either of us having to acknowledge it.

"Of value?" She caught my eye for an instant, then looked down at her own hands, half folded in her lap. "Oh, some personal stuff." She paused a moment, then looked back up. Her eyes were moist, but she wouldn't give in. "Some people in the course had a lot of grieving to do." Then quickly, "But I just don't agree with that. I mean you have to move ahead. That's what I believe. You can't look back. I guess I learned that from my father. You have to put the past behind you and move ahead."

She held my eye doggedly while she spoke, testing herself. In the end, she passed. She was not about to give me that much, and I was not at all sure I wanted it. Besides, we each knew enough for now. We backed down.

" 'Move ahead,' " I said as I leaned back. "What's that

mean for you? Where are you headed?" Her face broke into a smile and she turned, looking out the frosted window. Then, after a moment,

"Oh, be more myself, I guess."

"How's that?"

"Oh, you know, not getting jerked around so much by other people, not always worrying about what they think of me."

I smiled at the familiarity of her sentiment. "Is there something wrong with that?" The question was clearly loaded, and she responded with a fire I hadn't seen before.

"Would you believe my brother had a fit when he saw that stuff?" she burst out, pointing to the degree plan. "He thinks I shouldn't study anything but what I need to run his stupid business!"

So she was onto her own tricks: even as she felt the heat of her brother's expectations, she resented them. Clearly, there was an Emerald inside this woman who wanted to be her own person. That puzzling dichotomy, that struggle over the meaning of "value," maybe it was the echo of an inner conversation between an old and a new Emerald? It often seemed that the educational worth of a given subject was in an inverse ratio to its apparent usefulness. Perhaps the new Emerald was crying out for something that would allow her to escape from the ordinary, practical "realities" of a life grown absurd.

Suddenly the waitress was above us, wanting to know what we wanted. We ordered coffee, smiled her away, and I lounged back into the corner of the booth, wondering whether to go with Emerald's emotions or pursue my hunch. Plates clattered in the kitchen. I decided on the latter.

"Look, Emerald," I said, "Just suppose you could have all the money and all the time you needed to learn about anything in the world you wanted. No need to learn a job skill, no need to be practical. Just to go after a burning curiosity. What would you want to learn?"

"Religion."

It came back so quickly I was thrown again. But it was perfect.

"Ah, so that's what the Old Testament next fall is about?"

"Yes." (Isn't it obvious?)

"Well, what ... what, exactly, does religion mean for you? I mean, it seems so far from accounting and numbers and all that."

"Yes. That's what I like about it. It's so different from what I do all day long. I like to come home and do something completely different."

That made sense to me. After a long day in the left brain, we need to change sides. But somehow something wasn't quite right yet. I was beginning to get a sense of what the two parts were, of where they rested, but what linked those "completely different" studies? And where was Emerald in all this? I still needed a connection.

"What is it about the Old Testament or archeology or death and dying that is so different from accounting?" I tossed in that last, fingers crossed. But maybe she would connect it for us.

"Well," she replied, flicking glances at me like a chickadee, cautious but not at all frightened, "I want to learn how it all began."

"And you feel you can learn the answers by studying those subjects?" I was not at all sure where she was going with this. She was beyond the point of thinking she could find the meaning of life by looking it up in the dictionary. Yet she did seem to think the Answers were out there, that if she could just study enough, read the right books, get the right information, she would find them. Was that what she wanted?

"Well, archeology will give a kind of scientific answer, and the Old Testament course will give religion ..." She broke off and looked at me with a question. "Does that make sense?" Evidently it didn't quite, to her.

I replied that I understood her uncertainty, but I still needed to clarify something. Was this quest no more than a counterpoint to accounting? I floundered for the question, then blurted it out.

"So here you sit in your stuffy little office day after day with your numbers—your pluses and your minuses, your rights and your wrongs, your world of certainties—and suddenly you find yourself staring out the window at a cloud and asking, 'Is this all there is?' Is that what your quest is about?"

Her smile this time seemed almost a relief to her. She reined it in quickly, but the acknowledgment was there—as though it had all been a guessing game and I finally got it. "What do you really want to know?" I asked her softly. And she began to talk.

"Well, like I said, I want to know how it all began. I mean I got interested in this and started reading, and I want to know about how the earth originated and I want to know what were the beginnings of Man. All I had to go by was Adam and Eve, and I don't buy that. I thought the logical way to attack it was to go through religion; then I find out that religion only goes back to 3000 B.C. Darwin goes back a couple million B.C., and I wonder what's going on all this time. Surely Neanderthal man must have some thoughts about what's going on, sitting out there in the cave looking at the stars at night; something must be going through his mind, definitely. And when the thunder comes, he knows he didn't do it."

"That's a religious question," I said, echoing Robert Novak. "Who am I under these stars?" But she went on, unhearing.

"And the most difficult problem is, we have no concrete evidence. I mean nobody walks up to us and tells us point-blank, 'Well, I can tell you. I was there.' It's kind of difficult."

"Why do you want to know all that, Emerald?" I asked. "What difference does it make?"

She replied, "It probably doesn't make any difference. It's a good way to keep me busy." Then, as if dissatisfied with her own diffidence, she frowned and added, "It helps my understanding of the world around me, and I think that's pretty important." She went on to muse about how simple it would be to be an animal.

"How come," she asked, "the animals are so successful and we're so unsuccessful? We're the ones with brains." Emerald looked across at me, her face a question. Yet something told me she didn't want an answer—at least not from me. I nodded, holding her eye. She looked down again, shook her head softly. "It seems everything is in chaos."

I waited a moment for us both. Then, "What's to be done about it? Is your quest somehow a way out of it?"

She was silent for a long time, studying her own fingers on the empty coffee cup. "To find out," she said finally, passion sheathed in velvet, "or even touch on what the differences, what the hinge is, what the chaos hinges on."

I think we must have looked like lovers at that moment, leaning toward each other, eyes on something invisible between us, oblivious. But just then there was a loud bump and a screech as the door swung open and a huge checkered man burst through the steam and greeted the other two inhabitants of our world. "God*damn*, ain't it some cold out there?"

We both leaned back; the clock caught my eye, and I signaled the waitress. I had several more people to see before dark. As we awaited our change, I spoke of my own journey toward a way of being that I didn't understand. I did so, not sure what my words would mean to her but wanting her to know that I too needed and valued the part of me that wouldn't come out even. Then we arranged for another meeting, put on our parkas, and plunged into the dazzling cold. She gave me a quick wave, slipped into her car, and purred off to the south. Turning out of the parking lot, I noticed a bank of clouds to the west. "At least it should warm up," I thought, and headed north.

As I drove, my mind kept returning to the conversation with Emerald. I was intrigued with the way she used language—that extraordinary concreteness: a course in the Old Testament would "give religion," archeology would "give a kind of scientific answer," "Religion only goes back to 3000 B.C. Darwin goes back a couple million . . ." There was a coarseness about how she packaged the ideas in their words, yet a marvelous poetry in her vision: "And when the thunder comes, he knows he didn't do it." Did that tangibility have something to do with her intellectual growth, or was it simply her personality? Would education blunt her intrinsic sensibility? How could I honor her curiosity without harming her innocence?

And what did "growth" mean for her anyway? "Not getting jerked around so much by other people, not always worrying about what they think of me," she had said. Was that just selfishness, or was this thrust toward independence part of a larger pattern in her life? And did her return to school cause this new concern or was it the result? Clearly it was placing a strain on her relationship with her brother. How was it affecting her two children, her friends? What was cause and what effect in the game of hide-and-seek between Emerald and her world?

Then there was that astonishing drive for some sort of deeper meaning to her life. Was this a question she had always harbored and only now allowed to surface? Or did school have something to do with stirring it up? I wasn't sure how I felt about that. On the one hand, it seemed a positive thing for people to ask serious questions of their lives, yet on the other, it could be deeply disturbing for some to lose the sources of meaning that had sustained them for so long. Friends may be lost, and marriages suffer. Who was I to tamper with their inner lives? I was no psychiatrist; I wasn't trained in these things. Yet all I had done was to ask her about what she was learning and offer her my best version of an honest response. Was Emerald simply going through the kind of crisis of certainty that most of us have gone through as we continue our education, or was it something more?

The clouds had slipped beneath the sun as I pulled into Ed's place, a ragged farmhouse connected to the barn by a ramshackle chain of sheds. Ed still owned the land the house was on but had auctioned off the rest two years ago when his farm went under, a victim of economic forces he refused to understand. I had been appropriately sympathetic when he first told me the story, but I had been brought up short when he added that in a way he was glad it had happened. He had long since grown tired of farming.

"I needed the change," he said. "Farming hasn't much to do, you know, with growing things any more. Mostly it's fixing goddamn busted machinery. If I'da wanted to be a mechanic I'd have been one." Besides, he had begun drinking and only recently had dried out with the help of the local AA chapter. Now his wife was supporting the family, and he did odd jobs while he studied psychology. "I really want to work with peo-

ple," he had told me, "in the time I got left." Where he'd find
that work was anybody's guess. But there had been an urgency
behind his words that hinted of more than a desire for vocational training. In his early fifties, he felt time was running out.
Where was he headed? Would his educational voyage take him
where he wanted to go? Did he know what a terrible chance he
was taking? And what was my part in that journey? I parked
beside his old Ford tractor, hauled my briefcase out of the
backseat, and headed for the shed where the kitchen would be.
As I saw Ed's shadowy form through the frost on the storm
door and reached for the frozen latch, the questions still burned.

   Ed, Emerald, and thousands like them are part of a major revolution in higher education, a revolution that has seen the
proportion of older students in classrooms double within a single generation. Spurred by declining enrollments among traditional-age students and by a growing recognition that many
adults wanted to continue their education but lacked the
means, a number of colleges began to design special programs
during the 1970s to accommodate the new student. Because
most adults had jobs, courses were offered at night or on week-
ends, and degree requirements became more flexible; classes
were longer and less frequent. Because the majority were parents, part-time study had to be more available and financing
more appropriate. And because the age range of this new group
was considerably greater than that of traditional students, new
assumptions had to be made about how best to teach and support them. After all, the conventional curriculum had evolved
in response to the relatively innocent and distinctly different
needs of late adolescents. People like Emerald bore a breadth
of experience and a depth of emotional capacity largely unavail-
able to traditional college-age students. To attempt to teach a
thirty-five-year-old widow in the same way one would an
eighteen-year-old halfback did not make good sense.

   It is this last matter that has most intrigued me over the
years. First as teacher and administrator in a community college, later as external degree program mentor and researcher, I
have been struck again and again with the awesome differences
among adult learners and have long sought a better way of

understanding them. Why is it that at only twenty-eight Susan seems so much more able to handle complex ideas than Arthur, a retired businessman, even though her knowledge and experience are so much less? Is it background, gender, friends, intelligence (whatever that means)? Or could it be age? Is Arthur simply over the hill? Do our minds, like our bodies, just deteriorate over time? And why do so many women return to school in their mid thirties, so many men in their forties? What is happening in their lives or in our society that creates such a pattern? What are the special concerns of these groups that might give us a better basis for designing curricula? Is there any way to reconcile the pragmatic needs of these students for specific, job-related knowledge with their deeper needs for a more comprehensive understanding of their worlds?

I think I first began to entertain the notion that the metaphor of a journey might offer a useful framework during a conversation with Ellen, one of my first students. She was telling me about her experience of returning to school after a thirty-year absence.

"It's like a river," she said, and drew a line across the table between us.

> It's like I'm back there and want to get over here, and the only way I can do it is to cross the river. So I say, "OK," take a deep breath, and go. And I make it over here. And that's where you are; you are alive. Sometimes I get mixed up about the journey across the river; sometimes I think it's the worst experience of my life; other times I think it's the most fantastic experience ... but you know, when you get over here, you leave something—you have to—and sometimes I wish I was that person back there, but I can't be and I don't want to be. I mean I can't ever be that person again. Once you cross that river, the innocence is gone.

I was to hear the journey metaphor often after that, as I began asking people what it was like for them to *re-turn* to school. It was an extraordinarily useful way for people to get a handle on their experience, to name the feelings that too frequently kept them awake nights. Because journeys have destinations, it gave a sense of movement and purpose to what often seemed without meaning, helped them to understand that confusion, uncertainty, and fear may be a necessary, even valuable, part of educational growth. And it helped me to grasp the differences among them more readily. In a way, some had simply traveled more than others; some seemed never to have left home, while others had gone centuries away. But if my students were travelers, then who was I as teacher? If education was most about growth, what was my part?

What I was beginning to realize was that teaching is most of all a special kind of relationship, a caring stance in the moving context of our students' lives. Of course it involves knowledge; of course the teacher has to know *something*, but what we know is of value only as we are able to form it in such a way that our students can make use of it for their own evolving ways of knowing. I was keenly aware that I was a unique person for every student. Each saw me differently, and I needed to be different for each. Our students are always in motion, I was realizing, and our task is to honor that motion, to understand how each student sees education and his or her teachers in a different way at a different time. The job, it seemed, was not so much to individualize instruction as to *enrich education* so each student could take from it what he or she most needed at the time.

But occasionally the questions seemed overwhelming. What was that "loss of innocence" that Ellen described so eloquently? How did my own journey mesh with hers? If we were all in motion, what did timing have to do with the art of teaching? Is there some way of understanding this more clearly, so we can ask sharper questions, offer better suggestions, provide richer support?

This book is at best an interim report, an attempt to sketch some beginning answers to those questions lurking behind the storm door at Ed's house. For as they burned their way into my awareness, I found the outlines dimly swimming somewhere in the space between me and nearly every film or novel I encountered, each story I read to my children, every conversation with my students; they began to fuse into a single, deeper question: *What is my place in the growth of those I care for?* And as I held the question, not surprisingly I began to discover shards all about me—answers that have been with us since we were children.

Education as a Transformational Journey: The Role of Teachers, Advisers, and Mentors as Guides

> Not the least shyness, now, Telemakhos. You came across the open sea for this—to find out where the great earth hides your father and what the doom was that he came upon. . . .
>   Reason and heart will give you words, Telemakhos; and a spirit will counsel others. I should say the gods were never indifferent to your life.
>
> —*Mentor,* The Odyssey

If mentors did not exist, we would have to invent them. Indeed, we do so from childhood on. They come in an array of forms, from the classic bearded Merlin to the grandmotherly fairy godmother to the otherworldly elfin Yoda of the *Star Wars* trilogy. Myths, fairy tales, fantasy, and children's stories abound with mentor figures: Gandolf in Tolkien, Charlotte in *Charlotte's Web,* Utnapishtim in the Gilgamesh epic, Shazam in Captain Marvel comics, the spider woman in Native American lore, the Belgian doctor in *Tarzan,* the little old lady in *Babar,* Teiresias in Greek legend, the Skin Horse in *The Velveteen Rabbit.* They proceed from a place in us as deep as our dreams. Carl Jung tells us that the archetype, which may be of either sex or both, represents "knowledge, reflection, insight, wisdom, cleverness, and intuition." The figure appears in a situation where "insight,

16

understanding, good advice, determination, planning, etc. are
needed but cannot be mustered on one's own," often arriving
in the nick of time to help the traveler along the journey (Jung,
1958, p. 71).

Whether as close as the classroom or as distant as history,
mentors are creations of our imaginations, designed to fill a
psychic space somewhere between lover and parent. Not surprisingly, they are suffused with magic and play a key part in our
transformation. Their purpose, as Bruno Bettelheim says in *The
Uses of Enchantment* (1975), is to remind us that we can, indeed,
survive the terror of the coming journey and undergo the transformation by moving through, not around, our fear. Mentors
give us the magic that allows us to enter the darkness: a talis-
man to protect us from evil spells, a gem of wise advice, a map,
and sometimes simply courage. But always the mentor appears
near the outset of the journey as a helper, equipping us in some
way for what is to come, a midwife to our dreams.

We begin this chapter with a look at some ways in which
the term *mentor* has been used recently. In the decade since
Gail Sheehy popularized the term (Sheehy, 1976), mentors have
become a hot item. Success, we are told, whether in industry or
academia, is a lot slipperier without a mentor to show us the
ropes. A handful of books and dozens of articles now proclaim
mentors' virtues and defects (Speizer, 1981; Merriam, 1983).

However, relatively little has been said about the broader,
metaphorical context of the word. *Mentors are guides.* They
lead us along the journey of our lives. We trust them because
they have been there before. They embody our hopes, cast light
on the way ahead, interpret arcane signs, warn us of lurking
dangers, and point out unexpected delights along the way.
There is a certain luminosity about them, and they often pose
as magicians in tales of transformation, for *magic* is a word
given to what we cannot see, and we can rarely see across the
gulf. As teachers of adults, we have much to learn from the
mythology of the mentor.

In order to understand the mentor as guide, however, it
will be necessary to go back and look more closely at the journey itself. To do that, we will consider the importance of

"story" as a way of making sense of life's changes, focusing especially on a particular kind of story—the journey tale. We will then follow one illustrious mentor and his charge on their journey through *Inferno* together, deriving from this great tale of transformation some beginning principles of mentorship. Finally, as we consider how the principles of mentorship might apply to the real-life concerns of teacher and student, we will listen in on a conversation with Eric, an engineer hearing some unanticipated voices on his way up the corporate ladder and into midlife. The chapter concludes by suggesting that the combination of developmental theory and the journey metaphor offers a useful lens through which to view students like Emerald, Ed, and Eric.

Embedded in the chapter are a number of questions we might ask of ourselves as teachers or advisers: What changes do I want to see in my students? What kind of responsibility do I accept for them? How do my students see me, and what do they want from me? How do I respond to their hopes, their fear? And can I learn this or is it just so much magic?

But before we speak too much of magicians and mentors, teachers, healers and guides, I want to make it plain as daylight that there is nothing here that does not meet the eye willing to see or the ear ready to hear. Magic, as all true wizards know, is available to anyone willing to stand in the right place. Most magicians are simply people who have refined more than the rest of us the art of understanding how the world works. They know where lie the fault lines, the clefts, the barely visible seams in what we call "real." In working their magic, they simply scramble the line between imagination and reality, for they know that the greatest illusion is to believe we have no illusions. One need not meet students in wintry diners or seethe with love of Bach flute sonatas to make good use of the principles here. I have known fine mentors who lecture to classes of two hundred and never set foot off a campus. What distinguishes them has little to do with student load, or publications, or even popularity. Nor do they necessarily wear beards, outrageous outfits, or hearts on their sleeves. What makes the difference is their willingness to care—about what they teach and whom. They know they exist as teachers only because of their students; they know they are part of a transaction, a relationship.

Mentors

The original Mentor appears in *The Odyssey* as an old and trusted friend of Odysseus. He is appointed to look after the estate and, more to the point, Odysseus's son, Telemakhos. It is in Mentor's form that Athena, goddess of wisdom, speaks at critical times throughout the epic. Thus, Mentor is both male and female, mortal and immortal—an androgynous demigod, half here, half there. Wisdom personified.

In the story itself, Mentor serves as a guide to young Telemakhos in his search for reunion with his father. Mentor urges the boy on his quest, finds a ship, accompanies him on the first leg, and then departs, returning again at the end of the tale to assist father, son, and grandfather as they recapture their heritage and consolidate their return home. His part in the story is instructive, for he is a classic transitional figure, helping the youth achieve his manhood and confirm his identity in an adult world while helping the father complete his life's work.

Mentors, it seems, have something to do with growing up, with the development of identity. In one of the best and closest studies of the mentor-protégé relationship that I have seen, researcher David Zucker says with thinly veiled delight that "the most unexpected result [of the study] was that the structure of the mentor-protégé relationship . . . closely parallels the structure of the mentoring myth contained in Homer's *Odyssey*" (Zucker, 1982, p. vi). While we may share his joy in discovering the power of mythology to elucidate human relationships, we ought not be too surprised. The sample for most myths is, after all, rather large.

In a detailed, longitudinal study of the lives of forty men, psychologist Daniel Levinson found that many of his subjects had been guided and supported during their early adult years by older men whom he dubbed "mentors." Indeed, it was his research that informed Gail Sheehy's popularization of the term in *Passages*. Subsequent studies, especially in the business world, have pointed to the importance of a mentor for both men's and women's advancement in the organization (Roche, 1979; Hennig and Jardim, 1977; Phillips-Jones, 1982). Similar work has been carried out in academia, especially regarding the entry of women into the professoriat (Hall and Sandler, 1983). The gist of the research is that mentors are especially important at the beginning of people's careers or at crucial turning points in their professional lives. The mentor seems to manifest for protégés someone who has accomplished the goals to which they now aspire, offering encouragement and concrete help.

The term *mentor* has been used sporadically in higher education for years but first caught my ear when used formally by Empire State College, one of the nation's first colleges created exclusively for older students. Although mentors obviously continue to serve young people, the term has since come into much wider use as a neologism meaning "teacher of adults." Mentors generally have a wider role than conventional faculty advisers. They may or may not teach classes, but they are inevitably engaged in one-to-one instruction and are consequently more concerned than regular teachers with the individual learning needs and styles of their students (Thomas, Murrell, and Chickering, 1982).

Within the academy itself, mentors are understandably found most frequently among the ranks of the faculty. But unless there is some formalized process for assigning or recognizing mentorships (Brown and DeCoster, 1982), the process remains largely invisible—a German instructor spends extra lab time with a particularly promising student, or a biology professor and student begin to share problems of child care. More visible in this role may be the student counseling staff, who because their work is not to transmit specific content, are frequently more concerned with promoting the development of the student. But the range of possibilities is perhaps widest in those programs that view the learning environment as extending beyond the campus. External degree and cooperative education programs, for instance, frequently give formal recognition to supervisors and experts in the "outside world" who may often move into mentor status with their students. It is important for programs to recognize the potential of people such as these.

It is also important for institutions to acknowledge the centrality of the advising process, an activity that almost inevitably is viewed simply as a chore by overburdened teachers. Yet this is often the only point at which the instructor actually speaks individually with students and is inevitably the only time he or she is called upon to view a student's progress in a context broader than that of a single course. Even where teacher-student contact lacks the intensity or personal quality normally associated with mentorship, students can be powerfully affected by their teachers. Many of us carry memories of an influential teacher who may scarcely know we existed, yet who said something at just the right time in our lives to snap a whole world into focus. To a certain extent, of course, the timing of such moments is a mystery. Neither we nor the teacher can know when they will occur. But to the degree that as teachers we are aware of the shifting pattern of questions stirring the intellectual test tubes of our students' minds, we are in a better position to drop in just the right catalyst at the propitious moment to bring about the transformation we seek.

Mentors have no more meaning without students than answers have without questions. Just what are those questions? Here, Sam Keen writes of his mentor's advice.

> Once, in a dry time, Howard Thurman asked me: "What do you want, Sam? What are your dreams?" He had previously warned me about the proper order of . . . priorities. "The first question an individual must ask is 'What is my journey?' Only then is it safe to ask the second question: 'Who will go with me?' If you get the questions out of order, you will get in trouble" [1983, p. 172].

The first business of a guide is to listen to the dreams of the pilgrim. How are our students moving? What do they want for themselves? How do they tell their own stories?

Stories

We begin with stories. Children love stories. In the narrative structure is one of the most basic ways we make sense of our experience. But stories are important for adults as well, for in the great tales lies the syntax of our lives, the form by which we make meaning of life's changes. A good story transforms our vision of the possible and provides us with a map for the journey ahead. So we should not be surprised to discover that many major developmental theorists draw heavily on literature in their work. As James Fowler, a developmentalist theologian, notes, "Theorists of adult development have begun to play the role in our society that storytellers and mythmakers once played in primitive and classical cultures" (1984, p. 15). By suggesting the directions of growth throughout the life span, developmental psychologists are offering us "masterstories" against which to hold our own lives' tales for comparison and, perhaps, for revision.

It is a basic premise of this book, as of much current developmental theory, that development is more than simply change. The word implies *direction.* Moreover, development seems to happen not in a gradual, linear way but in distinct and recognizable leaps—in a series of spiraling plateaus rather than a smooth slope. Each plateau rests upon and represents a qualitative improvement over the previous one. It is good, I believe, to "develop," and as teachers, we cannot escape our part in this development. A ten-year-old does not simply know "more" than a four-year-old; she *thinks* differently. She can order things in sequence; her younger brother doesn't even try. She can classify objects into logical groups; her brother couldn't care less. And perhaps most important, she can tell (and appreciate) coherent stories because she has developed a sense of linear time; her brother remains adrift in a labile and essentially timeless world. As such, she has gained the power to array her fears, her wants, and her triumphs in some sort of order, while her brother is still subject to them all—buffeted by and almost wholly dependent upon his immediate experience. Is she, then, "better" than he for being at a later stage of development? Of course not. We can only be who we are at the time (and it's hard enough to do that well!). Yet because she has a capacity to construct a more elaborate interior "map" of the world, she is less likely than he to become lost if she finds herself in a strange place. She can rely more on herself and less on grown-ups to solve her problems. Because she can move beyond her immediate impulses and understand the motives of others more clearly than he, she is more able to anticipate their needs and thus serve her own. By virtue of her greater development, she is less subject to the demands of her environment and is consequently both freer and more powerful than he. In this sense, there are times when it is indeed "better" to think like a ten-year-old than a four-year-old.

I have watched with fascination as my children, two years apart, have moved through what Selma Fraiberg calls the magic years, struggling with profound fears of the unknown, of darkness, of powerful figures threatening to annihilate them. Their greatest weapon, as they grow, has been their increasing ability to give fears a context by placing them in time. They do this by hearing, acting out, and telling stories. For in a psychological sense, a story is simply our fears and triumphs given form in the context of time. Thus, preschooler Todd, with the help of a Spider Man figure, could battle with the Incredible Hulk, physically battering that hunk of green cheesecake while emotionally reassuring himself that he had the power to overcome his fears. Over time, with his father's exuberant storytelling, to say nothing of his culture's current penchant for escape fantasy, Todd learned to construct ever more elaborate scenarios with his little plastic Darth Vader and Luke Skywalker figures, while Kate, now a reader, could take yet a further step by consuming book after book. For children and grown-ups alike, stories allow us to control and form the inchoate, to give our lives meaning.

We are told that Zen masters often respond to the pleas of their students for "answers" by telling stories. Indeed, the tradition is honored among most great teachers, from Lao-tzu, Plato, and Jesus to the Hassidim, Kierkegaard, and T. S. Eliot. The reason is not just that these teachers want to keep things simple; they also know that insights always shine brightest for those who have them, that *truth* is a word we give to a pattern that makes sense to us, and that by offering a story teachers provide a common structure on which each of us can order his or her own experience. Great teachers know that to provide an answer is to confuse ends with means—a bit like flying a group of hikers to the top of the mountain when one person's reason for the trip is to learn to climb, another's to collect wild flowers, and another's simply to enjoy the day. A good story is a kind of hologram of the life of an individual, a culture, or a whole species. Each of us hears in it, with ears conditioned by our own history, what we most need at the time to understand.

Yet not just any story will do. Su Wen, the Chinese tell us, was a great physician. He could heal a thousand illnesses with a single needle by placing it in the right way in the right place in the right person at the right time. That's high art. The good storyteller does the same.

In his book *Ascent of the Mountain, Flight of the Dove* (1971), Michael Novak talks of the importance of "story" this way. In those moments when the world falls apart, when we lose a sense of meaning, stories can reconnect things for us, place our fears in context, help us to see new forms of meaning. They do so by offering a way out, not simply in the characters or the setting but in the very syntax of the tale itself, a syntax that seems almost universal. That seems obvious enough, but the point is that stories are not simply random recitations of events. They have an order in time, and to have meaning that order must go from somewhere to somewhere. It must lead the reader through some sort of journey. Stories, like human development, demand a sense of direction to be good.

The Journey

By no means do all stories actually tell of a journey, yet most do involve some degree of movement through space as well as time, and in many of these a common pattern reveals itself. The journey tale begins with an old world, generally simple and uncomplicated, more often than not, home. The Garden of Eden is a prototype. The middle portion, beginning with departure from home, is characterized by confusion, adventure, great highs and lows, struggle, uncertainty. The ways of the old world no longer hold, and the hero's task is to find a way through this strange middle land, generally in search of something lying at its heart. Christ's anguish in Gethsemane forms the dramatic counterpart to Eden in this sense. At the deepest point, the nadir of the descent, a transformation occurs, and the traveler moves out of the darkness toward a new world that often bears an ironic resemblance to the old. It is not the same, of course; it only looks that way. But the resemblance is no accident.

This mythic movement from an old, familiar land into the darkness of the nether world and back home transformed has been traced by Joseph Campbell from hundreds of myths and legends across numerous cultures and times. Calling it the "monomyth," he describes the heroic quest this way:

> The standard path of the mythological adventure of the hero is a magnification of the formula represented in the rites of passage: separation-initiation-return: which might be named the nuclear unit of the monomyth.
>
> The hero ventures forth from the world of common day into a region of supernatural wonder: fabulous forces are there encountered and a decisive victory is won: the hero comes back from this mysterious adventure with the power to bestow boons on his fellowman [1949, p. 30].

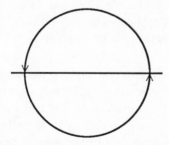

Along the way, a number of critical incidents may take place. The traveler may "refuse the call," preferring to stay at home after all; a mentor figure may appear to offer supernatural aid; a set of challenges must be met and overcome; an apotheosis occurs by which the traveler is transformed and empowered to return with a "boon" for his people; demons pursue him, but with help he escapes and becomes master of two worlds with a new freedom to live. The hero has been born again (Campbell, 1949).

The astute reader will note Campbell's language. Since most of the cultures from which he drew his information were patriarchial (including his own), his heroes are almost exclusively male; separation from "home" is essential to the journey. Contemporary critics (Bakan, 1966; Choderow, 1978; Gilligan, 1982; Belenky, Clinchy, Goldberger, and Tarule, 1986) have raised serious questions about whether separation has the same developmental meaning for women as for men, suggesting that the female journey may instead emphasize connection and care rather than isolation and hierarchy. We will continue to recognize this in later chapters. For now it is enough to note that the task facing both sexes is to reframe and understand in a radically new way the meaning of the world they once knew. This does not mean that the old world has been abandoned; rather, it has been incorporated into a broader awareness of its place. It is *seen* in a new way. The journey does not take away our old experiences, as we often fear before we embark. It simply gives them new meaning. This is the significance of the paradoxical Zen saying:

> Before practice, there is the mountain;
> During practice, there is no mountain;
> After practice, there is the mountain.

Nothing is different, yet all is transformed. It is *seen* differently. In that change of perspective, in the transformation of meaning lies the meaning of transformation (Mezirow, 1978). Our old life is still there, but its meaning has profoundly changed because we have left home, seen it from afar, and been transformed by that vision. You can't go home again.

The irony is that you also can't get there from here. That

is, for this sort of mythic transformation to occur, we have to get lost. By definition, there are no paths through the wilderness and no ways home save through it.

In one of the most richly imaginative of modern journey tales, *The Lord of the Rings,* Sam and Frodo, the central characters, are taking a brief break during their terrible journey into the Dark Empire of Mordor. Sam, lover of stories, is speculating with Frodo about whether their own tale will ever become part of the legends of their people. "I wonder what sort of a tale we've fallen into?" he asks.

"I wonder," Frodo replies. "But I don't know. And that's the way of a real tale. Take any one that you're fond of. You may know, or guess, what kind of a tale it is, happy-ending or sad-ending, but the people in it don't know. And you don't want them to" (Tolkien, 1965, pp. 407–408).

For each of us, tangled inside our own stories, the endings are hidden. Yet most of us spend the better part of our lives trying to assure ourselves that our tales are already told, even if not yet lived, and that they have a happy ending. The discovery that this might not be so can, in itself, lead to a profound transformation. But the appearance of someone who has already taken the journey can bring a sigh of relief to the best of us. That is where mentors come in. They have been there before, and we greet them with awe and, above all, hope.

So it was with Dante whose *Divine Comedy* is almost certainly the most brilliant and richly detailed account of a transformational journey ever written. It is the story of his descent through Hell and Heavenward through Purgatory accompanied by the Roman poet Virgil, a classic mentor. In their friendship is a prototype of the mentor-protégé relationship. Join us for a closer look.

The Deep and Savage Way

The central theme of the tale is Dante's quest for Truth, represented by his journey through Hell to Heaven in search of union with his love, Beatrice. The tale begins at midlife, a fitting time for asking ultimate questions.

"Midway through the journey of life," begins the epic,
Dante finds himself lost in a dark wood, terrified and fleeing in
desperation from wild animals. He has lost all hope when Virgil
appears, coming toward him through the gloom. Assuring Dante
that he is an envoy from Beatrice, who awaits him near the end
of his journey, Virgil leads the pilgrim through Hell on the paradoxical downward journey toward the light.

Virgil knows the territory. He is Mentor Supreme, alternately protecting his charge from threat, urging him on, explaining the mysteries, pointing the way, leaving him alone, translat-
ing arcane codes, calming marauding beasts, clearing away
obstacles, and encouraging—always encouraging.

At one point in the descent through Hell, the old man
takes the younger in his arms like a child and plummets down a
rocky embankment to escape a flock of vengeful spirits; at another, he snaps at Dante for becoming too absorbed in conversation with frauds and falsifiers. And finally, in his greatest single
act of instruction, Virgil bids the pilgrim gaze directly upon the
Emperor of The Woeful Kingdom himself.

> When we had gone on so far that my Master
> thought it good to show me the creature who was
> once so fair, he took himself from before me and
> made me stop, saying: "Lo, Dis, and the place
> where thou must arm thyself with fortitude."
> How chilled and faint I turned then, do not
> ask, reader, for I do not write it, since all words
> would fail. I did not die and I did not remain alive;
> think now for thyself, if thou has any wit, what I
> became, denied both death and life [1961, p. 43].

Knowing that explanations in the pit of Hell are generally superfluous, Virgil has the good sense to add nothing at the
moment. He has brought Dante to the brink of being and nothingness, bidden him look, and retired. The experience is transformative, for it marks a momentous boundary, not simply between life and death but between what Dante knows and what
he cannot conceive. It is a transformation precisely because it

goes beyond both life *and* death, making possible the unimaginable.

Then, telling Dante to grasp him around the neck, Virgil swings down the very haunches of the Beast, leading him beneath Satan's feet out a long pathway back, upward toward Purgatory just as the morning stars are fading. The first leg of their journey has been completed.

As they walk through Purgatory, the relationship between the two men grows softer. In Hell Virgil bore clear authority and seemed virtually invincible. In this Middle Kingdom both he and his protégé stand out less sharply from each other and from their surroundings. Here they are among peers, and despite Dante's continued respect for his guide, their relationship reflects this sense of growing equality. The sounds here are muted, the light less stark, and one has the sense that while earlier the pair had walked in single file along narrow pathways, here they more often stroll side by side. Whereas formerly they had been sightseers, largely detached from their surroundings, now they are participants engaging more fully with the inhabitants of the land as well as with each other.

By the time Virgil takes his leave near the end of the journey through Purgatory, Dante is ready for his next leap, his momentum beyond question. The proximity of the light draws him on, and Virgil's prodding is no longer necessary. At the brink of Heaven, the mentor offers his blessing, explaining that he can lead no further and instructing his charge to await the appearance of Beatrice. His task is complete. "Free, upright, and whole is thy will and it were a fault not to act on its bidding; therefore over thyself I crown and mitre thee."

A short time later, turning to his guide for support, Dante finds him gone. His pathway now leads beyond the vision of his mentor.

Here, in this extraordinary tale, is embedded all the richness of the mentor-protégé relationship as it moves from a beginning rescue to a downward journey toward transformation and through to a growing equality as the pair separate. What makes this such a powerful and enduring model? What does it have to offer us as teachers and advisers?

Virgil begins by *engendering trust, issuing a challenge, providing encouragement,* and *offering a vision* for the journey. In so doing, he helps to transmute Dante's fear of abandonment into the call of adventure. Throughout the journey, he alternately supports and challenges his protégé to keep moving, to sustain his quest.

By way of engendering trust, Virgil reminds Dante that Beatrice had sent him. He is thus an emissary of the light, a channel for truth, much as Mentor is a vehicle for Athena's wisdom. It is interesting to note that in these and other epics, a female figure is often closer to "the source" than men. Both Dante and Odysseus are journeying toward the feminine, as though unification with the female will constitute wholeness for them. Levinson's work, which we will encounter in the next chapter, describing the male need at midlife to rebalance an overload of youthful masculinity, makes sense in light of this mythic statement (Bridges, 1980).

It is noteworthy that both Virgil and Mentor are half-way creatures, residents of both this and the next world. As such, they are ideal guides for those in transition, human enough to understand this world, immortal enough to lead the way to the next. Yet they are only the embodiment of wisdom, never the source. This is a particularly important distinction, one too often forgotten by overly dependent travelers and easily flattered guides. No human being can be a *source,* and for either mentor or protégé to believe as much is to lead the journey dangerously astray or abort it altogether.

Notice that the mentor appears near the beginning of the journey when the pilgrim is most afraid and uncertain. Understandably, Virgil's power is considerable at this point, for there are good reasons why authority is important early in the journey. When we feel out of control, as Dante did, we need to believe that others are in it. We need something solid to hold to until we regain our balance. Returning to school after years away can be a deeply unsettling experience for many adults. Competent though they may be in their work or homes, they find themselves suddenly at the mercy of teachers sometimes younger than they and in danger of ridicule from fellow students who could be their own children.

Surrounded by forces that seem greater than ourselves, we are understandably anxious about those who wield power. Will they use it for us or against us? This is why mentors are sometimes feared at the outset or simply not recognized. And it is why, when they are known, they are welcomed with what may later seem a surfeit of adulation. For as Campbell observes, they are seen as "intercessors with The Powers" and as such must be carefully courted. Teachers of adults do well to recognize the anxiety experienced by many beginning students. It is often masked as bravado or scorn. But underneath often lies a deep uncertainty—about the ability to succeed "late in life," about losing face before other students or teachers half their age, about working in sometimes starkly unfamiliar realms. Knowing it for the fear it is, we can act to relieve it gently rather than attempting to overcome or deny it.

Not only was Virgil's timing good, but he was experienced. He had been there before. He knew the dangers and many of the enemies lying ahead. He could explain to Dante the meaning of his encounters and steer him clear of threats. Students often speak this way of their advisers: "She explained all the forms and bureaucratic detail to me," or "He kept me on the track so I knew I wouldn't get in trouble." In postsecondary education, the mentor holds the keys to membership in that other world of "the educated," a world that holds a good many more mysteries than those of us on this side of the threshold readily remember. Like Virgil, the academic adviser is a translator not simply of the arcane ways of academia but of the very words themselves: *credits, distribution requirements, liberal studies.* We tend to forget that like members of any specialized field, we cloak ourselves with mystery in the service of our mastery.

In addition to explaining the damned to Dante, Virgil also explains Dante to the damned—when they are not too preoccupied by rivers of boiling blood and similar infernal delights to notice. From this unique position between worlds, the aca-

demic mentor frequently finds it necessary to interpret to colleagues the special circumstances of a particular student's life,
explaining, for instance, why caring for three sick children and
a dying aunt somehow took precedence over Sheila's timely
completion of a term paper describing the esthetic properties of
a tenaculum.

For Dante, Virgil was a model poet. On the basis of their
common craft, Dante was able to trust his mentor and was
drawn toward him. For many students, the teacher serves as a
concrete manifestation of what they wish to become. The attraction may be specific—"I'd like to have that kind of a job
myself"—or general—"He seems to have a freedom I admire."
For others, especially women, a female mentor may seem to retain an alluring balance between responsibilities of home and
career (Erkut and Mokros, 1981). But all mentors serve some
sort of higher tradition. As keepers of the educational fires, as
the most accessible exemplars of what it means to "be educated," mentors embody answers to questions like "How does
she know so much?" "How can I become like that?" and
"What am I supposed to know?" Viewed from sufficient distance, it all looks like magic, and we ought not be too surprised
when we are treated like magicians.

As the journey progresses, Virgil offers great support and
encouragement to his protégé, shoring up Dante's courage again
and again. More than to any other aspect, when asked to describe the good mentor, students point to this. "He was incredibly supportive, and I really felt liberated by that." "Even
if she disagreed, I always knew she would help me get it right
because she went out of her way to see my point of view."
"Without his encouragement, I never would have made it." Un-
fortunately, this nurturant aspect of the mentor's job is often
shortchanged. Many men, especially, see this as "mere baby-
sitting," essentially unrelated to the "real business" of teaching. "By the time they are at this level they ought to be able to
take care of themselves" goes the argument. "It's not my job
to hold their hands." Yet if we are serious when we assert that
education is most successful when students "grow," that it is
intellectual development we are about rather than simply knowl-

edge acquisition, then the evidence is strong that emotional engagement must be a part of the learning process. The recognition that passion is central to learning and the capacity to provide emotional support when it is needed are hallmarks that distinguish the good mentor from the mediocre teacher.

At the same time, Virgil is no mere patsy. Along with the rest of his breed, he sets intricate tests and challenges along the way and does not hesitate to express disapproval of Dante's behavior if necessary. For mentors also "teach" in a conventional sense, offering new information, giving advice, testing, and frequently stimulating their students to take issue with them. "I disagreed with a lot of what she said, and I still do," said one student. "But I have to admit she really made me think." The result is to unveil new perspectives. Blinded by fear, Dante literally comes to see the world afresh—"He really opened my eyes," said one student of her teacher. Followers may be unable to discern where their guides are leading, but if the journey is a good one, they will learn, as Don Juan says of Casteneda, to *see* in a new way.

Finally it is time for Virgil to leave. At some point, mentors always depart, generally before the journey is over. The trip belongs, after all, to the traveler, not the guide—and the mentor has his own promises to keep. When the transformation has been accomplished by the student and accepted by the mentor, the departure may be smooth and caring. Sadly, such cases are frequently an exception. Current research suggests that many relationships end in indifference or hostility. Still, if the journey has taken its full course, the traveler has her own momentum. The power that seemed at the outset so overwhelming has moved inward, and the student has become her own teacher. If the mentor is also capable of letting go of that power so that the relationship can be genuinely reciprocal, the odds favor a lasting friendship. The paradox is that at the outset few students can imagine the relationship evolving to friendship. The idea of equality is literally incomprehensible. Yet afterward, it seems the only possibility. Describing such an ending, one student said of her mentor, "Yes, we're friends now, but there's still that respect; I'll always respect her. You know, I

feel that we are now much more like colleagues than we were."
The idea of "respect" has allowed her to hold both the earlier
hierarchical form and her new equality at once. She can continue to honor her teacher while cherishing a new friend.

Said another student,

> I used to think that I wanted more than any-
> thing else to be like Barbara; I wanted, almost, to
> *be* her. But I'm not, of course. I think I'm more
> myself now than I ever was . . . except that I'm not
> the person I used to be. Does that make sense? I
> think that's why we can be friends.

That "But" is telling, for it marks a fresh boundary between someone who once sought her identity through immersion with another and a person who now knows that she must
be her own author. Because she came to see herself anew, she
could reconstrue the relationship as well, and do so on a more
mature and equal basis.

Occasionally, both partners will be fortunate enough to
sustain the connection through its maturity. Of dozens of formal mentoring relationships, I count only a small handful in
my own life that have done so. Ella, a participant in some of my
early developmental research, was one such person, and she
wrote this about her experience at the time.

> My first impression of Larry was of an al-
> most-god standing above and apart from those of
> us in the [learning group], yet somehow tantaliz-
> ingly reachable if we chose the right road to where
> he was standing. . . . [Our relationship] progressed
> through the emotionally charged and draining
> phases of growth, rebellion, and separation into a
> tenuous state of autonomy fueled by my desire to
> prove both to myself and to him that I was finally
> "educated" enough to go it alone, thank you very
> much. . . . Luckily Larry said and did the right
> things at the right times to both push and pull me

through the process until some sort of level was reached between us.

That's a rare accolade, and I continue to treasure it, along with Ella's friendship. It was she, more than anyone else, who taught me about what is best in our work. Both of us are now off on our own paths, but they cross and cross again, and when they do, we find that we are learning similar things from our lives. The old hierarchical roles were shed back there somewhere, and in place of the earlier enchantment is a simple friendship—a whole new kind of magic.

So much for the violins. But long before that moment is reached, if it ever is, lie long hours of work—students struggling to understand difficult material and integrate it into complicated lives, mentors attempting to enter the thought frames of their students and help them pry loose their old assumptions on the fulcrum of a new idea. In the conversation that follows, meet Eric, an engineer in his mid thirties who has gone about as far as he can go, unless he changes direction. He has returned to school to do that, but with the help of Milt, a true mentor, Eric discovers that something more than his direction must change. In reading, try to sense the movement of Eric's life. In what ways does his journey parallel Dante's? What does his metaphor about trenches suggest about *how he conceives of his journey*? And finally, consider how both Milt and I provide for Eric a *vision* ahead, *encouragement,* and *challenge* as we guide him into his own deep and savage way.

Into the Trenches

The walls are bare, beige, almost baleful; the table and chairs fit together perfectly with an engineered elegance. Through the glass partition behind Eric, I can see people moving about the office space in utter silence: businesslike, correct, and very, very careful. We have met in the conference room of the small electronics firm where Eric works as an engineer to discuss his project for the adult development seminar that I am teaching.

"I'm still not sure what you want in this presentation," he says. A touch of impatience edges his voice. "Do you want me to go through the book and just give out Levinson's ideas? Hell, I can do that; I'm great at charts and that."

I don't answer right away. There seems to be an "or" coming, and I want to hear what it is. He holds his glance for a second and, not seeing an answer, leaps ahead.

"Or . . . or do you want me to criticize him, or . . . I mean, I can do that too if you want, but I haven't studied much psychology and I'm not sure I can . . . ," he falters.

"Sure, Eric. That would be good," I reply. "We've got three hours, and I'll need some time for an introduction and we'll want to discuss what you've presented, so I'd say you should put together roughly a two to two-and-a-half hour talk. Try to help us understand Levinson's theory, but you should also try to help us engage with it. Get us thinking about where it does or doesn't make sense in our own lives."

The "we" is deliberately ambiguous. I've been trying to encourage Eric to connect the work with what is happening in his own life, but with only limited success. He's extremely skittish about his inner life and has no intention of "pouring his guts out" as he puts it. At least not in public.

"Yeah, I guess I can do some criticism of it too," he says with an amiable but belligerent grin. "That shouldn't be too hard."

The belligerence, I think to myself, hides a good deal of fear about handling this sort of material. Much of what he has studied up until now has been related to engineering and business: courses, he says, that make sense. Now that he's being asked to deal with more fluid content, he's uneasy.

"Just remember," I remind him, "that this is just one of a whole handful of theories that we are looking at. None has 'the truth'; each is sort of like a slice of an orange—what you see depends on how you cut it. You don't have to worry about being 'correct' in the same way you might with calculus. What you need to do is first be clear about what Levinson is saying. Explain that to the class. Then, when you criticize, look at what kind of sample he used, what his assumptions are, and think about whether your own experience fits or not—or better, where it fits and where it doesn't."

Eric nods. He has heard all this before, but it is understandably still hard for him. Just over a year ago, fresh in the program, he and I sat in this very room and discussed his study plan.

"I just want that piece of paper," he had said, spiking me with a smile, at once friendly and dead serious. "I'll level with you. I've been in my current position long enough. I look around at some of the ding-a-lings that run this place and I know damned well I can do better. But they've got that piece of paper and I don't. So just tell me what I've got to do."

Everything about Eric said precision, from his neatly trimmed hair to his perfectly kept looseleaf notebook with every document and form in its place. For a long time after I met Eric, I would feel inordinately bumbling—sure I would trip over my briefcase, spill coffee on his registration form. Arriving five minutes late would find me trembling with guilt, angry at myself for leaving myself open to the judgment of his engineered intellect. And indeed, that was an application to which he freely turned his mind, sharply criticizing a current course at the community college as too "unstructured." "Why don't they get someone to teach that stuff who knows what she's doing?" he complained.

But in the months that followed, we had warmed up considerably with each other. For all of his cross-grained irascibility, I found his candor refreshing. There was something deeper driving that honesty. Eric knew something about himself that didn't square with the man he showed at work. One day, curious about Eric's urgency to get ahead, I asked him about it.

"Look," he said, "I've been spinning my wheels at this job for ten years, and I just don't want to keep spinning any more. I'm good at what I do, damned good." He fixed me with that competent look again and then turned to stare at the wall, as if trying to see through it, outside. "But I want to get doing what I *want* to do."

"What's that?"

"That's the trouble," came the reply, evenly; "I don't

really know. The only place I really feel good is when I'm out in the woods. Or fishing." And for the next half hour, Eric talked about his love for the outdoors, his skill as a bow hunter, his fascination with natural history, and his very considerable knowledge of local fish and game.

"Why don't you study that?" I asked.

"Hell," he shot back, "Nobody pays you to do what you want to do."

"They do me," I said.

"Sure. That's different. You've got all that education. You think I can afford to do that when I don't even have a degree? Besides," he added with a grin, "I couldn't live on what you're making." I laughed—somewhat bitterly—and agreed with him.

"Look," he said with a tinge of desperation, "I'm starting to feel a lot of pressure. Not just in my work but in other areas as well. It's like I've got this biological clock inside me that's just ticking away. And I figure I've wasted all this time in my life, and I don't want to waste the second half of my life. I've lived almost thirty-five years and I figure I'll live to be maybe seventy. Then, boom, that's it."

It was clear that there was a good deal more going on in this engineer's mind than little wheels and a quest for a piece of paper. So over the following weeks, we explored a number of other possible study areas for Eric than simply more engineering. Although a complete shift to environmental studies was one such possibility, we both decided that it would be too drastic. And as it turned out, during this time Eric pressed for, and received, a promotion to a managerial position. As a result, he chose to focus his studies on industrial management.

"More and more now, I'm working with people," he told me. "I need to learn more about what makes people tick." So that was how we ended up here, talking about Daniel Levinson.

"You know, reading this stuff is different from reading a math book," Eric is saying. "You have to pick and choose what's important." I grunt agreement and he goes on. "It's like this organizational behavior tutorial I'm doing with Milt right now. We read a lot of case studies, and at first I kept looking for the right answer, the right way you're supposed to come out on each case. But as soon as I'd say what I thought, Milt would come out with another whole point of view I hadn't thought of. I'm beginning to get the idea that . . ." And as he says this, he grins knowingly at me, "I'm beginning to realize that there's no single right answer. You have to try to put them all together and come up with the best approach."

Predictably, my own grin answers his, and I respond with mock confusion, "But Eric, I thought you didn't like Milt. You said he was nothing but a wishy-washy college professor."

"That's right!" he bursts out. "He was. But now he's changed. Must have been my influence," he adds with conscious irony, and we laugh together. I remember that first study. Both Eric and Dave, whose story appears in the next chapter, needed to study accounting, and I brought them together with Milt, a business instructor, in hopes that a strong bond would form among the three. It did, and although Eric had listened with open skepticism to Dave's praise for the liberal studies and fought Milt's discursive teaching style, it was fascinating to see how he was drawn back to Milt now, how the very same experience he had once thought too filled with "bullshit" and devoid of real content was becoming transformed into an experience he recalled with real respect.

"The thing about Milt," he continues, "is that he really helps you see that there's a lot of different points of view and that you have to try to make up your own mind for yourself about these things. There's no simple right or wrong answer when it comes down to dealing with people. Like, first there's the floor manager, then there's the boss, and then there's the production workers, and the union and all. I mean in their own way, they're all right. Or wrong," he adds, chuckling.

He goes on to talk about Milt and how shaken he has been by Milt's losing grapple with cancer. "He's come to mean an awful lot to me. You know, at first, he didn't even want to take me on. He said he would only do it as a favor to you. But since then we've gotten pretty close. He's shared a lot of things with me about his life that I don't even want to talk about." Eric stops and looks at his notebook, carefully framing it between his hands. "In a way, maybe it's just as well he is dying. Maybe I won't have a chance to see his warts."

We are both silent a long time, avoiding each other's eyes.

"Yeah," I say finally, "he's a rare man. He just won't let his . . . his condition get to him, will he?" Eric, who has been staring at the pale wall again, talks, almost to himself.

"You know, it's funny. This fall, during hunting season— I almost always get my deer the first day—this fall I ran into a deer. It was a big buck, twelve-pointer. He stopped right in front of me. Not ten feet away. And we just looked at each other. Neither of us moved a muscle. We just stood there . . . for a minute, two minutes, I don't know. Finally, he just turned and walked into the bushes. I never even lifted my bow. It's crazy. I don't know what's happening to me. Sometimes I'll put a fish back even though it's big enough to keep."

We're both silent again. Eric stares straight ahead, unmoving. At last I ask, "What's it about?"

He answers, still to the wall, "I dunno. Maybe it's because I don't want to stop something. I dunno," and then turns to me.

"You know, sometimes in your class I feel pretty dumb. When Susan and you get going about Jung and Freud and all those names I don't even know, I feel kind of shallow. Well, maybe so. Maybe I am shallow." He looks directly at me now, but there's no challenge there. Simple declaration. "But I've got deep trenches."

I smile, moved by his honesty and eloquence. We both take a deep breath and straighten our chairs. "We'd better finish up," he says, glancing at his digital watch; "I've got to get back."

We discuss his presentation for a few minutes more and then pick up to leave. He opens the door for me as I go out, and I remark that I hope I won't get a ticket for parking in an executive parking space. "I hope it wasn't yours," I say, "now that you're a fat cat."

"Hell, you'd never catch me parking in one of those places," he replies, the familiar grin back.

"Oh? Why not?"

"You wouldn't believe this place," he snorts. "It's like a bunch of goddamn baboons. They all scrap for the parking place closest to the boss. A regular pecking order. Same thing in meetings. Number three man has to sit next to number two man; number two man has to sit next to number one man. It's a crock." Then he sticks out his hand, grinning broadly. "Thanks." I return the handshake, but drive off feeling vaguely empty. In another place, another time, I'd have hugged him just then.

Clearly, Eric was "growing," although at the time I was not sure how. Not surprisingly, the more I have learned of developmental theory, the more complicated the picture has become, and with every new developmental scheme has followed a period of seeing through the eyes of this researcher or that theorist. To a considerable extent, as I write now, I continue to see different people through different lenses depending on which perspective seems to illuminate the most. But over time, I am beginning to see some common threads, to develop a clearer vision of what it is that happens when adults return to pick up an educational journey abandoned long before. Grasping developmental theory is more akin, I have discovered, to learning a language than it is to acquiring a new body of knowledge. More than the particular vocabulary, it's the syntax that matters; it's a way of seeing beneath the surface to the structures of growth. This is why the journey seems to work so readily as a metaphor for development. It gives us a model for grasping underlying structure in motion, of understanding in a deep way the meaning of metamorphosis as *the evolution of form.*

There is a tendency on first encountering developmental theory to think of stages as though they were a sequence of Procrustean operating tables onto which researchers clamp their subjects, lopping limbs with ghoulish abandon. (And I must admit, to overhear a conversation among serious developmentalists as they haggle over an interview transcript can be a bit disconcerting to the naive humanist: "This is clearly a 4MC; no 2 ever talked like that!" "You mean a Perry 4 or a Clinchy/Goldberger 3B?" "Either one. She has that flat Loevinger 3ishness all through.") But while research demands such precision, and some writing does seem to emphasize the tables more than the people, for teachers this is not only unhelpful and inappropriate, it is an inhumane way to think about the movement of our lives. It is the people, not the stages, the moving picture, not the snapshots, that should command our attention. This is particularly important in education because few teachers or mentors ever see a student through an entire journey. Rather, we accompany students along some legs of some of their journeys, and if we are to play our part well, we need to view their movement with a broader eye, to see whence they have come and whither they are headed. We'll need two or three good maps.

In the next chapter, we will eavesdrop on three more conversations. Each will illuminate a different facet of the growing adult. And each will provide an opportunity to view "growth" through a different lens. At the end of the chapter, we will return to Eric and look at him again through all three lenses at once.

Chapter Three ❧

Three Useful Maps
of How Adults Change
and Develop

> In order to understand anything well, you need at
> least three good theories.   *—William Perry*

It has never been any secret that we change as we age. The
only question is how. Cultures vary greatly in their answers to
that question, ranging from those traditional societies in which
age is synonymous with wisdom to our own high-tech belief
that to age is to become less valuable. (When was the last time
we had an American president we would characterize primarily
as wise?) It is an appropriate paradox, then, that ours should
be the culture that has generated the most careful analysis of
that question: What happens as we age? Perhaps precisely because of today's cacophonous change, we seek reassurance that
our lives do not, in fact, run downhill from the beginning like
some maverick alarm clock. We need to know that life is more
than our mechanistic metaphors would suggest.

Ed must have been wondering that, too, as I approached
his door that frozen December afternoon carrying my papers
and questions. Was his life simply winding down—or, for that
matter, was mine? Was his return to education just a desperate
attempt to forestall the inevitable, or might it promise a genuine
rebirth? And what did that mean, exactly, "rebirth"?

In this chapter, the reader is invited to join conversations
with three different people: Dave, a man struggling at midlife
with questions about what is important in his life; Sandy, at

43

thirty-three feeling the stirrings of a ripening independence; and Monique, a young woman caught in a conceptual world too narrow for her new aspirations. We will examine each conversation through the eyes of a different developmental theorist. Then we will re-view Eric, whose story appeared in the preceding chapter, through all three lenses. While the differences among the theories are important, all provide useful and overlapping perspectives. And all attempt to counter the implicit metaphor of the unwinding clock, which pervades so much of our conversation about aging. Instead, they suggest more profound and mythic metaphors: the seasons, an upward-spiraling helix, a journey.

Developmental perspectives of this sort can help to improve the quality of education in a number of ways. For administrators, knowledge of the real-life dilemmas faced by students like Dave can provide valuable arguments for enhanced use of the liberal studies to help adult students confront the existential questions of their lives and consequently enrich the depth of their learning (Gamson, 1984). Knowledge of the particular life issues of different age groups can sharpen marketing techniques (Aslanian and Brickell, 1980). Perhaps most important, these developmental theories raise into clear view the question "What is education for?" thus offering an alternative to the self-centered and frequently directionless relativism that has recently become such a bête noire among contemporary critics.

Meanwhile, in the classroom, as teachers come to recognize the motion of a person like Monique, they can supplant their understandable but probably inappropriate frustration with a more compassionte understanding of the range of ways in which their students make meaning, and devise methods to help their students see new choices. They can begin to design activities, exercises, and assignments that will challenge their students differentially, in accord with developmental needs. They will discover the educational power of controversial perspectives seriously debated, of placing theoretical constructs in a historical or cultural context, of flicking just the right question to just the right student at just the right time.

Finally, a ready set of developmental concepts can help counselors or professors, in their role as advisers, to hear the unique movement of each of their advisees and work accordingly. They might, for instance, encourage older students needing to confirm a lifetime of experience to undertake projects with younger people, exchanging their accumulated wisdom for insights through the eyes of a younger generation; midlife women might discover themselves anew through women's literature; young adults seeking identity might study family history or read biographical material. As we learn to see people in the context of their potential for growth, the possibilities for enriching their educational experience expand rapidly. As learners come to incorporate more complex and diverse information into their intellectual vision, they tend to seek more of the same. When the process is occurring smoothly, it seems to progress almost by itself. That, indeed, was what Dewey had in mind when he suggested that educational value ought to be measured by "the extent in which it creates a desire for continued growth" (1916, p. 62).

A concern about the meaning and experience of growth was hardly new to me, of course, when I read Dewey. In a sense, it had been with me all my life—at least since that day when I lay on my back as a child and watched a tiny cloud far above me dissolve with infinite grace into the blue, and felt a terrible sadness. It was important to me to know that we *grow* as we age—not just bigger but better too, in some way *better*. Later, as a high school teacher, I saw it happen with my own students, and then with participants in encounter groups and teacher training workshops, and finally with my own children. I knew people could make important changes, and I called these growth, but still I lacked a way to understand what I was seeing. It was clear that people were moving, but from where, to where? I needed a map.

Asked to imagine a map of America, most of us conjure up a vision of a multicolored United States—pink Massachusetts, yellow Texas, green Florida. But as every cartographer knows, a political map is only one of dozens of possible maps. A geographic map might ignore state lines entirely, emphasizing mountain ranges, rivers, and lakes; a historical map might draw boundaries in sharply different places than our more familiar

contemporary one; and a demographic or weather map would
look different in still other ways. What goes on a map clearly
depends on what interests the cartographer; and the map we
choose depends on what we wish to know.

The same goes for theories of human development. Although developmentalists, like cartographers, may assert at
times that their maps are value free or strictly descriptive, they
have made choices in constructing their schemes to highlight
some elements and to ignore others. Those choices inevitably
affect the traveler who is using the map. In preferring paths to
over another, travelers do not simply trace differing paths to
reach their destinations; they may often be led to a new destination. Thus, when Carol Gilligan (1982) offered women an
alternative map to the prevailing ones, suggesting that optimal
development need not mean ever-increasing separateness, she
caused many women—and men as well—to reconsider the importance of striving toward a stance of detachment and abstract
principle and to value instead those parts of themselves calling
for connectedness and relationship. The very existence of a map
stirs the traveler in our bones, and the places on that map color
our dreams.

Yet good maps also offer choice; they are not mere for-
mulas. And while developmental theories do imply direction,
none insists that the journey can be taken in only one way or,
indeed, that it be completed at all. Just as a map frames the setting for a journey, so does a developmental theory offer a context for growth. It indicates landmarks, points out dangers, suggests possible routes and destinations, but leaves the walking
to us.

One of the best-known maps is the one offered by Daniel
Levinson and his associates in *The Seasons of a Man's Life*. I
have chosen it here partly because it was Levinson who saw
most clearly how mentors help us through crucial times in our
lives, partly because the study sheds penetrating light on what is
going on in the lives of many men as they return to higher education, and partly because it is simply a well-written and insight-
ful book.

As a member of that family of developmental studies that

have come to be known as psychosocial or phase theories, the work is mainly concerned with the question "What happens to people psychologically as they grow older?" It is closely related to the earlier thinking of Carl Jung and Charlotte Buhler as well as contemporary research of people like Bernice Neugarten, Robert Havighurst, and Roger Gould. What unites this family is that each of these writers sought to understand common tasks that people confront as they face the problems associated with aging. The theories are thus chronologically and culturally determined to a significant extent. By the same token, few of Levinson's colleagues have locked life changes as tightly into specific ages as he has. Most have found considerably more room for variation according to gender, age cohort, life task, or ethnic and economic status (Knox, 1977).

A second map, offered in Robert Kegan's *The Evolving Self,* represents another major branch of developmental theory, often called stage theory. Jean Piaget is generally accorded fatherhood of this family through his contribution of the idea that we pass through distinct and qualitatively different stages in the ways we construct our childhood experience. This notion gained greater sophistication as applied to adults in the work of Jane Loevinger, Lawrence Kohlberg, and Carol Gilligan. each of whom suggested that as we develop, we move first from a "preconventional" stance, in which our own personal survival is paramount, into a "conventional" orientation, in which our main concern is to fit into and be accepted by society, and later (if our development continues) into a "postconventional" position, in which we derive our decisions from broader considerations than personal survival or a wish to conform.

What is exciting about this family of theory is that it asserts that growth involves more than becoming a well-adjusted member of society (moving from the first to the second level). It also means coming to see one's own culture from a critical stance and establishing loyalties that go beyond one's immediate community (moving from the second to the third level). In many ways, Kegan's book provides the most carefully honed elaboration of stage theory to date.

Most stage theorists focus their attention on a kind of growth that does not inevitably come with age. They are less concerned with the process of becoming older than they are with the question of growing wiser. That is, Piaget noticed that some children seem to be able to comprehend the world in more adequate ways than others, and he saw that the difference has less to do with static "intelligence" than with dynamic "development." The stage theorists extend this observation throughout the life span. Some adults seem to "understand" a complex world in a more complex way than others. Rather than see intelligence as a fixed condition, developmentalists suggest that we all have the potential to evolve toward increasingly integrated and differentiated ways of making sense of the world. Thus, while two forty-two-year-old men may share common tasks in relation to their culture, they may interpret that experience in sharply different ways, depending on the framework of the particular stage they are moving through. Because later stages are by definition more conceptually inclusive and discriminating, are "better" in some sense than earlier ones, this family brings with it both exciting prospects and considerable dangers.

Drawing on some twenty years of close listening to Harvard students talk about what they were learning during their four college years, William Perry sketched a third map, one he calls a "scheme of intellectual and ethical development." In many ways it is the most useful and engaging of the three. Its value is that Perry describes just the sorts of changes that liberal educators hope to see come about in their students, and he does so in a way that intuitively makes sense to anyone who has struggled to understand why some people seem so determined to see a shifting and multicolored world as though it were a black and white snapshot. As such, it offers us a beautifully articulated slow-motion film of the journey from naive and simplistic thinking to complex and relativistic reasoning. While such movement need not necessarily happen as a result of formal education, it seems evident that a good education increases the likelihood that it will happen and thereby fosters growth in a number of ways.

It is time now to look more closely at how the theories can help us to see and hear our students more clearly. Each of the following conversations highlights a particular question: What is important? Who am I? and What is right? But I hope it will be clear by the time we return to Eric that no single vantage point or theory can reveal the extraordinary richness of the human territory. Rather, it is from the interplay of many perspectives that the teacher can best know how to be for whom and when.

We begin with Dave, at forty-three struggling to understand why his priorities have begun to shift under his feet. In listening, consider how the liberal studies courses he took mesh with the turmoil of his midlife transition. Notice how he describes the direction of change in how he sees himself and thinks about what is "true." And take note of how these changes affect those around him.

Through the Hourglass

He looks tired. I nudge the tape recorder closer to his bowed head, hoping to be unobtrusive. It's unlike Dave to mumble, and I find myself straining to catch his words. He still speaks in that same somewhat inflated yet disarming style, and the passion is still there, but it is subdued in a way that astonishes me. He speaks to the floor, to himself.

> . . . a very, very dramatic change that I witness inside myself. No longer am I boisterous—you know, take an initial, active part. Not interested in that at all. Very quiet mannerisms as compared to very loud, robust type. I have an extremely hard time making decisions that I never had before, even though there used to be a lot of wrong ones. Now I don't make any if I don't have to. I wait as long as possible and think about it. That's what stands out for me.

We are sitting in the community college office where I

had asked him to come for an informal, follow-up interview. Dave and I have known each other since we met eight years ago. He stood out then, a tall, handsome man in his mid thirties, radiating confidence, a gunslinger of the construction industry. Owner of a highly successful small business, he had fathered three sons, was Little League coach, and a respected member of the church community. He had gone about as far as he could, learning on his own, and wanted to "get more formal-type learning." With the kids mostly out of the way now, he could. On the basis of an unusually high award of experiential credit, Dave entered the external degree program and became my student. At almost exactly the same time, to the consternation of his wife and friends, he sold his business and began work for a large industrial firm. He felt a need, he said, to "try something with more of a challenge."

Not long afterward, he was selected to participate in a study of adult development and gave us two intensive interviews a year apart. In the first interview, he spoke of returning to education as a way of "filling voids" in himself. When he had attained the knowledge he sought, he told us, he would achieve his goal: "peace of mind."

A year later, though still undaunted in his quest, Dave had begun to entertain doubts. For the first time, he spoke of an "internal" self that seemed to be asking unsolicited questions: Why change careers? Why go back to school? Why am I feeling these feelings?

> Internally I've been in combustion. I've been, I've got an internal upheaval, OK? Crazy thoughts, a lot of questions to be answered. Outwardly, I've been very, very energetic, trying something different. . . . I've always been in control of my external self. I thought about what I was going to say; my appearance was always right for the situation; I made sure the proper tools were always at hand . . . and suddenly, uncontrollably, the internal Dave Hyssop began to take ahold of his life. And all of a sudden the tools of the external weren't

important; they didn't do the job, they didn't bring me any of that peace of mind I've mentioned so many times. It was the internal that had control of me.... It kept reaching out and taking ahold of my life and shaking the hell out of me, OK? and saying, "No, you don't need this business, you don't need these tools, you don't need this appearance anymore. That's not what life is about."

I ask him about that now. How does he see his movement over the years since that conversation? How might he describe it? He looks at me sideways, wry grin baring a straight row of teeth, his eyes show our brotherhood. We both know the territory.

"I'd still sketch it with my old hourglass theory," he says, squinting out now through the dusty window of the old office building to the brick facade of a tenement hotel across the street. "You know, there's a coming into life so easily in the big bottom bubble.... I remember in my thirties being very self-satisfied with where I was going, and tremendous energy, confidence in myself and feeling of success...."

His voice trails off; there's a long silence for both of us. Finally, I ask, "When did it start? I mean when did you enter the neck of the hourglass?" More silence. Slowly, he turns to me, then back to the window.

"The hourglass? Oh, I guess, I'd say . . . I've been in there maybe five years."

"So you were about thirty-eight?"

"Thirty-eight. Yeah. And getting into the neck, I suddenly realized for the first time what an individual I was. I didn't need a lot of things that I depended on before. I began to question a lot of things that I was always taught to believe in or that always seemed to be right. I remember for a long time in there, just questioning everything."

We talk then for some time about what it's like "in there," for me as well as for him. He speaks of the struggle within himself between an "old self" that always seemed to be in control, and a "new Dave" who seems to be more passive. Yet while his former self was more decisive, it was also less genuine, obsessed with "tangible things" at the cost of the "general concern for humanity" growing in importance now. "I was a bastard!" he says of himself. "A real bastard." And I begin to realize that when Dave calls himself passive he simply means that he no longer feels such a need to control his outside circumstances. He is drawing back, making way for the emergence of a more "internal" self, a self he calls more real.

"Did your education have anything to do with all this?" I ask, not sure I want to hear the answer. He looks at me, a twinkle in his eye, jaw set.

"Well, I'm very disillusioned about it right now. I was extremely disappointed in what I thought my education would do for me in terms of where I was in life when I began, some of my objectives, I mean. It's not going to do much for me in terms of employment or money, and [long pause] I'm not even sure I like myself anymore."

Somehow I had expected this, perhaps because I've heard it enough before, and yet I hear a "but" coming. I nod and keep my mouth shut. After another long pause, it comes.

"The one thing it did for me is make me realize how little I know, how little learning I did have, and how much there is to learn and understand. You know, I read a lot more than I ever did before—all kinds of things interest me. I'm an entirely new person now, and I'm having trouble living with myself. Other people too—my wife and my kids." He smiles to himself. "The other day she said she wished I'd never gone to college."

"What did she mean by that?" I ask.

"Well, I'm not the strong man in the family anymore. She wanted me to tell Ted, our youngest, to mow the lawn, and when I asked him, he said he wanted to work on the basketball court first. So I said, 'Fine, but the lawn's got to be mowed.' I got home that night and the lawn was mowed—no big deal. Now my other kids, I'd beat their ass if it wasn't mowed right then and there. I was a bastard, I tell you. My wife got used to living with that."

We talk on about how much strain there is on our relationships when we are going through changes ourselves, how hard it is on marriages, on friendships. And he speaks of his own changes as a journey. I ask him what he feels he is moving toward.

"I'm beginning to see the whole world as being relative," he replies. "It's like, like . . . " searching for the words, "time means nothing to me anymore. Like Einstein, you know; it's only a measurement of space. It's got nothing to do with beginnings or endings." He falls silent a moment, then grins and shakes his head. "Man, you can go any way you want. You know, all of us, we get thinking about our thinking and we immediately start to judge our thinking—why we're thinking that way or if it's all right to think that way. And, you know, you suddenly realize that in your mind you can think about anything you want to think about. You're a self-entity, irregardless of what you were before or what you're going to be tomorrow."

"Sounds like you've been traveling."

"Oh yeah," he says, grinning broadly at me now, the old Dave back. "I've traveled a long, long ways. You know, my education was like a catalyst when I think about it. I always enjoyed that word: *catalyst*. I always thought it was fantastic ever since I took a science course in junior high—a catalyst, you know? Something that starts something, helps something burn brighter, or you know, gives something more energy. Yeah, that's what I think my education was, a catalyst."

"Can you describe that a little more?" I ask. "A catalyst?"

"I think it brought to the surface things that were probably always inside me," he replies, sending a chill down educational spines at least as far back as Plato. "Maybe I lived a kind of phony life before; you know, it wasn't the real me. My education, how I studied, working with other adult learners, that was a catalyst. You know, look in the mirror and be truthful with myself. At least I'm being truthful with myself because that's the real me. My education brought out those things; it provided me with the confidence and the freedom to see things as they are, truthful about everything, not hide and act other than the way it actually is."

The power of Dave's words leaves me drained. It's almost as though we have changed places—he now the active one, I sitting passive, in awe before the new Dave. We talk on a bit, and Dave speaks of his need to make new connections with the world. His frustration now is that he has left the old world behind but is having trouble finding a place in the new one. "You know," he says as we stand up, "no man is an island. And I'm an island. I guess it's time to make some connections."

Watching his lanky form disappear down the hallway, it strikes me that the irony is that he has not so much lost connections as redefined them. He still has his friends, his family. And they might well be the same as they have always been. But the image he holds of them no longer fills his inner spaces the way it used to. The spaces themselves have grown and he's feeling the gaps.

Dave's hourglass is a fitting metaphor for the midlife transition described in *The Seasons of a Man's Life* (1978). Levinson and his associates divide men's lives into four major eras. Like a stairway, they ascend through time, the risers representing periods of consolidation with relatively little change, the steps indicating disruption and what he calls structure changing (see the chart on the following page). As he sketches it, our lives move rhythmically back and forth through periods of building, breaking, building, breaking, and building again as we grow older and accommodate to the changing circumstances of our lives. (See Figure 1.)

Levinson pays particular attention to the middle two eras of the life span, the years from about seventeen to sixty. The defining task of the late teens and early twenties is to move into the adult world and become accepted on its terms. For men in our culture, this means getting a job, establishing a household, and developing a sense of competence. During the twenties, says Levinson, men devote their energy to exploration and tentative commitment. Many of those he studied began to form a "dream" of how and who they wanted to become—a kind of projected script for their lives. Often they would find a mentor who em-

Figure 1. Levinson's Developmental Periods.

```
                                           (Late Adulthood)
                    65

                        LATE ADULT TRANSITION
                    60
                        Culmination of
                        Middle Adulthood
                    55
                        Age 50 Transition          Middle
                                                   Adulthood
                    50  Entering
                        Middle Adulthood


            45
                        MID-LIFE TRANSITION
            40
                Settling Down
            33
                Age 30 Transition
            28                              Early Adulthood
                Entering the Adult World

2
    EARLY ADULT TRANSITION

7   (Childhood and Adolescence)
```

Source: Levinson and others, 1978, p. 20.

bodied that dream and who could help them move toward it. Mentors, in Levinson's ground-breaking research, are closely linked with the dream. They are living proof that it can be attained, and they usually help their protégés toward it. Appearing most frequently during one's twenties and thirties, mentors tend to be a half-generation older and remain in the role from three to ten years. Because much developmental research has looked at men and women in the workplace, it is perhaps not surprising that mentors are more commonly associated with the working world, with the building of competence and career rather than with development of the awareness and emotional maturity more appropriate to caring for oneself and others. Levinson's study of the lives of women will be published shortly, but whether it will deal with the meaning of mentorship for the whole lives of women remains to be seen.

The BUILDING period of the twenties ends with the midcourse correction that Gail Sheehy called "Catch 30." It is a time when we ask, "Is this really what I want?" and may be surprised to discover that when we thought we were asking the same question years before, we had actually asked, "What *should* I be doing?" In effect, we grow more serious about our lives, hearing an inner voice that urges us to make our commitments, "for soon it will be too late to turn back." Depending on the answer, this BREAKING period may be relatively mild or tumultuous, but typically it involves the act of self-assessment: "Is this what I want?"

This transitional time bridges our thirtieth birthday and comes to an end with the beginning of the settling-down time, around age thirty-three. Now we begin to act on the commitments we have come to, spending the next five or six years BUILDING again—establishing a business, settling into a job, raising a family.

Then, beginning in the late thirties and extending into the early forties, comes the notorious midlife transition. It represents the elbow joint of our lives, squarely in the middle, separating spring and summer from fall and winter. For many men the most dramatic transition, it prompts us to reappraise our life, not simply against our dream as we did years before but against our whole life span, cast with growing sharpness against the backdrop of our death. The neglected parts of ourselves call out more loudly to be heard, and for many, a longing for wholeness begins to replace the ideal of perfection. It is during this time, says Levinson, that we address more fully the polarities that lie within us like scales seeking their balance.

What tends to throw us off balance is our impulse to hold

onto one end of those scales. By midlife, their imbalance can be such that only a major jolt can right them again. Such a jolt has the twin possibilities of either deadening our systems entirely, sending us down the remainder of our lives in slow despair, or refreshing us and pointing the way toward something like wisdom. Writing about this possibility, Carl Jung termed it *individuation,* the process by which we differentiate (yet again) our selves from our surrounding culture in a way that leads not to isolation but paradoxically to a greater sense of membership in the whole. Levinson "operationalizes" the term by suggesting that individuation happens as we redress imbalances along four polarities. Although he discusses these in detail in the context of the midlife transition, he makes it plain that the stuff of each polarity is always with us, and each transition requires tinkering with our little imbalances. To the extent that we maintain a reasonable equilibrium through early transitions, our midlife crisis will remain relatively placid. The more fully we can throw ourselves into the tumult of one crisis, the more fully we will grow in our ability to cope effectively with the next. It is essentially like collecting parking tickets—regular glove compartment cleaning keeps the Big Fine down.

The tension between being at once both *young* and *old* is the first and most apparent polarity. To address it, we must first acknowledge that we have changed since we last looked. Since the change is inevitable and since at all ages we contain within ourselves some aspects of both youth and age, the important question is "In what ways am I older and in what ways young?" To retune the balance each time, we need to draw out those parts we call young and old and label them afresh. "The task in every transition," Levinson reminds us, "is to create a new Young/Old integration appropriate to that time of life" (1978, p. 212). A similar process of introspection and redefinition is at work with the other polarities: Creation/Destruction, in which we come to acknowledge our capacity for evil, Masculine/Feminine, in which we question a sexuality formed by earlier needs, and Attachment/Separation, in which we reassess the boundary between ourselves and others.

Different cultures tend to value one end of each polarity

more than another. In American society, for instance, youth, masculinity, creativity, and separateness are almost universally more weighted than their counterparts. To right the balance, to "develop" in Levinson's terms, then, implies that we must swim upstream against our culture. We need support for such action, and in this respect it is interesting to note that mentor figures are frequently androgynous (Mentor), ageless (numerous Eastern bodhisattvas), or both helpful and destructive (Merlin). They have transcended polarities and become transcultural figures, people who have moved beyond the "normal" limits into a barely comprehensible world that calls to us and into which they are uniquely empowered to lead us.

By the mid forties, Levinson writes, we have begun to move out of our midlife wilderness and we begin BUILDING a new "life structure" for the second half of our lives. It is time for the realignments that took place during the last transition to settle in and give more lasting meaning to our relationships, work, and spiritual commitments. There was great variability among the men studied at this period. Some, consolidating the gains of a lifetime, entered more deeply and richly into their lives than ever before; others seemed simply to be marking time until retirement; and still others seemed to find it a time of great pain, of "constriction and decline."

Although Levinson delineates several further phases, the work loses much of its power after this period, in part because the research grows thinner but primarily because the authors have outreached their own experience and simply lost their passion. In any event, those portions of the life span that they illuminate most thoroughly stand out with great vividness and provide guides and pilgrims alike with a valuable map.

There is, however, one important caveat. Levinson studied men. I find his work strikingly useful for understanding major aspects of my own and my male students' development, but its value for women is less clear. For one thing, women's life paths are different (Baruch and others, 1983). Our culture's expectation that they will take time out as mothers wreaks havoc with the neat, linear male trajectory. How a woman decides to juggle her "family responsibilities" has major ramifications for when she returns to school (Bernard, 1981; Evans, 1985). For another thing, recent (and long overdue) research is increasingly demonstrating that women define themselves in relation to others differently than men do, placing more emphasis on connectedness, less on separateness (Choderow, 1978; Dinnerstein, 1976; Gilligan, 1982; Baker-Miller, 1976; Rubin, 1983; Klein, 1985). This fundamental difference holds major implications for education, implications that are only now being spelled out in a call for a "connected education" to counteract what some consider an undue emphasis on detachment as a prerequisite to "rational thought" (Belenky, Clinchy, Goldberger, and Tarule, 1986).

But Dave too seems to be feeling the effects of too much separation. Let's return to him and consider what we see through Levinson's overlay. It should be apparent that Dave was squarely in the midst of a rousing midlife transition. The hourglass metaphor was a unique and effective way to make sense of what he was feeling as he moved from the confidence, self-satisfaction, and tremendous energy of his early thirties into the neck of the hourglass, a time he traces to his late thirties when he sold his business and returned to school. Though he physically remained at home, in a metaphorical sense, he had left. His friendships fell away; he spent more time with studies and work, less with his family and community. In a real sense, he found himself wandering alone in a wilderness of questions, dancing, as he put it, in a twilight zone.

It was during this time that the sea change he describes as a shift from active to passive occurred. Although there are hints in his description of Levinson's male-female shift, the change seems more profound than this, more encompassing. Dave links the changes in a number of aspects of his life: from interest in tangible to intangible things, from material to humanitarian considerations, from external to internal concerns, and from being in control to being out of it. He describes an "old self" who was a "bastard" and a "new Dave" whom he's not sure he likes but who is at least much more "real," no longer obsessed with appearances. And although he acknowledges that he is not as satisfied as he once was, he is more content now than he has ever been. A superficial happiness is no longer the goal of his life. Dave is clearly hearing new voices in himself and is listening with rapt, if sometimes uneasy, attention.

Transformations rarely, if ever, come about abruptly. Rather, they slip into place piece by piece until they become suddenly visible, often to others first, only later to ourselves. Yet it is possible sometimes to see key moments that seem central to the change. In Dave's case, the discovery that "in your mind you can think about anything you want to think about" is such a moment. Able now to think about thinking (a capacity Piaget considered of critical importance for the higher stages of intellectual development), Dave realizes perhaps for the first time, that *what he thinks can be separate from who he is*—that he can *have* his ideas rather than simply *being* them. This new capacity is both liberating and frightening, for while he is free to have his own thoughts, he can no longer hide behind the old beliefs. All at once, the givens of his life—patriotism, the work ethic, his boyhood religion—come up for scrutiny. With confirmation that "the whole world is relative" comes a new kind of responsibility. Dave's reluctance to act impulsively, or even decisively, is grounded in this discovery.

What is the place of education in all of this? After all, with or without his further education, Dave would have confronted his midlife transition. What difference does a theory like Levinson's make in how we work with adult learners? At times, the connections between Dave's transition and his education appear so organic that it is senseless to try to tease them apart. Yet it seems clear that his educational experience changed the quality of his transition in significant ways. A course in anthropology helped him to gain distance on his own values, to see his own conditioning in a fresh way; a psychology course encouraged his capacity for self-examination; an esthetics course put him in touch with universals in human experience; conversations with his mentor helped him to name what was happening and gave him permission to do it. However familiar, his own term *catalyst* has a fresh power as he uses it to describe what his education was for him: something that starts something, helps it burn brighter, gives it more energy. So while the inevitable midlife transition brought on the questions, his education gave them a broader context, legitimized them, and allowed him to draw on far wider experience for answers.

"I learned it was OK to ask those questions," he told me later. "Everyone else was going through those changes too. It was those liberal studies that really pulled me through, no doubt about it. Funny. When you told me I ought to take so many of them, I can remember thinking, 'Now what the hell do I need those for?' I guess you must have known something, eh?"

Did I? There certainly was no formula. Dave's particular track was utterly his own. Yet because his life had led him to ask fundamental questions of meaning, studies that welcomed such questions without answering them would clearly hold promise. But how to connect the student with the study? For as Dave's remark implies, this is often a good deal clearer to teachers than students. The teacher's art lies in helping to bring those questions to the surface: in giving them legitimacy and the student permission to go about answering them.

A quite different set of questions confronts Sandy, at thirty-three working hard to replace her old roles as daughter, mother, and wife with a new relationship to her family—one that includes herself as an independent person. As she talks, listen to her description of where she is coming from and where she is headed. Note the function of her studies in that movement. And try to see how she is redefining the boundary between herself and others.

Joining the World

Although it is only three in the afternoon, what little light the day has to offer is fading fast as I shut off the engine, hoping it will start again in the subzero cold. I step over a frozen snowbank and stiffen against the sound of branches crackling overhead. To my relief, Sandy opens the door quickly and gestures to the kitchen table where I sit, a bit too far for comfort from the compact woodstove against the far wall.

"That's where I do most of my work," she says, smiling toward the table with gentle irony. "Coffee?"

We make small talk for several minutes, and then feeling the press of the growing darkness outside, I remind her that I have stopped by to listen to her talk about what it is like for her, at the age of thirty-three, to be back in school studying again after twelve years. She explains that she had spent much of that time after acting school trying to find work, to prove to herself that she could be a successful actress. She had also married and borne a child. At her husband's urging, she began to think about resuming her education. Staying at home seemed stifling to her; she felt an intense desire to "participate in the world." The program in which she had recently enrolled seemed right. She liked its flexible structure, liked being treated as a unique human being, felt that "it was time," she says, laughing somewhat self-consciously, "to prove to myself that I wasn't dumb."

"Has it worked?" I ask, drawn to her laughter.

"Well" she pauses, catching a breath, hearing it as a serious question, "yes, I think so. I mean I'm finding out that I have my own thinking process and I have my own way of learning and that I have my own way of understanding myself and learning how to deal with things in life. I'm finding what that is now. I think that I had previously . . . I hadn't developed that side of myself at all. I feel like that the way I guided myself through life was to go back to my family and say, 'Tell me what to do. Am I OK?' you know, rather than seeing, looking, understanding how *I* operate and finding out how *I want* to think and *I want* to deal with myself and how *I want* to treat other people from my own perspective and my own point of view."

I'm struck, as I listen, by the contrast in her voice, dark and somehow burdened as she speaks of that earlier self who turned so often to her family and to others for guidance, hardening to a kind of driven urgency as she tells of her new self, underlining *want*, nailing it home, setting each word of "my own point of view" up on end for display.

"And I feel like that it's just happening. I'm starting to see who I want to be, and it's really, it's getting away from my family and getting away from all that security. I was really cowering late in my twenties and realizing I had to find a way out or I was going to get smothered by it." Her voice drops, and she looks down at her hands, laughing softly, wryly. "And I don't know if I'd like that."

"Away from all that security?" I ask, curious about the tension in her words.

"Well," she replies, "my last study was about family systems, and I know my family has a definite system of how it operates to keep its members secure. There's a loyalty in families that gets so ingrown and so protective that its members all stop growing. And I've had to find out what my philosophy is and how I want to live as a separate person. It's all in letting myself think and feeling secure enough to think."

She goes on to describe her experience with feminism, her struggle to understand it not simply as a woman's issue but as a source of power for both women and men. It has changed her relationship not only with her husband but also with her family, separating her from them in still another way.

The language of movement suffuses her speech. At one point, I ask her whether some of the changes she describes have been easy for her.

"No, but it's been forward moving; it's been exciting; it's been ... more and more I feel that I'm being pulled with a current. I'm connected now with where I'm going, and I wasn't before."

"Where's the current going?" I ask.

"Well, I guess that what I *want* is to feel that I am ... to know that I am independent. And that I am responsible for myself emotionally and intellectually, and that I stand alone." She is choosing her words carefully now and rounds off that word "alone" like a sculptor her clay. "That I can support myself, support myself and my kids if I have to, that I'm not at the mercy of greater forces, that I've got some control, and that I've got a vehicle to express myself—you know, to participate in the world rather than isolating myself and putting it down. That's what I want: I want to be a *legitimate member of the world.*"

She laughs at this, disarming the considerable power of her speech, but I can feel the chill on the back of my neck. Perhaps she senses it too, and we both fall silent for a moment. On cue, the phone rings, and I take a deep breath.

The conversation goes on for some time after that, illuminating corners like a flashlight in the attic. Sandy's sense of motion is striking, the more so as she chooses to describe her adviser as a guide, moving ahead under some mysterious force, leading the way on a voyage she cannot take alone. Her use of the journey metaphor is quite explicit. She sees herself moving toward a clearer sense of independence, a self defined more by her own actions than others' expectations, away from a security that no longer protects so much as constrains. Far off, too dim to make out, there might be an edge to the horizon of independence and self-rule—a kind of reblurring of distinctions, a new sort of legitimate dependence. But it is dark off there, and she can't be sure. For now the struggle is to feel responsible for the shape her life has taken, for what she does in her life, for her-*self*. Never again will she allow someone else to do that for her.

How best to understand this drive toward independence so powerfully described by Sandy? It is a movement familiar enough to those of us in traditional higher education, accustomed to watching our late-adolescent students using the new-found world of college to bridge away from their families into the world of full adulthood. But are we then to understand Sandy as somehow "retarded"? Simply because she followed a different schedule from her more conventional sisters seems scarcely reason to think of her as an aberration. Isn't there some better way to characterize Sandy's movement than "out of step"? Besides, what does it mean to be a "full adult"? Are we to believe that all adults think and function as autonomously as Sandy? Ten-year-olds value independence too; is this the same thing? While Levinson's work and the findings of those who have studied women's lives in a similar, age-linked fashion will tell us much, these psychosocial theories seem to stay on the outside, to cast light mainly on the boundary of the person and his or her culture. To see more deeply inside, we need to turn to the stage theorists.

Although the stage theorists share the recognition that development continues throughout the life span and does so in a series of plateaus rather than a smooth progression, they differ from the phase theorists in their assertion that each successive stage represents a qualitative *advance* over a previous one. As we grow older, they would suggest, we may or may not grow wiser. Their "stages" are an effort to describe what happens if we do.

"Wiser" is clearly a loaded word. I know of no leading stage theorist except Erikson who uses it formally. Most are much more careful, following the lead of the biologists and general systems theorists who have inspired much of their thinking, speaking of "development" as a sequential series of adaptations to the interaction between the organism and its environment. For "wisdom" they might substitute something like "increased differentiation and integration of the cognitive structures." In effect, we "grow" through engaging with the world, changing and being changed by it. We become ever more discriminating in our ability to see the world on its own terms, or as others see it, and ever more able to make sense of it despite its growing complexity—able to make sense of it in ways that both retain our own sense of meaning and yet respect its diversity.

One of the clearest thinkers in this field is Robert Kegan, like many developmentalists, a former literature scholar turned psychologist. In *The Evolving Self* (1982), he describes with charm and eloquence his vision of the meaning of growth. Although clearly derived from the work of Kohlberg and Piaget, Kegan's model avoids the sometimes boxy quality of the earlier theories, substituting for the ladder metaphor an upward-spiraling helix. Beginning stages (Kegan prefers to call them balances, a term that better catches the dynamic nature of development) are characterized by impulsiveness and self-centeredness; these yield to a more "other-centered" stance, in which interpersonal relationships and mutuality are paramount; this in turn gives way to the birth of a new and more separate self, from which finally evolves an "interindividual balance" in which the tension between "self" and "other" reaches a new synthesis. From this position one is able both to maintain a clear sense of self and yet to merge with others, dissolving and reforming one's separateness when appropriate. If this sounds a bit abstract, yet vaguely "wise," this is the case with most stage theories. Their highest stages tend to fade into the mist—or is it light? In any case, it seems necessary that this be so, for their creators can only see so far "beyond" themselves, and as a critic once observed, doesn't one reach a point when all this is irrelevant? After all, the exemplars of these "advanced" stages— Martin Luther King, Jr., Mohandas Gandhi, Mother Theresa— were not, to my knowledge, developmental scholars.

Several things are worth noting about Kegan's map (see Figure 2). First, what is important for our purposes here is not the particular balances so much as the overall direction of movement. That is, as we cycle through these levels, we go through times when we are preoccupied primarily with our relations with "the other" and times when we are mainly concerned with our "self," apart from the other. In an important sense, our lives can be understood as a series of transformations of how we see ourselves in relation to others, how we negotiate the twin claims of what David Bakan has called agency and communion (Bakan, 1966). Thus, the early stage "impulsive" child is unable to distinguish his own impulses and wants from those of anyone else. We *are* our impulses, says Kegan; we don't *have* them. It is very difficult, as any parent knows, for a four-year-old to see through any eyes but his own. The "imperial" ten-year-old, however, knows what motivates her younger brother because she is more able than he to get outside of herself. She understands the importance of reciprocity (and the power of bribes) in a way he cannot. More self-possessed than her brother, she *has* her impulses; what she can see less clearly are her needs. With movement into the interpersonal balance, however, we open up in a whole new way as we seek to redefine ourselves through others, often as teenagers but frequently later in life as well. This is the time of falling in love ("I am *nothing* without you"), of conforming to the ways of the tribe, and of transforming the earlier mutual back-scratching morality into a more communal group ethic of trust. A more fitting paeon to interpersonal virtues than the Boy Scout law would be hard to find: trustworthy, loyal, helpful, friendly, courteous, kind, obedient, cheerful, thrifty, brave, clean, and reverent. Now we *have* our needs, but we *are* our relationships. With the swing back and up-

Figure 2. Kegan's "Helix of Evolutionary Truces."

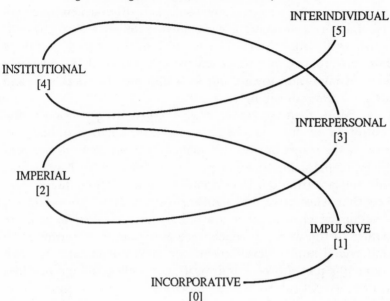

Psychologies
favoring
independence

Psychologies
favoring
inclusion

Source: Kegan, 1982, p. 109.

ward toward what Kegan calls the institutional balance, we "zip up" in a sense, drawing our boundaries more clearly, struggling (often against the inner and outer voices of our culture) to define ourselves in terms less borrowed from others than earned of our own effort. Loving becomes more an act of will than of self-denial; responsibility is redefined to include oneself; loyalty to the tribe is based less on friendships than respect for abstract principles; and guilt replaces shame as a form of social control. Finally, we swing back in a new yielding to something greater than ourselves, dissolving our boundaries once again as we work to let go of a self that may have grown too narrow. We reach out again to others in an effort to heal the wounds of too much separateness with a new compassion and often a new spirituality. Each transformation, each move involves a swinging outward, away from the familiar world into the strange, a leaning into uncertainty, a risk. Often we experience that move as a kind of impulsion toward our own opposite, our dark side, and we go at times unwillingly.

More than any other stage theorist, Kegan respects the motion in our lives, and he has focused the chapters of his book not on the stages but on the quality of the transitions between them, emphasizing how our movement involves both a reaching out and a letting go. Development is not a self-contained process that takes place inexorably. How readily we grow—indeed, whether we grow at all—he says, has a great deal to do with the nature of the world in which we transact our lives' business. To understand human development, we must understand the environment's part, how it confirms us, contradicts us, and provides continuity. Of this we will see more later as we look more closely at how mentors function: crucial parts of the "holding environment" (Winnicott, 1965) within and because of which we grow.

Most returning adult learners are moving through Kegan's interpersonal balance toward the institutional stance. Without benefit of developmental theory, Malcolm Knowles has made a career of describing this shift among adult students. Among those changes he describes as "dimensions of maturation" are moves from dependence to autonomy, passivity to activity, subjectivity to objectivity, and selfishness to altruism (Knowles, 1970). Each of these corresponds to Kegan's "three/four" shift.

Because stage changes take years to accomplish, we generally see our students only during brief sections of their passages. Our task is not to peg them into particular stages but rather to see them in their movement and to help them understand what may lie ahead. Consider Sandy again.

Clearly, her story tells of transition out from the "security" of her family—an interpersonal world that defined her for years—toward the "security" of a more self-conscious and deliberately constructed identity. Her tale reverberates with the voices in numerous current feminist writings about the struggle to define a new self apart from the reflections of a male-dominated society in which her place was to keep her place. Alice Koller's *An Unknown Woman* is a particularly effective portrayal of the anguish this can entail. As such, the appeal *and importance* of feminism to Sandy should come as no surprise, for the movement is a powerful cry for an ideology of self-affirmation to enlarge the personalized world of face-to-face contact with family and friends. It calls us to identify also with people we do not know, thus defining a new and broader sense of our place in the world.

But beyond this, Sandy's frequent return to the theme of separation, of emergence from embeddedness in her family's expectations, of a sense of breathing again after being almost "smothered," is striking in its evocation of liberation. There can be no doubt that she is moving into Kegan's period of self-authorship, feeling her oats, reveling in the new promise of independence, of control, of participation in the world. This is the time when people think of career rather than simply job; goals and a sense of achievement take on a new power; a feeling of purposefulness and the capacity to achieve what one sets out to do makes itself felt more strongly than ever. Those who return to school at this time tend to see the value of education not as a means simply of gaining new status (a concern more strongly felt at earlier stages) but as a way to achieve career goals or sometimes as a way to expand and develop that precious new inner self that they are beginning to discover and value so highly. All of these are movement "out" as the inner self comes more clearly into view. At the same time, recall that "separation" for women at this point may have a different quality than for men. Carol Gilligan's work suggests that Sandy may not so much be splitting herself off from her family as attempting to redefine her relationship so as to include *herself* as one of those deserving of care. We will return to this when we meet Sandy later in the book.

Ahead for Sandy lie a new career, new friends, and perhaps a new basis for friendship. Her marriage may experience strain as she redefines the terms of relationship, taking her own needs into account in a new way. Her mentor might do well to stand back and watch carefully before moving too precipitously, for Sandy needs her head. Her question is about who she wants to become, and she must answer that by herself.

This three/four shift is the single most common transformation among women returning to higher education. Like Sandy, many women do well in high school and are headed for college when they fall in love and marry instead. While their husbands may be able to complete the break with family and begin to confirm their worth in the outside world, the women remain inside the home, caring first for the husband and later for the children, enmeshed in a web of relationships that often (though not inevitably) simply continues the earlier patterns of dependency and self-sacrifice that characterize the interpersonal balance. For such women, the return to school—triggered perhaps by the children's departure from the home, or the dissolution (impending or accomplished) of a marriage—is the reaffirmation of a self long postponed. Often coupled with an outside job, the shift toward that independence of which Sandy spoke so powerfully can be a heady and disruptive experience as she struggles with the conflicting demands of work, study, and family. The three seldom mesh smoothly. One of the most important of all our interventions as teachers and advisers of adults is to acknowledge in our female students the poignancy of that struggle.

In our third vignette we meet Monique, a twenty-six-year-old secretary. She became one of my first students, and the conversation that follows occurred early in our career together. The central question for Monique had to do with how one distinguishes between good and bad, right and wrong. As you read, take note of how she views authority; consider the way she construes the nature of knowledge; and notice how she views herself as a learner. What lies behind her misunderstanding of the assignment on sexuality, and what made for the breakthrough at the end?

Leaving Home

For a woman with little formal education, one of the few ways to edge out of the pervasive poverty of the Northeast Kingdom is to become a secretary. For a few years, money for job training was available to employers in these parts, and a number of women seized the opportunity to ground their meager high school secretarial skills in solid experience. As soon as she could, Monique began to take college courses, seeking to expand her knowledge and move into a more important administrative position. It irked her that people with less experience whom she considered less competent than herself held authority simply because they had "that piece of paper" and she did not. As far as she could see, the sole difference lay in that college degree. It did not—indeed could not—occur to her that perhaps another difference might lie with the way she thought, interpreted her experience, made sense of the world.

After she had been in the program for a couple of terms, taking courses in office management, business communication, and the like, she decided, quite on her own, to take a weekend course entitled The Challenge of Sexuality. I was a bit surprised but encouraged the choice, feeling it was important for her to move outside her narrow vocationalism. The instructor had designed the course in a loosely structured discussion format, providing some basic information but restricting his part chiefly to guiding the class in its own discovery of the values that society places on sexuality and gender. This might be a good chance, I thought, for Monique to gain some distance on a topic about which I knew her to have strong opinions.

She could not have been back home more than a few moments after that first weekend when she called.

"I'm not going back! That Bill must be sick. He must get his thrills by making people tell all about their private sex lives. It was nothing but a sex counseling session. I learned nothing. Nothing!"

I listened for some time. Knowing Bill, I was quite certain that he had more conventional means of excitement at his disposal. Apparently Monique had run squarely into a deep prohibition. To discover an authority who ought to know better, using such obscene words as *penis* and *vagina* in public was profoundly disturbing.

She had been required, she went on, to write a fifteen-page paper about her private sex life. "There's no way I'm going to do that for him. No way. That's for sure."

When I asked her for the specific wording of the assignment, it turned out that it was "to discuss your own life in terms of what you have been taught about sexuality." Assuring her that I too would be reluctant to discuss my own sex life with a stranger, I explained that the assignment was simply to examine her own beliefs about sexuality, not to tell about her sex life. She cooled down at this, and we talked of how she might go about writing the paper.

Although she put it off until the last moment, she did eventually complete the assignment and was delighted several weeks later to receive very good comments on her work. "For days after she got that paper back," said a friend, "she was a new woman—Monique at her best."

Curious about the impact of the experience on her way of thinking, I arranged a meeting in a nearby restaurant for an afternoon snack.

"So how are things going with your courses?" I ask.

"Well, the photography with Armand is going pretty good, I guess," she replies, speaking softly with a slight French-Canadian lilt beneath the Muzak. "You sure were right about him. He's a really sweet guy."

She giggles a lot when she is uncomfortable. Giggles now.

"What have you learned?" I ask, overanxious to move from him to her.

"Oh, a little bit about how to make a picture pleasing, I guess. A little bit about photography, the different styles, you know." But when I ask her what particular styles, she is stumped; she has forgotten the names of the photographers. She does recall several particular shots but seems to have no way of talking about more than one photograph at a time. Everything is isolated. She likes this, doesn't like that; remembers the content of a picture, but nothing of the form. "How does she make sense of this?" I wonder, and ask her if the course was worth taking.

"Armand did a pretty good job, I'd say," she begins, and I signal the waitress for more coffee while Monique describes Armand and what he did. Again I try to move from him to her, less gently this time.

"OK, Monique, that's a description of what *he* did, but what do you think made it a good course?"

"Well, let's see now [pause]. Well [seductively], I liked his individualized style of teaching. I liked the content. I liked learning that a photograph should be a piece of art. I liked learning the history. I liked learning how to run a camera."

After another ten minutes of this, Monique is on her second piece of pie and I decide it's safe to broach discussion of the beast with two backs.

"How would you compare your two courses this term?"

"Well, I guess they were both interesting," she says slowly, then giggles uncomfortably. "But I liked Armand's better than Bill's." She giggles again and flicks a cautiously knowing glance in my direction. Armand's course, she explains, had a lot more facts in it. He lectured more and gave her the feeling that he would take care of her. He seemed to care for her personally, though her one criticism is that "he was too much of a mother hen."

"Bill's course didn't have enough facts," she says, avoiding my eyes. "Still, I guess he did the best he could. There's no way he could have done much differently than he did, either."

Looking for her sense of how she has changed, I ask her to recall how she felt about the course at the beginning. Does she feel differently now?

"I didn't like his whole approach," she replies, turning dark. "Some of the language in the class was too much for me. I didn't like the talk. I didn't like the discussion of sexuality; it made me feel as if I didn't even want to be in the room." And, indeed, she contracted a cough that first weekend and found herself leaving the room frequently. I sympathize with her, acknowledging how difficult it can be when people say or do things we feel are wrong.

"I wish he'd given us more facts or maybe even some opinions from other experts so I could make up my own mind. Well, he did have some facts but not really enough." Without saying a word about herself, she is saying volumes about how she thinks. The word *experts* catches my ear.

"Were there any ideas from experts in your reading?" I

ask, looking for a vein. "People you disagreed with or who disagreed with Bill?" This time we hit pay dirt.

She pauses and looks down, thinking hard, then looks up with a frown. "Well, one psychologist thought that children should be given a special room in the house where they can experiment with, you know..." Looking away, she giggles incongruously. Is it embarrassment or anger? "I'm gonna let my children do that?" Her voice rises and she holds the appalled expression an instant too long, to make sure I get the point.

"Do you have any idea why an expert would have suggested such a thing?" I ask, wondering how clearly she can see into that darkness. In reply she sinks back deflated against the padded Naugahyde of the booth. What was the matter with me? Couldn't I see how ridiculous that was? After a long silence she looks up from the empty pie plate, glances past my face, and fixes her gaze toward the plastic flowers on the jukebox against the wall.

"I suppose it might be a way of letting them get out their frustrations. Maybe he thinks it might be good for them?" She looks over, checking. I agree and then go on to restate what I imagine to be a more complete rationale. Then I add, "Now this man's an *expert*. How can you possibly disagree with him?"

"Well, he's just too idealistic. Those ideas are all very well in theory, but he doesn't understand the way things really are—the practical aspects." She goes on to explain that experts sometimes do disagree with one another and that there's really no right or wrong anyway.

"Do you really believe that, Monique?"

"Well, there's no *one* answer. You have to look at all the facts and then make up your mind."

"Did you used to believe there was a right and a wrong?"

"I don't know. I think there might have been. I'm afraid I still have some old principles there that go down pretty deep." The boil has burst. She speaks softly now, concentrating on the space between our plates. Pensive.

"You're 'afraid'? What's wrong with the old principles?"

"Nothing. It's just that they're conservative."

"Is there something wrong with being conservative?"

"Not really. It's just that I'm trying to see things in a broader sense rather than in a narrow-minded way. I'm gettin' there, but some things still go down quite deep." I'm with her now. Gentle.

"What are those things—that go quite deep?"

"Well, thoughts about sexuality, I guess."

"Can you remember some of those things that you feel quite deeply about?"

"Well," she pauses, takes a deep breath, and plunges on. "There's one that I might be more liberal on now: no sex before marriage and no outside activities. I used to feel that there should be no sex before marriage and that if you live with a guy before marriage, that's terrible. Now I can recognize—at least see—their point of view and not even bat an eye about it like I used to. So I guess I'm relaxing a bit about that, and I'm not judging, which I would have judged before. I think I'm . . . relaxed more, more tolerant of other people's ways of doing things."

We talk for a while longer, and I focus on the word *tolerant,* a key word for Monique now. It's her word, and I underline it for her. I tell her I want her to use that word and to think about things in that way as often as she can so that when she finds things that bother her, she make an effort to see things through others' eyes, to try to imagine how they might explain what they did. Perhaps that will help her continue to grow more tolerant.

We walk silently together back to her office. At the door, she flashes a quick smile and goes inside.

While conversations like this are not everyday occurrences, they do happen often enough to keep me alive; they're the stuff of my work, and for the insight, the credit goes to William Perry, who has done more to illuminate important dimensions of the intellectual growth of college students than anyone else I know. Disarmingly simple, Perry's scheme offers a powerful way of understanding the struggle that Monique and students like her go through as they attempt to make better sense of what they think is right and wrong, and under what circumstances.

Much of the appeal of the theory is that it lends itself so readily to the metaphor of a journey. Indeed, in Perry's book *Forms of Intellectual and Ethical Development in the College Years* (1968), it is described as a "pilgrim's progress." Although the framework first grew from the stories of a highly select group of traditional undergraduates as their ways of understanding evolved during four years at Harvard, the model has since been widely applied among students of all ages and backgrounds. The initial formulation has held up generally well.

Briefly, the tale begins in an Eden-like garden where good and evil are clear and where Authority unequivocally divides right from wrong. Knowledge is concrete and readily available if Authority is properly courted. As students at this early point, we tend to see ourselves as passive vessels to be filled with Truth by authoritative teachers. We can become quite frustrated if teachers do not live up to this expectation.

But as we travel, clouds begin to roll in and obscure the light. Some things appear to be more readily provable and, hence, more true than others. In time, as authorities visibly clash before our eyes and as we lose the simple vision that once so clearly divided right from wrong, we find ourselves in a dark and, for some, forbidding Gethsemane, torn from the plain truths that once both blinded and preserved us. At one moment we are buoyed by a new kind of freedom; at another we are submerged beneath the weight of our own uncertainty. Some of us, unable to bear the dark, turn back to the safety of earlier truths; others, bemused and numbed by the swirl, temporize; and still others, blessed perhaps with courage—or simply desperation—forge ahead through the forest of simple relativity toward a new apprehension of truth. We discover that though there are many truths, not all are of equal validity, nor do they exist in isolation. Each has its own context, a meaning, connections that rest on certain assumptions and contain their own inner logic. We too have a context from which we construct our own reality. In fact, everyone does. With this realization, we have negotiated the shift into contextual relativism and our view of the world is transformed. It remains now to acknowledge our place in this new world, to begin to make—and later unmake, and make yet again—commitments to values, work, people, despite our bone-deep knowledge that the rock we once thought the world rested upon has been replaced by some sort of manufactured substance: attractive perhaps, maybe practical, but fabricated and surely not permanent. On it, nonetheless, we build our church.

With this in mind, the conversation with Monique, and perhaps the source of my frustration, grows clearer. I had known Monique for some time before and knew that she tended to color the world more black and white than gray. At the same time, she was a perfectly intelligent, capable person, and I knew that she felt driven to make sense of the new information she was picking up. Perry's model suggested that an exploration of Monique's notions about authority and about how one tells right from wrong would reveal how she was making sense of diverse and conflicting information and, more importantly, how her meaning making was changing in response to the new knowledge. That was what lay behind my questions.

It was clear that knowledge for Monique was fairly concrete and discrete. If the instructors in the two courses had attempted to make connections for her, she had evidently been unable to hear them. It is not surprising that things seemed so fragmented. She was still some distance from a position that would allow her to place such disturbing information in the context of a particular set of assumptions about human nature. She was simply incapable of making such abstract connections without help. Perhaps because of this and perhaps because of her consequent high need for external authority, Monique attempted to give meaning to her confusion by discussing the instructors—comfortable territory—and the extent to which they provided meaning for her in the form of "facts." Although I repeatedly asked her to discuss the course itself, she stuck like hot bubble gum to what she felt about her teachers. Far from being a detached examination, evaluation at this position was a matter of personal feeling: one likes or dislikes the object in question. One cannot both dislike and consider something good

at the same time. Given so personal an identification with the
source of knowledge and a strongly traditional upbringing, it is
no wonder that she found it difficult to handle the course on
sexuality. She simply lacked the capacity to decenter herself
from the ideas, to *have* her own ideas rather than *be* someone
else's. She thus found it easy to feel attacked when her ideas
came under question. And this is why she was so quick to assume that Bill wanted her to describe her sex life rather than to
discuss and evaluate *her ideas about sexuality.*

Perry's formulation all began, he tells us, when as a literature teacher he asked his students what they believed he wanted
from them. Upon receiving the responses, he discovered each to
have a quite different teacher. To some, he was a pleasant fellow who wanted them to think for themselves; to others, he was
an imposing authority whose job it was first to inject and later
to extract from them the right answers; and to still others, he
was an exponent of a particular point of view arguing for a coherent set of interpretations of literature. How to make sense of
all this? Like several others who later turned developmentalist,
Perry had been influenced by the massive study of authoritarianism carried out in the postwar years by Nevitt Sanford and
his associates. It was clear to Perry that some of his students
showed distinct authoritarian patterns. Yet over time, they
seemed to change. Because he interviewed his students every
spring, his experience of students was more akin to a motion
picture than isolated snapshots—there was movement here. In
most cases, the authoritarian students *changed.*

With his colleagues, Perry began to listen to students' answers to the least-loaded question they could devise, one borrowed from Robert Merton: "Why don't you start out with
whatever stands out for you about the year?" Interviews typically lasted about an hour and commonly centered around how
students made sense of the diversity of new information and
experiences that college brought them. It took some fourteen
years in all before Perry published the group's findings in a
book with the outrageous title *Forms of Intellectual and Ethical Development in the College Years: A Scheme.* The basic
map of the journey, a nine-position continuum, appears in Figure 3, with a description of the itinerary.

Figure 3. Perry's Map.

```
  1      2      3      4      5      6      7      8      9
 |-------|-------|-------|-------|-------|-------|-------|-------|
```
Dualism . . .   Contextual Relativism
       Multiplicity
                    . . . Commitment . . .

Perry's Main Line of Development

Position 1: The student sees the world in polar terms of we-right-good vs. other-wrong-bad.
Right Answers for everything exist in the Absolute,
known to Authority whose role is to mediate
(teach) them. Knowledge and goodness are perceived as quantitative accretions of discrete right-
nesses to be collected by hard work and obedience
(paradigm: a spelling test).

Position 2: The student perceives diversity
of opinion, and uncertainty and accounts for them
as unwarranted confusion in poorly qualified Authorities or as mere exercises set by Authority "so
we can learn to find The Answer for ourselves."

Position 3: The student accepts diversity and
uncertainty as legitimate but still *temporary* in
areas where Authority "hasn't found The Answer
yet." He supposes Authority grades him in these
areas on "good expression" but remains puzzled as
to standards.

Position 4: (a) The student perceives legitimate uncertainty (and therefore diversity of opinion) to be extensive and raises it to the status of an
unstructured epistemological realm of its own in
which "anyone has a right to his own opinion," a
realm which he sets over against Authority's realm
where right-wrong still prevails, or (b) the student
discovers qualitative contextual relativistic reasoning as a special case of "what They want" within
Authority's realm.

Position 5: The student perceives all knowledge and values (including Authority's) as contex-

Figure 3. Perry's Map, Cont'd.

tual and relativistic and subordinates dualistic right-wrong functions to the status of a special case, in context.

Position 6: The student apprehends the necessity of orienting himself in a relativistic world through some form of personal Commitment (as distinct from unquestioned or unconsidered commitment to simple belief in certainty).

Position 7: The student makes an initial Commitment in some area.

Position 8: The student experiences the implications of Commitment and explores the subjective and stylistic issues of responsibility.

Position 9: The student experiences the affirmation of identity among multiple responsibilities and realizes Commitment as an ongoing, unfolding activity through which he expresses his lifestyle.

Conditions of Delay, Deflection, and Regression

Temporizing: The student delays in some Position for a year, exploring its implications or explicitly hesitating to take the next step.

Escape: The student exploits the opportunity for detachment offered by the structures of Positions 4 and 5 to deny responsibility through passive or opportunistic alienation.

Retreat: The student entrenches in the dualistic, absolutistic structures of Positions 2 or 3 [Perry, 1968, pp. 9-10].

Perry is fond of pointing out that "the first characteristic of any theory is that it is wrong in any particular case." He does not exempt his own scheme from this and advises that it be viewed with caution. On at least one occasion, having taken his audience of several hundred earnest academics and administrators through his marvelous description of the scheme, he announced impishly, "Now, of course, you realize that this is all nonsense." People do not live, he emphasizes, inside little boxes marked with his position numbers and development does not occur in a straight line; rather, those who have made the journey may think dualistically in some areas under some circumstances, multiplistically in others, contextually in still others. Nevertheless, we will function predominantly in one range or another, and although a contextual thinker may on occasion operate dualistically, a dualistic thinker will not think contextually. In accord with other stage theories, Perry's positions are hierarchical and essentially invariant: each rests on the one before it, and there are no shortcuts. At the same time, however, people may move through two positions in a brief burst, or remain for long periods at a single position. Occasionally they even retreat to an earlier stance.

Position 1, basic dualism, is essentially a construct necessary to anchor the scheme. It is at position 2 that the movement begins. Things start to fall apart, first as the student discovers that there is more than one answer for most important questions, then as she discovers that authorities may differ in what those answers are. But the process may be a slow one. For many, it takes years. No one begins at the absolute beginning; almost all of us have discovered at least some moral ambiguity in our lives, even though some find it harder to accept than others. This is especially true of adult learners, some of whom have spent sixty or seventy years feeling its cold touch.

My own research (Daloz, 1981) suggests that most adults returning to college arrive carrying some degree of dualism and a good deal of multiplicity. That is, they are moving away from exclusive reliance on external authority as the source of "truth," toward skepticism of such authority (albeit sometimes rather dualistic skepticism) and the belief that any opinion is as good as any other. This is when the journey gets exciting, for it is during this time as the old foundations begin to crumble that the footings are laid for the transformation that Perry describes as the 4/5 transition, the central transformation of his scheme and very probably of a good college education. Let's look more closely.

In the midst of multiplicity, that yellow wood this side of

contextual relativism, two paths diverge. One route (position 4a on the map) is characterized by the belief that in the absence of authority any opinion is as good as any other. Since nothing can be known for sure, one's own experience is the most reliable guide. Asked how he tells right from wrong, a person in this position is likely to respond as this student did: "Just my own intuitive experience, I guess. No one's gonna be able to tell you, and you just have to rely on your feelings." Hard work, which often served as a criterion of value before, seems pointless now. Said the same student a moment later, describing a literature course: "There's no end to how much I study, you know. I can work thirty hours and pass or two hours and pass." The classic stance of the 1960s hippy, which in many ways typifies this position, is as much a developmental statement as a sociological one. If there are no ultimate values, why work anyway? This is often disparaged as "mere moral relativism," unattractive to observers on either side. To those who have yet to venture, it looks anarchistic, sacrilegious, unkempt, and terrifying. To those who have moved through, it can appear spineless, destructive, cynical, and self-indulgent. One of the values of a developmental perspective is that it allows us to acknowledge all of the above and then go about the business of helping people move along, for there is no better place to begin rebuilding meaning than when all previous structures are in shambles.

The other route (position 4b), somewhat more worn, is also more docile. Here the paradigmatic student is one who begins to realize that "they (the authorities) want us to think for ourselves" and who proceeds to do what "they" want. Procedures such as use of evidence, weighing both sides, and testing hypotheses are seen initially as the "right" way to do things; later they are relativized and become a "better" way. Perry sometimes refers to this as the Trojan Horse effect: we take into our midst a foreign way of thinking that ultimately brings about the transformation. Less a giant to be slain than a benevolent voice urging its own demise, Authority paradoxically becomes the bridge to its own overthrow, a bridge as delicate as a spider's web: "It seems to be some loyalty to truth, a feeling that if the truth is really dubious, it is better to have a dubious truth than a false certainty" (Perry, 1968, p. 108).

Understood as a transitional stance, intellectual diffidence is important, confusion, benign. If we help our students to accept the confusion and uncertainty, to feel safe with it, if we encourage them to enter the darkness, to explore those terrifying opposites fully enough, there is a good chance they will begin to move through them on their own and begin to discern a meaning in "the starless air." As they find it safe to let go of their self-evident ways of making meaning, discover the considerable limitations of common sense, and begin to risk seeing through the eyes of other people, other cultures, other times, they will begin to construct a world first of multiple opinions but eventually—and more importantly—of multiple ways of arriving at those opinions. The discovery that things can be related, that connections can be made rather than truths found, begins to dawn, and the world is reborn on a whole new level. In short, our students begin to think about thought itself. It is this recognition that lays the groundwork for the critical shift from multiplicity to contextualism, for the essential difference between the way Monique thinks and the way her teachers think.

But she is not there yet. Indeed, her thinking seems most like that found in late dualism, early multiplicity. Consider her approach to authority. Perry found it fruitful to ask how students dealt with conflicting authorities. Monique recognized that experts might legitimately differ, but she stopped short of standing up to them herself. (Full-blown multiplicity allows us to do this by denying that *anyone*, expert or not, "really" knows anything.) Instead, she resorted to the old that's-all-very-well-in-theory ploy, asserting her own expertise to reside in her direct, practical experience. And because she was unable to imagine how an opposing point of view to her own might be constructed, she was powerless to argue against it except in the ad hominem way she chose. This is one reason why it is so important to encourage students to articulate positions different from their own. Until they can do that, they have no way of constructing an argument on the basis of reason rather than their gut.

Nonetheless, it was at this point in the conversation that we began to move. Her assertion that "there's no such thing as right and wrong," struck me as a bit facile, knowing her as I did, and I questioned it. From there, she was able to recognize important elements in her own growth and see that although she did, indeed, continue to hold some strong "principles," she was becoming better at seeing some parts of the world through others' eyes. By continuing to practice suspending judgment, by holding that word *tolerant,* she would continue the direction of her growth toward greater understanding.

This episode drove home to me the meaning of Perry's wry observation that "Too early a moral judgment is precisely what stands between many able students and a liberal education" (Perry, 1969, p. 105). To remain ignorant, judge everything. By sealing great chunks of the world into boxes marked good and bad, right and wrong, we effectively choose to remain ignorant about large areas of our experience, saying, "I will learn from this but not from that." In this way, the kind of "entrenched dualism," as a colleague calls it, from which Monique is emerging has a self-fulfilling quality, for by defining in advance the lessons we will learn, we safely protect ourselves from both nasty surprises and useful lessons. This is not to say, however, that the obvious course for enthusiastic mentors is to set about shattering dualism wherever it occurs. Monique's stance, like all of ours, represents a delicate truce with the "truths" of her life. We all presort what we let into our lives. The task is not to stop sorting; rather, it is to seek ever finer and more fitting instruments. For Monique, the time has come to retire a tool that is no longer up to the task and to forge something better.

"I'm getting there," she says, and quite by herself comes up with exactly what she needs: "tolerance." Clearly, she has a sense of her own direction despite what she herself acknowledges is fierce resistance. She knows her question is about tolerance. Our job in cases like this is least of all to push. Rather, what we can offer is simply a little light in the right places and lots of support. Monique can take it from there.

In concluding this chapter, let us return to Eric, whom we met earlier, and consider his story in light of the three maps we have just reviewed. We begin with Levinson's perspective.

In the adult development seminar that I had set up for several of my students, selecting particular theorists for particular students, I had chosen the Levinson study for Eric. Several years before, he had begun to realize that his present career path had taken him as far as he could go. He had prepared himself in his teens for an engineering career that took him through his twenties. But by the thirties transition, he had come to see that if he wanted to continue to move ahead, he would have to make a leap into management, a field in which a degree would be a virtual necessity. Right on schedule, he returned to school in search of the ticket. But as Levinson says, transitions are times of the breakup of old structures. If Eric were to rebuild a new structure adequate to his thirties, one that would allow him to secure a satisfactory place in the adult world and to become his own man, he would need to make some qualitative changes, letting go of some of the assumptions that got him through the earlier decade. *More* education wouldn't do. He needed a *richer* education, one that would provide the breadth of understanding necessary for leadership. It took a while for him to realize this fully. Surely it was not clear when he first came into the program, at that first meeting. But over time, especially through his association with Dave and Milt and to some extent myself, he began not only to see that he would need to change but that he could and that it would be all right to do so. A good deal of that change had to do with Eric's willingness to let go of the tough facade with which he had first greeted me and that he had always used for protection and advancement in his career. Human development is rich with ironies, and it is no accident that Eric was most able to move ahead in his career at precisely that point when he could let go of the single-mindedness that had brought him to where he was. It is a lot easier to let go of one thing when we are holding onto something else, and for Eric that something else was the positive quality of his other, more reflective self—the Eric who drew his strength from being alone in the woods. That's the extraordinary impact of his experience with the deer, his readiness to respect another life in a way he had not done before. What he did not want to stop, it seems to me, is the delicate emergence of a new, more vulnerable Eric.

In Kegan's terms, this looks like the leading edge of the
institutional self, the fresh determination to define ourselves in
our own terms rather than as we would have others see us. To
be ten feet from a deer and not shoot *is* crazy in the eyes of the
prevailing and conventional ethic of hunting. "You just don't
throw fish back in when they're big enough to keep," says the
voice of the culture. "Well *I* do!" retorts Eric. He is listening
more and more to a new voice, one that has been inside him for
years but only recently able to find ears. It's still tender, needs
plenty of privacy, but in the right setting, where it is safe, the
voice yearns to be heard. For his final paper, I encouraged him
to write a personal application of the various theories he had
studied. He was reluctant at first and asked if he could submit it
in longhand since he did not type and wanted no one else to see
the work. I agreed, and he later told me that he had spent hour
after hour of intense concentration writing pages and pages,
many of which he was unwilling to show anyone, including me.
He had discovered the journal, and at last he had a friend in
himself who would listen. For people like Eric, at that delicate
transition from conventionality to a new independence (a point
that Jane Loevinger insightfully terms the self-aware stage),
self-disclosure can be both extremely threatening and extraordinarily powerful. The journal, with various safeguards for confi-
dentiality, is an effective device for helping people find their
voice at this period.

Eric's course in organizational behavior was important in
giving him a new perspective on his workplace and a language
with which to describe the pecking order of his bosses. But the
emotional force underlying his description, the relish with
which he declared their simian proclivities comes, it seems to
me, from the new voice. Because he was strengthening his roots
in soil other than the work world, finding new nourishment in
an inner self, acknowledging openly the love he bore for the silence of the outdoors, he was able to view his job with more
detachment and was consequently able to make his decisions in
greater freedom. "I'm just not as attached to that place anymore," he told me later. "I know there's so much more to me
than that now."

For Perry, an important dimension of development is a movement from reliance on externally validated "truth" to internally coherent explanations. Such momentum is clear in Eric's story, and an important road mark is his willingness to see varied and competing approaches to the same problem. Working with Milt, coming to trust him—largely thanks to the older man's willingness to be open about his own humanity—Eric was able to let go of his need for a single "right" way of doing things. He grew increasingly able to acknowledge that other points of view may also be valid, have their own inner logic. His current way of addressing a diversity of solutions is "to try to put them together and come up with the best approach." This has about it the ring of intellectual compromise and lacks full recognition that "the best approach" might be more than simply an amalgam, but Eric has come a long way from the simple expectations of his earlier days. His current stance still maintains that absolutes will always exist in some fields—engineering, for instance—but he is quick to affirm that "there's no simple right or wrong answer when it comes to dealing with people."

Given reasonable faith in the maps, the journey ahead is clear. In his work life, Eric will need to consolidate his new position of leadership. Assuming that the administrative climate surrounding his job is sufficiently flexible to acknowledge his broader perspective, Eric should be able to flourish and move ahead as the cultural script dictates. If he can continue to care for his new self as he moves up the corporate ladder and if that self maintains its respect for the legitimacy of his working world, his path ought to be fairly smooth. As he grows more familiar with his new, inner self and becomes more willing to share it openly with others, he may find a growing capacity for intimacy. His family and his close friends may take on a new meaning for him. And as he is able increasingly to listen as well as talk, he will gain a deepening appreciation for the complexity with which others live their lives. In time, if he can remain open to the continuing challenge of the new diversity that his growing openness reveals, he will grow more adept at building bridges, making connections among people, ideas, differing values. And if his teachers can reveal to him their own fears and uncertainties, their own humanity, he will come to see that they too—even mentors—are creatures of their contexts.

All this, of course, is laced with "ifs" as any prognosis must be. Maps can never substitute for the journey itself, nor can they ever be more than representations of the territory. People, Perry reminds us, are always bigger than our ideas about them. And those deep trenches of Eric's do not lie on anyone else's charts. They are his own, and the choice to enter them is his.

Chapter Four 🎼

The Unsettling
First Steps of an
Educational Journey

"Thou hast so disposed my heart with desire for
the journey by thy words that I have returned to
my first intent. Now go, for but one will is in us
both, thou leader, thou lord and master."

Thus I spoke to him, and when he set out I
entered on the deep and savage way.

—*Dante,* The Divine Comedy

As they head off on the first leg of their journey, students often
sense that their educational travels will require them to let go of
old ways of seeing. They react in a variety of ways to this discovery. For some, ready to make changes in their lives, the new
demands bring a welcome freshness. For others, the journey can
be a stiff challenge, one they complete only after considerable
turmoil. And for still others, the pressures prove too great; they
turn back to the simple haven of a home too safe to leave.
Understanding the precise nature of the demands we make on
our students and calibrating our expectations to their particular
strengths and weaknesses is a special art, for what is a snap for
one may prove a challenge to another and overwhelming to yet
a third. In this chapter we will listen to the voices of these students as they head down "the deep and savage way."

Opening with a discussion of the emotional tenor and intellectual stance of the first part of the journey, we then meet
three students as they and their mentors attempt to sustain a

fruitful balance among the challenges and supports of their educational work. We will meet Betty, who despite her teacher's best efforts, chooses to retreat to the shadow of her former worldview; Jean, who struggles with mixed success to free herself of the tangle of family relationships; and Richard, who almost reluctantly manages to break through his own dogmatism.

Like all of the examples in this book, these "cases" have emerged from my interviews and personal experience over the course of several years. They describe real people who did not always deem to follow the scripts written by theory. The reader is advised not to see these as polished illustrations but rather as the kind of coarse approximations that reflect most of life's refusal to behave itself, and in searching for lessons, to look not simply at what went "right" or "wrong" but rather at what happened. What these vignettes have most to offer is not a set of neat generalizations but a model of a certain kind of passionate relationship, a relationship in which mentors care deeply about their students' welfare, win or lose. The greatest practical value of this book is that it offers some new ways of asking questions—of students and about them. This chapter concludes with a set of concrete suggestions for how to do this.

Let us begin then by asking what motivates adults to return to higher education. Why do they begin the journey? There are, of course, as many reasons as students, but the vast majority do so because of some transition in their lives (Aslanian and Brickell, 1980). For women, one of the most common precipitating events is when the children leave the house, either for school or for good. Said one mother, as she began to build a new career:

> I had been very busy raising my kids, and I loved it. My youngest son was going to kindergarten, and I think it occurred to me that I wasn't doing a darned thing. Somehow I wasn't satisfied with that; it was depressing me; I didn't like it. It wasn't the way I wanted to spend my days, and I thought, "Another ten years of this?" Something had to give.

For men, the event more frequently revolves around work. Like Eric, this man had reached the limit in his job. To advance further, he needed a college degree.

> I work for the state. And in order to advance
> it is always beneficial to have a degree. I have gone
> quite far without one, but to go further I need to
> go back to school and get that piece of paper. One
> day I saw an ad in the paper about how it's never
> to late to go to college, and so I called them.

People working with adults in transition have heard variations of these stories many times over. And the tales extend far beyond the classroom, for when tales of transformation are told, they often begin with a glimpse of a simple, happy scene just before the descent. King Arthur was a wise and successful ruler; Cinderella was of unparalleled goodness and sweetness of temper; Adam and Eve were naked and not ashamed. Yet usually there is a cloud on the horizon; the serenity is flecked with portent. Something doesn't quite fit, and so they move toward the threshold, impelled outward.

As anyone who has ever stood on such a threshold knows, however, the excitement we feel is usually mixed with a good dose of fear. A glance at departure points in many great tales reveals travelers often almost paralyzed as they face the unknown terrors ahead: Dante on entering Inferno, Christian before his pilgrim's progress, or Gilgamesh and Enkidu before the events that were to make of their lives an epic.

So it should not be a surprise that the most common emotion experienced by adults as they return to the classroom is fear. I once asked a group of students to write about their educational experiences using the metaphor of a journey. What were they feeling as they set out? More than four out of five described fear in one form or another. At one level, the fear is born of a simple anxiety about an unknown future. For many of these students, school is a reminder of a former failure and understandably carries grim memories. But there is more to it than that. Whether in terms of Levinson's life structures or

Kegan's balances, transformation involves both a breaking down and a rebuilding. Since we can rarely see far ahead, we are much more aware of what we are about to lose than what we might gain. Fear of the unknown may be irrational, but it is not unreasonable. Here Martin talks with Joanna, his mentor, about it. She has asked him whether he learned anything new in his psychology class.

Martin: I think the biggest thing that comes to mind was that before the class I had an idea that psychology was similar to a technical field where a molding machine in Denver was the same as a molding machine in Boston, and by that sense a psychologist in Orange County Mental Health would believe the same as someone who had the same training any place else in the country.

Joanna: And the training would be the same?

Martin: That's right. And where now I see it as, there really isn't anything that's black and white that you can cut a piece out of. And as you go through, two people might seemingly have the same ideas and agree on the same things, but if they were to write it down, it would be different. I guess that's probably the biggest thing I learned—that nobody really knows what's right or wrong, best or worst, good or bad.

Joanna: Do you have as clear a sense of what's right or wrong as you did before?

Martin: No. When I talk, when I say no, I'm talking about right here, sitting here today. Last week or even last month might have been completely different. I can't even remember. But I know that right now, no, I don't.

Joanna: That must be unsettling.

Martin: Very much to me right now. Yeah. It's hard for me even to admit to myself because I've always had at least one foot firmly planted somewhere, and I always knew where it was. And, gee, it's sort of like jumping from one iceberg to another. You don't really know how solid the next one's going to be when you jump.

Joanna: Does that feel exciting or is it all negative?

Martin: I can't . . . I can't put it together. It's [long pause] I just can't get my hands on it.

Joanna: You feel as though you're in the middle of quicksand right now?

Martin: Yeah. And it's . . . kind of frightening really.

No nineteen-year-old sophomore, until recently Martin was a prominent official in the Presbyterian church. At thirty-seven, he is the father of nine children, holds an important industrial management position, and is well respected in his community. But along with many of his fellow students, he feels an old, dualistic world breaking up under him. He has left home, and he's scared.

Being human, when we are afraid, most of us turn to other people for help. It is fitting that we seek Mentor just as we need him. Dante found his Virgil; Martin, his Joanna. Joanna was of immense importance to Martin as he proceeded to negotiate those ice floes in the following year. During the passage, he said he could not imagine doing it without her, was extravagant in his praise. Had he been the only student to speak so glowingly of his mentor, this book would never have been written. But we heard it again and again.

The early phases of the relationship are frequently characterized by adulation, though occasionally by terror or a paradoxical failure to recognize the mentor at all. To understand this, it is important to recall that fear both blinds and paralyzes. When we are frightened, we don't *want* to see too much. At such times, mentors can appear, lantern in hand, helping us to see the way ahead, perhaps strengthening us in our downward journey, promising in some way to help us fill the void left by the loss of our former certainty. At such times, we need to think of them as part divine, and it comforts us to believe that they have been here before, that they can see the way through. Most of us are in no hurry to learn that our teacher is only human. That can wait.

The speed and quality with which the mentorship "levels" seem to depend to a great extent on the student's ability to grow a conscious inner self that can mediate conflicting information effectively. Students at early positions seem to need to invest the mentor with power as a defense against the fear of rampant uncertainty. Until they can develop their own inner voice to sort "right" from "wrong," they understandably rely on external authority. This correlation between Perry's dualism and a high need for authority has been well documented (Adorno and others, 1950; Perry, 1968). Teachers, advisers, mentors are all important authority figures during this period, and it is a safe bet that regardless of how we name ourselves, we will be called on to fulfill this need for some students. Consider for a moment what Perry has observed about how students in early positions view authority.

> From this position, a person construes all issues of truth and morality in the terms of a sweeping and unconsidered differentiation between the in-group vs. out-group. This division is between the familiar world of Authority-right-we, as against the alien world of illegitimate-wrong-others. . . . Morality and personal responsibility consist of simple obedience . . . of committing to memory, through hard work, an array of discrete items . . . as assigned by Authority. In this structure's most primitive form, Authority's omniscience is so taken-for-granted that no distinction is made between Authority and the Absolute. "Truth" and "what They say" function as tautological alternatives of expression, as do "right" and "what They want" [1968, p. 59].

Few adult students are so naive as to believe that only one source of authority holds all truth, though for some the Bible comes close. Most acknowledge at least several authorities. These students know their teachers to disagree with one another and tend to side with their favorites. They may further attempt to resolve conflict among authorities by dividing them into good authorities and bad ones—thus maintaining the essential dualistic structure. This tendency to consider some teachers good and others bad, of course, persists for all of us. But the reasons differ tellingly. In early developmental stages, good teachers are those who really know the subject and tell us what is right and wrong. The others either do not know what they are talking about or refuse, for their own arcane reasons, to come clean. And because knowledge is concrete, good teachers provide lots of facts.

But teachers are not the only authorities in a classroom. A classic conflict arises when a teacher and a textbook differ. The dialectical movement begins to heat up as the student shuttles back and forth between, and later among, authorities, trying to find out which one is right. The breakthrough comes when she is able to realize that perhaps there's something amiss in her basic formula, in the assumption that there must be a right and a wrong in the first place. At this point, something—usually a very small something—shifts, and she finds herself allowing that perhaps in some areas (like literature or art) there are no absolute answers, at least not yet.

With this realization, the student is forced to reevaluate her view of authority as well, for how can one authority be better than another if there is no single truth to know? So, seeking some basis for judgment, she turns elsewhere. Good teachers are the ones who want you to figure it out for yourself. (Ah, so that's why Dr. Scruggs never gave us the answers.) They may or may not have a lot of facts, but good teachers *care* about you, they try to get you to learn. Sometimes, as this student had it, "[they] let you do things your own way. Maybe if you're writing, they let you break a rule or something in English to make your point. They let you do your own thing. They don't make you adhere strictly to the rules."

There are still rules, note. But as the old structure thaws, good teachers become more permissive. Like you, they are searching for their own truth and are no more dependent on authority than you are. Accordingly, they are less concerned now with grading. After all, if there is no right or wrong and if what really matters is your own personal experience, how can they grade? Good teachers are supportive and nonjudgmental. Among psychology students, Carl Rogers (through no fault of his own, we might add) attains new heights of popularity. He becomes truly a teacher's teacher because he *seems* to say that all you have to do is let people do their own thing and they will learn. Wow.

Perry notes that as the former structures break down and as authority loses its hold, some students turn to cynicism and bitterness. Teachers who once were seen as paragons of knowledge may now appear pompous and empty. For adults like Martin entering this intellectual sophomore slump, it can be a time of considerable trial, demanding patience and care from the teacher. A good deal of anger may well up to fill the void left by authority. It is a hard time for families, and given the welter of stress on adult students, the loss of such fundamental security can be a backbreaking straw.

It seems likely that the bridging away from authority that goes on at this time is paralleled by a tentative shift away from the assumptions about proper behavior and conventionality that have held people up to this point. It may gain early impetus in a countercultural thrust, a "pushing away from the dock," as Sharon Parks (1986) puts it in her important and engaging study of this shift among young adults in college. But older students have often been a part of that conventional culture for years. It may take a profound jolt to help them see for the first time that others may not only differ from them but may do so *legitimately*. As long as we have to be right or wrong, it is difficult to question our culture's givens and to form our own *considered* value position.

It is characteristic of the journey metaphor that mentors may be seen as gatekeepers as well as guides. They stand at the boundary of the old and the new worlds and, as such, hold the keys for successful passage. They understand the cryptic passwords and, like Virgil in Hell, seem to be able to move undaunted among the inhabitants of that frightening world. That they are in a position to make judgments and to select or reject us gives them considerable power. Their refusal can be a terrible blow; their acceptance of us, a tonic of magical force. Though some take to it more readily than others, such power makes most mentors uneasy. Handling it is delicate work, for to dissemble too soon can lead to confusion and even resentment from students. Yet to accept it too easily or to hold to it too long denies the student his or her own power. Indeed, the management of power over the life of the relationship is a central problem for both partners. Almost always, the relationship begins in a "complementary" mode in which the mentor is clearly dominant (Bateson, 1972). As the partners come to know each other more intimately, there is pressure for the relationship to become more symmetrical. But the movement is seldom smooth; sometimes one, sometimes the other partner resists. In many cases, the strain is too much. One partner moves too fast, the other is unwilling to change, or the changes are inappropriate, and the relationship collapses. Betty and Ken are a case in point.

Searching for the Rock

Student and teacher in a special-access program for adults who have been away from education for a number of years, Betty and Ken first met when she enrolled to take Dimensions of Learning, the centerpiece of the program, a course explicitly designed to provide a review of basic learning skills as well as to promote student development. In it, students practice solving problems, taking tests, reading analytically, and writing. The book list includes Plato's allegory of the cave from *The Republic, Revelations: The Diaries of Women,* and *1984*—all readings intended to promote the ability to carry on thoughtful discussion of matters existential and epistemological—a skill considered by Roger Cranse (1982), the program's designer, to be "more basic than basic." Classes are kept small, the atmosphere personal and supportive. The teacher's role includes acting as formal program adviser to students in each class, so the teaching load is relatively light.

Betty's ruddy appearance belies the strain of her forty-three years. The central fact of her life is that two years ago she "threw away [her] life to Jesus" and was born again. Her faith has been the galvanizing force for a life gone tragically awry with her husband's conviction for incest, the consequent destruction of her twenty-year marriage, and her forced departure from the family home where she had spent most of her life. A Christian fundamentalist group took her in, and she felt cared for in a way she had not experienced since childhood. Through them, she obtained work in a nursing home and returned to college to learn the skills she felt she would need to hold her job.

In our first interview, she explained that her former life had been "communistic," a term she used to mean "evil" rather than to describe a social system. Now that she had "come to Christ," she knew that certain things were right and others wrong; the Bible was an absolute authority in these matters. At the same time, she was fully aware that not everyone agreed with her and they had a right to their opinion, even if it was wrong. Furthermore, she did not believe "we're stuck with saying everything is bad or everything is good." Some things were gray, and good things could come from bad. Her own life had taught her that.

Her job as a student was to listen carefully to what she was told by her teachers, to respect their authority, and to do the assignments faithfully. Yet she did not always expect her teachers to tell her what to do. Sometimes they wanted her to learn for herself from her own mistakes. She held Ken in high esteem as her mentor. He was "very knowledgeable" and spoke distinctly. His chief responsibility to her was to "lead me into clear understandings," and she joked about being in love with him "in a girlish way." Asked to describe an ideal mentor, she said it would have to be someone who was "so perfect I wouldn't have to find flaws in his life." Although Ken was not that perfect, it was extremely difficult for her to be critical of him.

As an anthropologist, Ken prided himself on his blend of scientific rigor with deep caring for people. Developmental theory held a special fascination for him, and he enjoyed the "magic moment" when a student would move from belief that her own point of view, her "campfire," was the only one, to a recognition of "multiple campfires."

His role as teacher was to help students to see a complex world more intricately by exposing them to "a world bigger than they know . . . in a gentle, supportive way." While emotional engagement with his students was essential because significant learning required trust, it was important for just that reason that a certain separateness be maintained: "There are boundaries that we all have to accept."

Ken's greatest satisfaction as a mentor would come when a student became aware of herself and "took off," by which he meant "grow philosophically, begin to explore bigger, more complex, and less self-centered questions." His job was to be a catalyst, helping students to develop a "multiple campfire perspective." The student's part was chiefly to be "receptive" and to "want to fly." An ideal relationship would be one in which the student and the adviser would grow progressively closer and in which the student's respect for the teacher changes from "blind" to "earned."

He held a high regard for the power in his position and was cautious about "intervening with people who are reasonably content with their lives." He did not wish to risk hurting people by forcing change upon them. On the other hand, helping those ready to fly was what teaching was all about. "For us to grow, we have to help other people grow. You have to give it away to get it."

When Ken first met Betty, he was impressed by her openness, that New England charm, the intelligent wit. He was aware of her Christian fundamentalism but felt confident that she had sufficiently sophisticated ways of reasoning at her disposal to reconstrue her religious experience in less narrow and dogmatic patterns without losing her faith. She was, he believed, ready to fly.

A year later, disillusioned with Ken and discouraged with her work, Betty talks of dropping out. "I guess when you come right down to it, what I want to be is more mother and things like that than a working woman." Work with the elderly no longer holds a reward for her, and thus much of her reason for study is gone. In addition, she failed a psychology course, an event that she acknowledges was "more important than you want to admit."

The lecture format of the class had moved too fast, and the instructor and the text did not always agree.

He spewed out all his knowledge, and I was writing it down, and what he told us and what the book had sometimes was different stuff, so you had to study all your notes from him. So I knew I wasn't going to do that great. . . . It was like "how can I do anything but flunk this class?"

Moreover, much of what she was hearing conflicted with her faith, and she resented "being put in a block" and "having to fit their pattern."

Although during the previous semester she had not taken a class from Ken, she had seen him occasionally and recently had a long talk with him. She felt she was talking to her father. Asked what that felt like, she replied that it was having somebody who knows things she does not, someone who could guide her, give advice. "My father usually saw things that I didn't necessarily see," she said, and broke into tears. She later explained that she was feeling "homesick for parents I don't have."

Betty strongly feels she needs a guide now, and while Ken has "been there all right," their relationship has not been what she had hoped. She knows he feels that "probably religion got in the way." But she cannot separate her faith from other aspects of her life as he would have her do, and she feels that to do so would be "like building a house on sand that's going to sink and fall in; it's there but it has no foundation."

If anything, her religious faith has strengthened during the past year. When she "came to know Christ," she became a new person.

By doing that I feel free to be myself, and I wouldn't want to give up being free to be myself anymore because I'm no longer my own. I was bought by a price and I think Christ paid a dear price on the Cross to die for me, and now I'm on that road of seeing that, I would never want to change it. . . . There's something that's going to make this life worthwhile regardless if it's a hard

life all the way through. So I'll never turn back
and I'll never look at anything probably the same
as I did before . . . such as evolution.

She feels she has been protected by her conversion against
the danger of future error; her faith gives her a kind of sterile
environment guarding her against intellectual infection.

Yet she does not feel that religion has been a barrier to
her relationship with Ken. On the contrary, it has freed her to
be more herself, more objective about what she reads and
thinks. And although she finds it difficult to believe that "baboons turn into people," Betty goes on to say that "it is possible there is something to evolution. . . . There could be reasons
that God allowed some evolution. . . . I often feel like God has
not revealed any answers to some things specifically for us just
to trust."

By the end of the interview, Betty made it clear that although she was discouraged, she would not stop learning. What
had changed was her certainty about future training; it was beginning to look as though her education might take a lifetime.

Riding on the surf of his own midlife transition, Ken describes the past year as having brought tumultuous growth:
"I've been living more for the present . . . gaining some modi-
cum of humility . . . becoming less self-absorbed . . . a better
listener." All of this has narrowed the gap between vocation and
avocation, a positive development, he says.

His views about teaching and learning have not changed
significantly, though he acknowledges that his humility may
have some relationship to the experience with Betty. He shares
her disappointment, describing the association as "difficult,
challenging, and fairly unproductive."

"She's a very bright woman, very observant, has a good
sense of humor, a great deal of charm and potential." But he
found it difficult to deal with her fundamentalist religion.
What he saw as her "reluctance to move away from a kind of
safe haven in her religion" ran against his own belief in the value
of multiple perspectives. Whenever he attempted to discuss
ideas that were at variance with her interpretation of the Bible,

"switches began to shut down." That might have been all right except that she would turn to Scripture for support rather than her own powers of reason whenever a tough question arose.

He suggested that she try reading materials from other religious traditions in order to strengthen her Christianity, but she "saw this as a very dangerous area." At one point Ken tried confronting it directly.

> Betty, we've got two tanks in our head. One is our *faith* system, one is our belief system that can't really be tested empirically. We all have that. Whether we're Communists or Capitalists or Christians or Buddhists, we have that. We believe in *something* even if it's only ourselves. We've got a faith system. And the other is the *logical* system, the observable world, the observable, knowable universe of cause and effect relationships. We're not talking about theological stuff.

Betty listened politely and then replied:

> You can't separate the two. It's either God's way or it's not God's way. It's either right and just in God's way or it's not. And frankly, there are things in this class that are not God's way.

At about this time, Ken realized that he had run into "a blank wall." And although he felt considerable frustration, he was reluctant to "get out the pry bar" and increase the pressure. He saw Betty's belief system as an important "stability factor" in her life and felt it would be wrong to "mess around" with it.

> I'm not a faith buster. I'm not a reprogrammer. I don't deprogram and reprogram people. . . . I see nothing sinister or unacceptable in a firm Christian belief. I find my own spirituality is quite well developed, and I respect the spiritual develop-

> ment of others, but there's so much in the way of
> knee-jerk   response ... unthought-out   response
> among fundamentalists. . . . [They] think in terms
> of black and white extremes.

So he chose to "pull away from it," hoping that over time some of what he had said or she had read would settle in and she would feel more willing to extend her reason into presently unquestioned areas.

But there was another reason things fell apart. Partway through the first semester, Ken came to believe that Betty was infatuated with him. It was a painful situation, for not only was it one-sided but he felt it would be ethically inappropriate for him to reciprocate in any event. She was very vulnerable at the time, and he did not want to hurt her feelings.

> I tried to let her know in every way that I
> could, in every civilized, gentle way, that I was un-
> available. I kept her at arm's length. And this led
> to a downturn, too, because I couldn't see her in
> the same light as a protégé after she started de-
> claring this romantic interest in me. So that further
> flawed the relationship.

At the time of the final interview, the relationship had tapered to the point where it was "not quite as warm or respectful as it was." Ken is saddened by this, but resigned. Betty's case, he feels, was an exception.

What happened? Clearly Betty's traumatic experience of betrayal contributed to her subsequent immersion in religious fervor. It might well be argued that we are treading here on the borders of psychotherapy, theology, or both—territory conventionally off-limits to educators. Ken felt that way, and his intuitions and respect for Betty's delicate balance led him to back away from a situation he feared was beyond him. At the same time, it is apparent that Betty's capacity as a student and her potential for intellectual growth—both concerns properly within educational bounds—were linked to the event and her way of dealing with it. The putative separation of intellect and affect is too often a convenient excuse to avoid asking hard but important educational questions. It takes but the slightest deepening of focus to see that both education and religion are centrally about growth of the spirit, and it is no accident that in less specialized societies healers, teachers, and priests are often the same person.

In any case, Ken felt that Betty was using her religion as a protective device, however necessary, to keep her from asking the sorts of questions that would lead to greater intellectual flexibility and complexity. When he sensed her precariousness, he backed away. At the same time, he has noted that someone with Betty's own religious sensibilities and somewhat less dogmatism might be able to help her "loosen up." His use of that phrase is interesting, for like someone wounded by a flying object, Betty is suffering from spiritual injury. As with a laceration in which the area around the wound stiffens to protect it from further harm, so did she stiffen her epistemology against further insults. Recovery would seem to involve a gradual loosening of the area as the traumatized region shrinks.

In certain ways, the healing metaphor is appropriate here. Betty found herself in a spiritual intensive care unit, a caring community that gave her the support she desperately needed when she needed it. The question, of course, is "Does she want to recover the flexibility?" And can she do so without either rejecting her community or losing her faith? Ken had hoped she could and would. It was apparent to him that her dualistic bifurcation of the world was limited to certain particularly sensitive areas. She was willing enough to acknowledge that some things were intrinsically gray, and on the whole she was probably more multiplistic than dualistic. Perhaps he could help her recognize those areas and then, bit by bit, transfer "horizontally" her gray areas toward the injured zone. But she found it difficult to handle a class in which there appeared to be two differing authorities and felt helpless. Her tendency to see the instructor as a fount of knowledge rather than herself as a source of learning meant that she found it hard to organize the material in ways that made sense to her. After all, what good would that do? Her task was not to make sense of disparate information; it was to learn the truth. Given that, she was right. How could she but flunk? It wasn't that she *did* something wrong; it was that she understood the situation inappropriately.

And then she got sweet on him. Transference, as the psychoanalysts call it, is what gives the mentor-protégé relationship its fire. Commonly understood as the process by which patients project their fears and aspirations onto the therapist, it occurs in modified form in virtually all mentorships. Therapists are taught to use it to help patients move through their particular problems. Ken had no such training, and for him it was simply an inappropriate infatuation. He did not wish to "use" it for anything. He just felt uncomfortable and wanted out. One can hardly blame him, for it appears from Betty's association of him with her father that her expectations were substantial. Ken's reluctance to play that part may contribute to her own discovery that she can care for herself, that she doesn't need a perfect mentor to protect her. If she can accept that and learn from it, she will continue to heal.

As every teacher knows, love in its many forms is central to the whole enterprise. It only becomes a problem when it moves in some way out of bounds we consider legitimate. That seems to happen in close situations of this sort rather frequently. Occasionally it works, and things go smoothly, but far more often one or the other partner—usually the student—ends up hurt. Some (though by no means all) of the growing number of sexual harassment cases now emerging on campuses may chronicle such relationships gone bad. And though it may sadden us, we ought not be surprised that sexuality so frequently becomes an issue; mentorships have a special intimacy, and the bounds are not always clear. Because the teacher holds the power in the situation, the primary responsibility for drawing the line falls in his or her hands. The decision can be painful, for we know that in the intensity of the connection lies the power of the teaching.

Still, neither Ken nor Betty has entirely shut off the relationship, even though it seems to have gone into temporary storage. It would be a mistake to assume that nothing has happened. Indeed, Betty could use much of what has occurred for her own healing. Whether she will or not remains to be seen, and for now she is very much in the wilderness, wandering, as she acknowledges, on sand, unsure of her footing, still believing that somewhere there must be solid rock.

For his part, Ken wound up feeling frustrated. He had chosen not to challenge Betty beyond a certain point for fear of hurting her delicate balance, but he found his efforts at support misinterpreted. The result was a stalemate.

But sometimes a student's difficulties lie outside the bounds of the relationship. Sometimes the only thing a teacher can do is be present when she is needed. It can be helpful at such moments to be able to step back and know that the best "intervention" is simply to be there. This seems to be what happened with Jean and Dolores.

Family Ties

Three years before our first interview, Jean's husband had been disabled, and in order to support the family she was forced to leave the home where she had raised four children into their teens. She took work as a chambermaid in a local resort, but soon dissatisfied with menial labor, she began secretarial studies at the local community college. Though the decision had hardly been free, she says, "it was something I always wanted to do," expressing a deep desire to "better" herself. Jean is now thirty-five, and her children are well along in school. "I feel it's time—it's now or never."

Most of her courses were job-related: typing, office procedures, shorthand. But she also enrolled in Dimensions of Learning, a course she entered with great fear, feeling "very, very lost." Here she met Dolores, her teacher, who turned out to be "super easy to talk to." Dolores's job, as Jean saw it, was "to get everyone through," and she was "fantastic" at it. Dolores seemed to know everything, was very patient, committed to her work, and loved reading. "She's got it all together, and I definitely haven't." Yet this did not mean Dolores was perfect; Jean might disagree with her teacher on occasion.

Math class was fairly comfortable because it was "pretty black and white; there's a set way to do it and that's it." Dimensions, on the other hand, "has a lot of levels of doing it right." Anyone's opinion there could be as good as anyone else's, though some opinions didn't make as much sense as others because they lacked the facts "to back them up."

Jean felt a good deal of frustration with herself for "always doing the things [she was] supposed to do" rather than what she wanted for herself. She admired her teacher's independence and looked to Dolores to help her set goals and to keep her "on the track." As long as she remained attentive and honest, she felt confident that Dolores "would be there."

For her part, Dolores loves her work, and talks with matter-of-fact amazement about her first class. When she first asked if anyone knew who Plato was, a hand shot enthusiastically into the air: "He's a dog, ain't he?" *and nobody laughed.* They all agreed.

Dolores didn't laugh either. Her job was to provide a climate where students could talk freely without embarrassment, think aloud without being put down, and experiment with sometimes frightening ideas. Education ought to help students to see themselves in a new way. It should move them from "narrow rights and wrongs" to where they could "work with ideas and not have to see the world as black and white." To do that, they had to feel safe from scorn. Her part in that was to act as a "sounding board for ideas, one that encourages rather than ridicules."

The term *mentor* had only recently come into her vocabulary, but she liked it. It had a reciprocal, two-way quality that appealed to her. Far from placing her on a pedestal, she felt the term allowed her to reveal her clay feet. That was important, for she was put off when students idolized her. They needed to see her survive errors so they could learn to do the same. As long as they were hooked on their failures, they would have difficulty seeing their successes.

Dolores had a special fondness for Jean. Like herself, Jean seemed to be honoring an inner voice that said it was time to care for herself. And Jean's curiosity, eagerness, enthusiasm, "inner sparkle," appealed to her. Dolores was aware of her student's insecurity, her fear of the journey she was undertaking, so it was Jean's courage that Dolores admired most of all—her "determination to get on with her life plan despite horrendous family problems." She held great hopes for Jean.

> She's so ready to push ahead with some new ideas. . . . She's going to move into doing a lot of independent thinking; she's going to be doing a lot of challenging because you can see it now, just those little sparks. I think she'll be able to move tremendously. . . . She's just standing at the threshold.

A year later, after mixed success in her secretarial science courses, Jean is confused, discouraged, and frustrated. She is still "hanging in there, still battling," but more than once she has almost quit. The reason, she insists, is not so much her schoolwork as her homework. Her husband has not made the progress she had hoped he would in recovering from his disabling accident, her nineteen-year-old daughter has moved into the house with a baby, and Jean feels almost completely without support.

> Last semester I tried getting out of the house to do my homework, but that didn't work because my husband was upset because I was gone so much. And I'm trying to do my homework around the telephone ringing and the TV going and the radio going, not having any room to go into by myself; or even if I go in and close myself in the bedroom I find that they're coming in and interrupting me even when I'm in there and even after I've asked them not to. . . . They don't feel how important it is for me. You know, they haven't even begun to grasp that yet, how important it is for me to do this.

Her frustration is all the greater as she feels the impact of her education, both *what* she is studying and *that* she is studying. She enjoys being with other students, feels as though she is "into the world" and "participating in something." And although she is not sure she is "on the track I was when I started," this does not worry her. There seems to be something more to it now than just learning how to be a secretary and more to her life than being "only a mother."

Knowing she will be heard has allowed Jean to gain a greater sense of her voice during the past year. She is no longer as afraid as before to speak up in class; she feels freer to ask questions. If someone calls her on the phone, she feels "more authoritative," more self-confident than she used to. And although she is ambivalent about it, she sees her goal as somewhat closer now, feeling that even though her family may not know (or care), "inside myself, I'm growing."

Asked how she would resolve a situation where two experts offered conflicting opinions, Jean says:

> I would probably go with the one that was closest to my own opinion, if I had an opinion on it. If not, I would just weigh the evidence and then state who I feel was right. . . . We act on the evidence we have right in front of us. We take a step in that direction. If everything comes out all right, we feel it's right. If it doesn't, we feel that it was the wrong choice and just learn from it and try again.

Faced with a difficult real-life moral choice, she may not have an answer. Pressed, she would turn to the religious principles she was brought up with. She believes in God, but is not "overreligious." "I guess I basically live by the rules," she says. "That's been set for us from generation to generation, and it was there for me."

Jean has not seen her mentor much since the Dimensions class ended, even though Dolores has invited her to drop by numerous times. When they have talked, however, it has been "refreshing." Jean has never failed to feel Dolores's interest, concern, and warmth, knowing she can talk to Dolores about anything, "not just the school." At the same time, Jean senses that her teacher will not tell her what she has to do but rather will let her make her own mistakes. She values that.

Despite their relatively minimal contact in the six months preceding the second interview, Jean has felt that Dolores was not far away, that the choice was hers to make if she wanted to talk. Even in absentia, she says,

> I see her supporting my goal, and I see her challenging, because she's where I want to be some day—not, say, this given job but her emotional attitudes toward her job and everything. I see her being where someday I want to be.

Dolores represents for Jean someone who has been where she wants to go. Her mentor incarnates her dreams and gives her encouragement to see beyond her immediate surroundings. She has begun to wonder whether the track she set out upon is the best one for her and has begun to dare to imagine something more.

> I'd like to be able to carry on a conversation with somebody and know what I'm talking about, have opinions—not like it's a math problem, right or wrong period—but just being able to give an opinion and know that it's really my opinion because I know what I'm talking about.
>
> In the back of my head I've always wanted to go back to school just to learn and to be more qualifying, to be more worldly about what's going on in the world. Not just the history of the world and how are math problems done, but just to be more learned about what's going on in general—everything.
>
> I was beginning to feel like I was just a

mother, and I felt important to my kids and to my
husband, but outside of that house I felt like a
stranger. And I don't have that feeling so much anymore.

And yet the questions raised by her family remain, not
only whether to study secretarial science or literature but
whether to continue studying at all.

Dolores shares Jean's sense of frustration. She wishes
they could have had more time together and fears that "things
have fallen apart" between them. Yet to an astonishing degree,
she is aware of Jean's difficulties despite what she feels is in-
adequate contact.

. . . limited finances, family problems caus-
ing severe barriers to her own education . . . resistance from a spouse who feels threatened not
only by her intellectual growth and curiosity but
by her being away from where he can see her and
exercise that sort of control he feels he needs to
assure himself that she'll stay with him. . . . And
there's an alcohol problem.

In addition to occasional phone calls and passing conversations, a current work-study student and friend of Jean's has
been acting as an intermediary between Dolores and Jean: "A
lot of messages from Jean come to me through Anne. . . . We
send messages back and forth through her."

Describing her student's past year as a journey, Dolores
has this to say:

It's a journey with a lot of potholes and
trees across the road, and thunderstorms, and needing to take detours. Last term she really had to
take a detour, and maybe she's had to fill in a couple of potholes this year, but she's underway again,
still moving ahead.

What is her responsibility as a guide to Jean?

> Maybe just trying to be there with the flash-
> light and keeping the door at various places of the
> journey open when she wants or feels that she is
> able to make it in . . . helping her find balance,
> looking at the different piles of stuff in her life
> with the old flashlight and saying, "Where are you
> going to add this chunk called school? How is it
> going to balance you?"

It is particularly important as she works with Jean, as
with all her students, Dolores says, to keep in mind the whole
of Jean's life, not just her academic curriculum. There is a temptation "to steer students into courses you 'know' would be
good for them," without regard for their capacity to handle the
work, given the rest of the forces in their lives.

> I need to understand Jean's whole life; I
> need to be able to see all the pressures on her. . . .
> We can't assure everybody success, but I think we
> can work with the whole framework, the holistic
> approach, so that the chances of success are going
> to be much greater than if we don't focus on the
> whole picture of the adult.

Dolores has heard her student's growing concern with
larger questions, and it frustrates her to think that Jean may be
unready to nurture that movement in herself. Yet she recognizes that her student needs practical training right now, and
she respects that need. She sees the distance that Jean has already traveled, but she also senses the threads that hold her
student, and from that perspective comes the wisdom to decide
when to support and when to challenge her student.

Jean's story is all too common. Her tale of trying to read
in the midst of whirling family life—often at the kitchen table—
brings a grimace of recognition to her sisters everywhere. For

most adult learners, the return to study, however exhilarating at moments, entails long hours of sheer drudgery, often at cost to family life. Dolores's recognition of the importance of seeing the *whole* student cannot be overemphasized. This is particularly true for female students who tend to be more concerned than men about the effect that their study may have on other people in their lives for whom they accept responsibility. Recent research on gender differences would seem to suggest that when study is seen as demanding a choice between cost to others and benefit to oneself, women are likely to sacrifice their studies more often than men (Evans, 1985).

Frequently, campus-based teachers fail to recognize that their commuting students live very different lives from residential undergraduates. And while no one (least of all the students themselves!) seriously argues that we should relax standards for these students, it is imperative that the boundaries that make sense for eighteen-year-old full-time students be reexamined for their usefulness to the growing number of working students of all ages. Class hours can be changed, completion deadlines made more flexible, study methods made more appropriate, and a range of more dramatic and imaginative reforms introduced in order to provide the kind of supports and challenges appropriate to students whose lives are demonstrably different from those for whom colleges were earlier designed.

But there is more than institutional rationale for attending to the whole lives of students. Knowing what is important to our students as individuals, we can more readily help them find connections between the lives they live and the subjects we teach. Effective advising is more than simply spewing out distribution requirements and interpreting regulations. A colleague describes his job as "accountant, lawyer, and philosopher king." Thus, we may shuffle credits and distribute requirements, but more important is our support and advocacy for the student, and more important still is our loyalty to a tradition of learning and intellectual accomplishment. When the first is allowed to eclipse the other two, we have prostituted our students and betrayed our commitment.

In the end, it is simply *better* to see human beings as

wholes rather than isolated minds, bodies, or souls. It is phe-
nomenologically better because it recognizes that the world is
intrinsically connected and respects those connections *before*
sundering them for purposes of analysis, not after. It is intellectually better because it allows a more complex and dynamic
understanding of living phenomena in flux, a grounded and contextual grasp rather than the abstract and conveniently frozen
vision of a cadaver on a table. And it is ethically better because
it represents a stance at least approaching a loving, caring respect for the inherent worth of the other person.

Having said all that, let's return to Jean's words. She says
she has "grown" even though others in her family may not recognize it (and, she implies, may not want to). But has she? Few
people, if asked, will deny that they have grown in some way;
our culture smiles on the word. Indeed, Jean's way of thinking
about knowledge seems essentially as it was a year earlier. She
said then that some things like math were black and white,
others gray; and she seemed to have no particularly sharp tools
for deciding whether something was right or wrong. After a
year, she acknowledges that she would "weigh the evidence"
but is still some distance from the kind of ease with the tool
that characterizes contextual thinking, and pressed to make an
ethical decision, she would finally turn back to her upbringing
rather than forward to her own developing principles. Those
seem to lie still ahead for her.

And yet, speaking of her "voice," she is unmixed in her
assertion that she has become stronger in important ways. She
speaks up in class, she disagrees where she would earlier have
buckled, and she can talk with others now about things she earlier would have bottled up. Especially among women, "voice"
has been shown to be a particularly clear metaphor for growth
(Belenky, Clinchy, Goldberger, and Tarule, 1986). Jean confirms this resoundingly. And her movement is echoed as she describes her new sense of self on getting out of the house and
"into the world." As she moves out, her angle of vision ex-
pands, and secretarial study no longer seems the only choice before her. Although her voice has yet to find the strength of
Sandy's "I want to be a legitimate member of the world," it is

the same song, no doubt about that. Whas has to happen is for the *figure* of the outside world to become *ground*. That is, moving out of the house is still an aberrant act for Jean. The house is where her home is, and under stress she will retreat there rather than stay in the world where her supports are still so tentative. In time, perhaps this will reverse so that the world will become the background, her house a special case. That day is some time off, of course, and may never arrive. But that is what lies over the horizon toward which Jean is trekking. As she continues to move, the choice will become increasingly real.

Dolores's part in this is difficult to see at first. Like many mentors, she feels she could have done more. And yet it seems clear that Jean didn't ask for more. She had ample opportunity to see Dolores and decided not to. As near as we can tell, this had nothing to do with negative feelings between the two. On the contrary, each speaks warmly of the other. Rather, it seems to be a mixture of Jean's own guilt about her family struggles and her strong inner sense that she can handle things by herself. Given that, Dolores offered perhaps the best gift she could: her caring presence.

By remaining receptive and available to Jean when she was needed, Dolores let her student know that she mattered enough to be cared about by someone important in the world. That's potent tonic, even on the shelf. Dolores's mere presence seems to have been a powerful support for Jean, for she knew that she could not drop out with Dolores around, she knew that someone who cared was watching her, and she knew that Dolores would be there if she really needed help. Mentors sometimes seem to function this way, as guardian angels, invisible but present and guiding. And just in case she needed to check to see if the angel was still there, Jean could send her friend Anne, the intermediary, to make sure.

But if Ken thought it unwise to challenge Betty's beliefs and Dolores found her steady presence to be her best choice for Jean, the next case illustrates what can happen when the situation is ripe for a happy blending of challenge and support. Notice how Hank supports his student by encouraging him to speak in his own voice, yet challenges him to hear other voices as well.

Growing Doubt

Richard had dropped out of college his freshman year. Ten years older now, something about him still appeared younger than his age. It was not his long hair and earring that set him off so much as a certain forced carefree quality. Many of his fellow adult students were well ensconced and even advanced in their careers. Richard was still undecided. Commitment, he maintained, was OK for some people, but he believed in freedom. During his years at large, he had lived in several communal situations. None had worked out very well for him, yet he would spend hours in conversation with fellow students arguing the superiority of such collectives over private living arrangements, which he labeled "selfish" and "archaic." Other students soon tired of the game, however, and complained that he rarely had anything fresh to say; whenever someone questioned him, he would revert to his "party line." This was particularly true when he spoke about education. "Schools should be abolished," he would say. "If we just let kids alone, they'd grow up much more healthy; people should be free."

He rejected the idea of authority, saying that it was responsible for "all the wars of history." If people would just be free, there would be no war. Asked what it meant to be free, he replied, "Well, you have to reject authority." For him, Summerhill, the progressive English school, represented the only legitimate form of education. He counted A. S. Neill, Baba Ram Dass, and Marshall Parks, an obscure anarchist, among the few thinkers he respected. "It's not because of their authority," he explained; "it's because they know the truth." He looked forward to his independent study on educational philosophies with Hank; Hank would understand.

"It's almost as though he sees me as a potential convert," was Hank's opening description of Richard. "He seems to need confirmation of his beliefs so badly."

Hank made these remarks on the basis of a brief conversation with Richard and twenty years as a teacher of adults. His early training had been in English, and like many of his colleagues fascinated by underlying thought structure, he had been drawn toward adult development theory in recent years.

"One of the intriguing things about all this stuff," he said wryly of the growing body of developmental research, "is that knowing about it doesn't keep it from happening." He was emerging from "a tumultuous midlife crisis" that had seen the end of his fifteen-year marriage and "an astonishing new freedom." Yet Hank's idea of freedom differed sharply from Richard's. "Freedom is like breathing," Hank said, "You have to keep doing it all the time . . . and there are times when you wonder if it's worth it." For him, the end of education is the enhancement of freedom. A good education should free people from their past, from their own cultures, without depriving them of either.

The most important thing that he had learned over the years about his work was how to listen. For him, listening well meant "actually trying to enter the world of the other person, see through his or her eyes as clearly as possible, without making assumptions or judgments. Just plain 'get' their world as they see it." In this act of listening, one could not only understand better how to work but "listening like that is teaching in the profoundest sense."

Hank described mixed feelings about his first contact with Richard. He was at once attracted to the young man's sincerity and passion; he liked and agreed with Richard's views, yet found them "remarkably rigid," and was disturbed that an idea as important to him as freedom could be so casually made into what he called "a canned religion."

Six months later, at the conclusion of the study, Richard is noticeably subdued. Asked about this, he replies, "I guess the biggest thing that stands out for me is that I'm not so sure of things anymore." This is not bad, he goes on, "only that I'm not so confident now as I was, you know? There are so many sides to things. It kind of makes you think."

The study had gone "really well" at first. He had decided with Hank to look at a variety of different ideas about freedom and education through history and in different cultures. The idea appealed to him because he saw it as an opportunity to confirm his views about society's destructive effects on the young through educational institutions. What happened?

> It turned out a whole lot more complicated than I had expected. I mean you look at a guy like Plato and it's pretty obvious . . . that he put society ahead of the individual, you know? But then you start looking at why you have to do that sometimes, like in Tanzania, for instance, or what happens if you have too much freedom.

Pressed for conclusions, he replies that "there just isn't any way to know for sure." He guesses that it "might depend on the situation" as to what would be the best approach. Perhaps surprisingly, he is not particularly uncomfortable about this. He seems to take a kind of new refuge in his tentative intellectual diffidence and denies that it is a major change for him.

> I don't think I've changed my opinion all that much; it's just that I have to think more about whether my opinions are, you know, any good. [What is a "good" opinion?] Well, I guess one that has some facts behind it, maybe some research to back it up. That's what I mean by "think"—you have to consider something from all its aspects before you make up your mind. And I kind of like that, you know? I mean it almost feels better to not know about something than to know it. Does that make any sense?

At one point, about midway through the study, Richard felt "pretty discouraged." He had begun his work with considerable momentum, but as his reading progressed, he began to realize that there were more sides to the problem than he had realized. He found it extremely difficult to write his second paper, a description of Plato's view of the role of education. In part this was because the language was difficult, but more, he found it almost impossible to describe a position different from his own, as Hank had specified, without injecting his own opinion. In the end, he had written a largely subjective reaction and had not received a favorable response from his mentor.

He was angry at first, but Hank's critique had not been wholly negative. "He said that what I had written was OK; it just wasn't the assignment, and he pointed out particular passages in the reading that I should go over again for the meaning." The second time Richard tried, he said, "I got much better comments." He was beginning to get the idea of distilling someone else's ideas, though he wasn't sure he saw the point. "I remember thinking, 'Why should I use these guys' ideas instead of my own?' and it sort of got me." As the term's work progressed, however, he found it easier to understand the readings, and by the end, he was able to produce a final paper that combined the ideas in his reading with some of his own. Did he reach any conclusions? No, he explains, but "I think I learned a lot—about how much there is to know."

Hank was pleased with the study. "Richard came a long way," he says. "I think what he learned most maybe was some humility." The first assignment had been simply a paper about Richard's own ideas—"a strictly personal statement" in order to let him feel that what he had to say was important but also to give both Hank and himself a starting point from which to see what difference it would make, as Hank wryly notes, "if he learned anything."

Like Richard, Hank considers the rewriting of the second paper to be a critical incident. "I think that's when he began to get it that his own subjective impressions—which were really not his own but were cloned from his countercultural heroes—were not going to be adequate." But Hank emphasizes the importance of his having provided positive support along with his criticism of the effort: "I tried to tell him that it wasn't *what* he was saying that was the problem, but *how* he was thinking about the question. He was still looking for answers from authorities, even though he outwardly rejected the idea."

The support was particularly important, Hank says, because he was really asking the student to let go of "some pretty

important external supports" in his preexisting doctrines, and
he had to be willing to be leaned on for a while during Richard's transition to "self-propulsion."

Hank is less sure that any substantial changes occurred in
Richard's view of freedom, a goal that he had held at the outset
of the study. The final paper did not deal very thoroughly with
the topic, and Hank's feelings about this departure are mixed.

> I guess you can only expect so much. He did
> loosen up a whole lot, and the final paper was a
> classic case of sophomoric multiplicity, where you
> have gotten the idea that there are a million ways
> of seeing but haven't yet figured out how to make
> them cohere. . . . I think he still believes freedom is
> some sort of Nirvana, and Baba Ram Dass is still
> on his throne, I think, but the world has gotten
> more complicated for him, that's sure. And—isn't it
> interesting—he's a whole lot quieter.

Richard's movement was clear and fairly direct, if un-
dramatic. As he acknowledges, he loosened up from his doc-
trinaire stance, allowing himself, with Hank's help, to move
around and look at the phenomenon of education from several
vantage points. In doing so, he discovered that the floor did not
fall away when he took a step out; he could immerse himself in
a different way of seeing and still return if he needed to. His
world, initially cast as an island of freedom surrounded by hostile authority, began to lose its harsh edges as the study developed. And although the movement stopped short of a complete
transformation of his idea of freedom, it is apparent that as
Richard's thinking becomes more complex, this idea too will
grow richer.

When their collaboration began, Richard viewed Hank as
the only teacher who would be sympathetic to views that he
considered too radical for most faculty. This was not because
he knew what Hank actually believed but rather that he saw
Hank to be more open, less judgmental—and consequently less
threatening—than the others. In this sense, Richard never ac-

tually saw Hank at all in the beginning. It was only as the study got underway that the young man realized that he was under some sort of pressure. Initially encouraged to express his own views, Richard could then invest himself in the work in a way he almost certainly would not have under more conventional circumstances. Hank was wary of his student's tendency toward counterdependence, a stance that Sharon Parks (1986) describes as still a part of reliance on authority. He did not want to get thrust aside with all the other jetsam in Richard's wake.

Richard is not clear about his feelings during the difficult middle of the study. Off the record, Hank acknowledges a certain sadistic twinge as he sent Richard's paper back. He knew it would be difficult for the student. Yet Richard simply describes himself as "quite upset." He seems unwilling to acknowledge anger toward his mentor. Later, as he began to "get it," and as the praise became more abundant, his esteem for Hank grew. By the end of the study, he sees Hank as "incredibly supportive, I mean just incredibly. He seemed to know just what I needed, and when I needed it. I couldn't have made it through without him." It's almost as if he has forgotten who threw him in in the first place!

Richard seems to have made the kinds of change we tend to call progress. He moved undeniably toward greater multiplicity, his thought grew more complex, and considering where he was coming from, the decrease in self-confidence is healthy for him. This part of the journey often witnesses such change, as uncertainty becomes more prevalent and legitimate. He was fortunate in having a teacher who was both skilled and sensitive enough to make the right moves at the right time. Although the change in their relationship is not dramatic, the two men certainly moved closer together in the course of the study, coming to know each other better even if there is no indication that they will continue the friendship after the formalities are over.

Yet as we have observed, it would be a mistake to consider the other two relationships to be less successful in any profound sense. For if a collaboration between mentor and student is fruitful, its primary task is to enable the student to work with the business she has before her. What is important in Betty's case is that she learn to be more comfortable in the uncertainty that surrounds her. If it means that she must wander for a while and do so alone, then perhaps that is what she needs. As long as she can know that someone will be there when she is ready to move on, it need not be Ken. There may be another, or perhaps she will find she can travel by herself.

Joan's movement is fragmented, not at all uniform, but she has spoken strongly in her new voice, and while the way ahead is dark, it is clear that she knows Dolores is there for her when she needs her. In Perry's language, she is temporizing. Some part of her knows it is not yet time to move on. Yet the foundations of her former world are shifting. As of this writing, although she is still a stop-out, it is significant that she has retained contact with Dolores and with college. It is almost as though she is just waiting until the ties that still hold her to her family slip a bit more, until she can move into a new family and new self without forsaking the old.

Richard's next step is to continue working with his new insights about the complexity and multiplicity of truth. As he does so, he may well begin to ask, perhaps with some anger, what right the institution has to make any judgments at all about him or his work. Like Emerald, the accountant we met in the first chapter, he is at a vulnerable if occasionally exuberant position, and it may be a while before he is able to move ahead and make the sorts of clear commitments that some of his fellow students have made. But he has finally broken the stuck place of his earlier fundamentalism and with care and support will be able to move ahead without retreating to the safer but less adequate world he has left behind.

It is important to note that all three students are moving. With the help of their teachers, they have lost their balance, and each is struggling to regain it. With the possible exception of Betty, when they do, they are virtually certain to find that they are no longer standing in the same place.

But these cases are all situations where teacher and student worked closely together. Are there lessons here for those in the more traditional classroom? Clearly the answer is yes, but

I want to emphasize that the lessons do not require individualizing instruction. Rather, they involve enriching our teaching so that each student can take from it what she or he needs. Here are some thoughts.

First, there are few college-level subjects in which there is no legitimate controversy. While it may, indeed, be wise to emphasize a preferred approach, teachers should attempt to *present a range of different perspectives* on their subjects and on the topics within subjects. What are the great controversies in the field? How do the antagonists support their positions? What are the differences in methodology? Practitioners in the field can be invited as guest speakers to present controversial positions. This is not simply so that each student can seize on a preferred approach. It is so that all students can recognize that there may be many paths up the mountain. That is where the developmental press occurs (Knefelkamp, Widick, and Parker, 1978).

Second, teachers can strive to provide a broad overview of their subject. What are the assumptions underlying the field? Is it possible to imagine other assumptions? Are the "truths" universally accepted, or do other cultures handle matters differently? How did the subject evolve through history? How was knowledge accumulated in the field? How is it related to other subjects? What impact has technology had on the evolution of methodology? Who are the "experts" and how did they get where they are? In short, we can *provide a context for our subjects,* a map of the field to remind students that all knowledge rests on a web of assertions, not some absolute, immutable Truth. Regardless of how practical or applied the field may be, graduates who see the big picture and can think independently on their feet are invariably more valuable than those who can only do things the "correct" way. This point is driven home for subjects as diverse as engineering, business administration, and education in Arthur Chickering and his colleagues' *The Modern American College* (1981).

Third, ample *opportunity to discuss and debate* the material is important. One of the greatest values of class discussion is the chance that it offers for students to role play positions with which they may overtly disagree. An avowed liberal might be asked to present impartially the conservative position on an issue, for instance, or members of different ethnic groups might reverse roles. This need not be done in a formal or artificial way. Rather, the instructor can periodically ask one or another student to assume a fresh stance in addressing a question. "I know you are a feminist, Alice, but how would a supporter of Jesse Helms respond to this issue?" "How do you suppose an inner-city black might react to what you just said, Nathaniel?" Development is closely related to the enrichment of inner dialogue, and class discussion helps students to process material, to hear different accents and to try speaking in new voices.

Finally, a quick survey of age, sex, and interests of a class, informed by a knowledge of developmental patterns, can help us to make some reasonable guesses about *the tasks confronted by our students*. Readings and written assignments can emphasize issues of concern to each group. Sharan Merriam (1984), for instance, has compiled a useful set of readings from literature around major themes of adulthood.

It is a given that what distinguishes Betty, Jean, and Richard from their teachers is not the size of their brains. Nor is it their age. The students simply think in ways that fail to match the complexity and intellectual dexterity expected of a college graduate or demanded by their expanding worlds.

It is a given, too, that these folks *can* change, though their teachers may well despair, and it might take more drastic alterations in their lives than simply attending courses to bring change about. In many ways, the traditional ages of college attendance are ideal for the sorts of change we value in liberal education: greater independence from authority, a new perspective on one's culture, and the capacity to think hypothetically and contextually. For this is the time of separation from family and upbringing, of the enhancement of formal operations (Inhelder and Piaget, 1958), and of the making of new commitments in a new environment. As Chickering (1969) has richly illustrated, campus life is ideal for the development of an autonomous identity. But for adults, few of whom live on campus and all of whom are deeply embedded in real-life relationships, such change comes with a good many strings attached. In a case like Betty's or perhaps Jean's, those strings may just prove too constraining.

Therefore, as teachers and advisers there is much we can do to help our students decide how far, in what ways, and even whether they will continue the journey. We can seek to understand the ties that hold our students in their present lives so that, like Ken, we can better judge how much challenge is enough. We can work to extend our respect for their struggle and communicate our support regardless of whether we happen to approve of how they are conducting it. We can encourage our students to look clearly at their own motivations for returning to college, to ask themselves the hard questions, and to respond as honestly as possible to those questions. We can do this individually in conversations after class or in comments on written work; or we can take time to encourage classroom discussion of the impact of class content on the "outside" lives of our students. Whichever way our students finally decide to go, we owe it to them to help their decision be a conscious one, chosen in the fullest light we can cast between us.

Before we move next into the heart of the journey, here are some guiding principles that have emerged thus far.

The primary task is to *engender trust.* One of the best ways to do this is to listen well. This means suspending our own agenda for the moment and attempting to enter the student's world. It also means asking questions that will move the student's reflections onto a level where the meanings are made. "Why have you come back to school?" is often a good starter, allowing both teacher and student to understand the place that education occupies in a student's life. "What are you learning?" can open the discussion more fully, followed by questions ("Why is that important?" or "How does that relate to what you said earlier?") that move beneath the content answers that frequently come first. "Can you tell me about a good teacher you have had?" is another question that moves to issues of authority and what is worth learning. Needless to say, the task at this early stage requires that we simply acknowledge the legitimacy of the answers, not that we judge them.

It is important in the early phases to *see the student's movement*. During an opening conversation, we can make a rough assessment. How is she moving? away from simple blacks and whites toward gray? away from tribal anonymity toward a more visible self? Or is she rebuilding a frame of meanings in a more contextual and interrelated way? And how does the return to education fit with life, her family, his work? This is a time for an initial diagnosis in which we look not so much for "strong" or "weak" points as for growing and withering edges as new perspectives succeed old like cells on a growing organism. It can be helpful to remember that narrow thinking is less an affront to us than a limitation of the relationship. It is a place to begin.

Throughout, we need to *give the student a voice*. As in any dialogue, it is important to grant space to the student's own views at first. This can be done individually or with classes. One accounting teacher tells of an early assignment in which he asked students to write a brief paper on what most people don't know about accounting. This yielded material with which he laced subsequent lessons and allowed him to connect the subject with the lives of his students in numerous fresh ways. Not only does this allow the teacher to learn more of the student but students then have a clear record of their own opening position in the dialogue, and they know they have been heard. In courses or studies where there is reasonable latitude for individual exploration, questions like "What would you like to learn about if you really had your choice?" or "What burning question would you like to pursue in this subject?" can often help students find an emotional core with which to fuel their investigation.

As trust is established and a way charted, it may be time to *introduce conflict*. An appropriate dose of conflicting or counterintuitive information can raise questions about the student's givens. This might be done by calling attention to the major disputes in the field or introducing data that do not fit the prevailing paradigm. Or one might ask the student to take an unfamiliar perspective or to explain in a sympathetic manner a position with which she disagrees. A subject like history, which places our absolutes in the context of time, or anthropology, which does the same across space, has special power because it can relativize our cultural givens and force us to construct new ways to hold the conflicting "facts." A historical or crosscultural perspective introduced to any subject from engineering to business administration can have this effect and help students to learn that before they agree or disagree with a position, they must first *understand* each side fully.

As students respond to the questions, in conversation or writing, it is important to watch for the growing edge, like a coach to photograph their forward movement and replay it for them. This may mean being very explicit about what students have done well. It is generally more effective to show people when they are on track than to tell them where they should go or to criticize when they have strayed. *Emphasize positive movement,* underline it, restate it, praise it. By spending undue time on the negative, we run the risk of simply helping our students to construct a vision of the impossible when our job is to help them imagine the possible and then move toward it. Always we are guides, encouraging movement.

Throughout this part of the journey, it is valuable to keep *one eye on the relationship* itself. Most often, as student and teacher come to know each other better, the distance between the two that characterized the early days narrows. As greater intimacy develops, some of the student's unreflecting deference to authority may diminish. No longer based on superficial trappings, the relationship has the potential to be transformed into something more profound and powerful. This has major implications for the growth of both partners, as we shall see in the next two chapters.

Chapter Five 🍂

How Learning Changes the Learner

> ... the person is most of all a motion, a motion
> that neither we nor she can deny without cost, and
> a motion which includes experience of balance and
> imbalance, each as intrinsic to life, each a part of
> our integrity, each deserving of dignity and self-
> respect.   —*Robert Kegan,* The Evolving Self

The purpose of this chapter is to take a closer look at the meaning of the word *growth* and to suggest some useful ways to
understand it. We will consider two questions about growth:
"What is its direction?" and "How does it work?" We look first
at how the word has been used normatively by stage theorists;
we then cast more broadly, turning to a discussion of the idea
of dialectic, emphasizing the importance of an understanding of
underlying structure; and we conclude with a conversation with
Irma, who chose to move through her fear to land upright on
the other side.

What lies ahead for Betty if she heals enough to take up
the quest again, for Jean when she resolves the bind of divided
loyalties, or for Richard as he lowers himself into the cauldron
of uncertainty? What happens when we ask ourselves the difference between right and wrong, who we are, or what the meaning of our lives is? What goes on down there in the dark anyway?
Recall what Simon in *Lord of the Flies* saw as he gazed
into the mouth of the Beast.

> "Fancy thinking the Beast was something
> you could hunt and kill!" said the head. For a mo-

ment or two the forest and all the other dimly appreciated places echoed with the parody of laughter. "You knew, didn't you? I'm part of you.
Close, close, close! I'm the reason it's no go? Why
things are what they are?" [Golding, 1954, p. 148].

Simon saw himself. Like Pogo, he met the enemy and saw
that "he is us." Then he was inside the mouth and lost consciousness. When he regained his senses, he knew exactly what
to do. Clearheaded alone among all the boys on the island,
Simon the mystic climbed the mountain and discovered the true
nature of the Beast. For that he was summarily executed by the
tribe.

Framed this way, the answers are avowedly dramatic. At
the heart of the mythic quest lies utter loss of meaning, often
symbolized by the death of the hero. Like Parzival, we cannot
gaze upon the Holy Grail and live. In Zen's famous series of ox
paintings depicting the journey toward enlightenment, there
comes a point where both ox and self disappear; the frame is
empty. We have so fully entered our opposite that the system
self-destructs and the screen goes blank. An old self dies so a
new one can be born. That's what goes on down there in the
dark.

In his book *Transitions,* William Bridges points out that
major changes require "the transformative experience of the
neutral zone," a time in which we welcome emptiness and sur-
render to Chaos. "Chaos," he reminds us, "is not a mess, but
rather it is the primal state of pure energy to which the person
returns for every true new beginning" (1980, p. 119). Likewise,
Carol Christ suggests the need for an "experience of nothingness"
to mediate woman's spiritual quest for a "new awakening" and
a fresh naming of her self (1980). In popular songs, in mythology, in religious canons, in literature, the three-part syntax of
transformation seems everywhere.

But even if we acknowledge that *growth* has something
to do with a "plunge in the refreshing waters of emptiness" as a
friend puts it, we still need to know more about what the word

actually means, what changes it entails, how it works, how you
know it when you see it.

Transformation—The Meaning of Growth

The problem with the term *growth,* as commonly con-
strued, is that it implies a continuous, rather unbroken process
of "more-ness." For the first eighteen years or so of our lives,
as Topsy had it, we "just growed," getting bigger. The word
seems to offer few intellectual crevices. It has a seamless and
rather magical quality about it. Yet clearly growth is not simply a matter of quantitative increase; there is a qualitative kind
of change as well.

Since the term is so closely identified with living creatures, it is not surprising that biologists have led the way to a
closer understanding of it. It is clear, after all, that living things
pass through a number of quite radically different forms as they
grow. A dandelion is at one point a seed, at another a rooted
cluster of new growth, then a golden flower, then a balding
headful of gray seed, and again a cluster of leaves. Likewise, an
egg and sperm become androgynous embryo that then differen-
tiates to a male or female fetus, later emerges as an androgynous
child, again transforms to a young man or woman, and finally
matures to a new androgyny. In fact, we change structure dramatically as we grow. That notion applies equally to our mental
and spiritual growth as to our physical maturation.

Drawing on his early training as a biologist, Jean Piaget
laid the groundwork for much of the extraordinarily fruitful
marriage of organic metaphors and epistemological speculation
that has since spawned developmental psychology. He understood growth to emerge not from the individual in isolation, nor
simply in response to the environment, but from interaction between the two. Organisms function in equilibrium with their environment. To maintain that equilibrium, they must *adapt,* they
must change in some way as the environment changes. They can
do this in either of two ways: either they modify the environment (by eating part of it, for instance) so that it *assimilates* to
their structure, or they modify themselves (for example, by extending leaves to photosynthesize sunlight), thus *accommodat-*

ing their structure to that of their environment. Growth involves the simultaneous interplay of both assimilation and accommodation as the organism adapts to its shifting environment.

Intellectual growth, says Piaget, proceeds in a similar manner. As a child develops, it moves through a series of accommodations, transforming the way it organizes information in a regular and predictable sequence from relatively simple, global, and self-centered ways of making meaning to increasingly complex and differentiated forms as the world it encounters grows more diverse and complicated. This doesn't happen, however, simply in a series of forward froglike leaps. Rather, the child will make a new conceptual breakthrough in one area at a time (say, in counting objects), remaining at an earlier stage in other areas. By a kind of sideways movement that Piaget calls horizontal décalage, the child gradually extends the power of the new insight to other parts of his or her experience. This concept is particularly helpful in explaining why some adults seem to be so "aware" in some realms, but so "behind" in others. And as we shall see later, it explains why the quality of the environment is so crucial to how we develop. Under stress and threat, we tend to hold to those earlier parts of ourselves with which we feel safest; conversely, when we feel safe, we can trust our growing edge more fully. The irony is that we often react with primitive behavior to environmental changes that demand all the adaptive capacity of our better selves. This seems to be as true dealing with an intransigent neighbor as with the Russians. Those who have developed the capacity to feel relatively comfortable with change seem to be those who can most productively cope with its demands.

Piaget's model deals primarily with intellectual growth and comes to a culmination with what he calls formal, abstract thinking somewhere in the teen years. Some researchers building on his work have suggested that many adults never attain that level whereas others continue to develop beyond it. The stage theorists mentioned earlier are among these researchers. Although I have chosen to discuss only Kegan's and Perry's work in any detail, there are others whose research is of special value in helping us to understand what growth looks like.

Probably most familiar is the work of Erik Erikson, whose

eight stages of man constituted the first major effort by a psychologist to work out a systematic scheme of stages throughout the life span. Erikson seems to be neither stage nor phase theorist, falling somewhere in between. But I have found his work of great power, especially his emphasis on basic trust, identity, intimacy, and generativity. Erikson describes a sequence of "crises" that each of us must resolve as we progressively engage with the tensions of our lives. Though they are age-linked, we cycle through them again and again as we mature (Erikson, 1950.)

    For Erikson, growth is fundamentally seated in a sense of basic trust, a capacity learned in the parent's arms but arching through a lifetime of progressive reaching out to others. To the degree that we can find that sense of basic trust in ourselves (a touchstone to which we must return again and again), we are enabled to take the growing risks of defining ourselves, sharing ourselves, giving ourselves to our children, and finally affirming meaning where there is only uncertainty.

    In the late 1950s, Lawrence Kohlberg, then a doctoral candidate at the University of Chicago, began asking schoolchildren to tell him what they thought was right and wrong. To do this, he told them several little stories without endings and asked them to talk about them. One of these hypothetical dilemmas has attained a certain limited notoriety since then. Known as the Heinz Dilemma, it tells of a man (named Heinz) whose wife is dying of cancer. He cannot afford the only available medicine and is unable to borrow money. What should he do? The case is designed to force a choice between stealing the drug (thus breaking the law) or obeying the law and allowing the woman to die. The actual answers the children gave were less important to Kohlberg than the *reasons* they offered for their choice. On the basis of the forms of reasoning that they used to reach their judgments, Kohlberg was able to construct a series of levels, a hierarchy that he later argued was in fact a sequence of moral development. Thus, "It's wrong to steal because he might get caught" is a less sophisticated answer than "It's wrong to steal because it's breaking a law and society needs laws." Kohlberg's stages move from early self-protective and manipulative levels (an act is wrong because you might be punished) through those dealing with maintenance of the social order (an act is wrong if it is against the law, and we must obey the law) to those based on loyalty to overarching and, he argues, universal principles (an act is wrong if it violates the principle of justice). Needless to say, the scheme is highly controversial (Gibbs and Schnell, 1985). Yet it has been employed in various forms in schools, prisons, and youth programs around the country for some years with considerable success. And it remains the sharpest and most thoroughly argued of recent attempts to spell out a direction for growth.

Influenced by Kohlberg, Jane Loevinger, a psychometrician, worked out a sequence of six broad stages and several sublevels based on lengthy analysis of a sentence-completion test (1980). Like Kohlberg's, her scheme runs from early stages characterized by impulsive and self-protective orientations through middle positions typified by conventional morality to higher, more autonomous stages. Her work has proven of particular applicability to understanding the movement of adult learners as they return to higher education. Rita Weathersby, for instance, found that people in early positions tend to seek education as a means of making up a deficit; education is a "thing" to "get." People in middle stages see education as a way to "be" someone; it will help them get a better job and enhance their status. With further development, however, people come increasingly to see education as a way to enhance first their sense of competence and ability to achieve, then their own inner growth. Education becomes intrinsically valuable rather than practically useful (Weathersby, 1981). The general movement of development for Loevinger is from early impulsivity toward later autonomy and integration. It is interesting that although Loevinger's methods differed from those of her colleagues, her stages closely parallel theirs.

An early protégé of Erikson and Kohlberg, James Fowler has constructed a particularly intriguing sequence of faith stages —"transformations along the journey of faith"—moving from essentially childlike mythic and literal interpretations of our place in the universe toward more conventional understandings and on through universal and self-transcendent expressions of our relationship with "the ultimate environment." Fowler has done more than any other stage theorist to acknowledge and explicate his indebtedness to other developmentalists. His major work to date, *Stages of Faith* (1981), contains a delightful set of imaginary conversations about human development among Erikson, Kohlberg, and Piaget. And an earlier book, *Life Maps* (1978), with Sam Keen (whose own book about stages of loving merits a careful reading as well), explicitly correlates each of his stages with those of other major theorists.

Although there are important differences among these theorists, all agree upon the broad direction of growth: toward greater autonomy and ability to act separately from the demands of one's environment. In 1977, an article in the *Harvard Educational Review* rang a resounding challenge to the idea that growth must be toward increased autonomy and "principled behavior" as Kohlberg had suggested (Gilligan, 1977). The author, Carol Gilligan, had worked for years with Kohlberg and knew his work intimately. Over time, she grew uneasy with the fact that disproportionate numbers of women seemed to fall into his third stage, a position in which "the good" is conditioned by the actor's intentions (rather than an abstract principle) and by the expectations of others (rather than by one's own inner ethic). Unwilling to accept the implied slur, she questioned the theory itself. The emphasis on autonomy and separateness as the "logical" end point of development, she maintained, betrayed a fundamentally male bias. She went on to develop this notion in her groundbreaking book, *In a Different Voice,* in which she drew on an impressive array of evidence from interviews, mythology, literature, and psychology, arguing that in contrast to the male vision of a "hierarchy of power," women view the world as "a web of relationships." Thus, to be "on top" and separate is less important to women than to be a part of a fabric of interconnected associations. And while the greatest sin for a man is to violate his personal integrity, to a woman the greatest evil is willfully to hurt another person (1982).

Gilligan then proposed a sequence of "perspectives" that

she argues more adequately describe developmental movement for women. While she adheres essentially to the notion that we move into, through, then beyond our culture, she rejects Kohlberg's implicit ladder metaphor, suggesting instead an involuted, organic form. As women develop, they spiral through a three-level evolution of responsibility to themselves and others. The early orientation is characterized by primary concern for one's own survival in the face of powerlessness. This gradually gives way to a stance in which one equates "the good" with caring for others; self-sacrifice is considered the highest virtue—the antithesis of the earlier perspective. The synthesis is attained with the recognition that "It is OK to care for myself as well." The self, as she puts it, becomes "a legitimate object of care." Out of this insight emerges a "morality of nonviolence" grounded in the ethic of care (1982).

The importance of Gilligan's work is only now being recognized, for she has righted a critical imbalance in how we have tended to think about development. By demonstrating so powerfully the profound importance of a sense of connectedness with and responsibility for others as well as oneself, she has affirmed for women the value and legitimacy of a way of being that has traditionally been undervalued, and she has reminded men that growth toward full humanity includes acknowledgment of our own needs to care, nurture, and retain connectedness with others. Justice, we are reminded, must be tempered with mercy—a willingness to let go of our "rules" long enough to see, truly see, another human being in pain and to hear from our own hearts the call of compassion.

Yet despite differences, common to all of these theories is the idea that growth proceeds from an early "preconventional" way of seeing in which our primary concern is with self-preservation in a narrow sense, through a "conventional" stance where we are moved as much by how others see us as by our own needs, to a "postconventional" position in which we work to resolve the tension between our own needs and those of others. For the most part, this final level entails a certain willingness to flout both authority and convention in the service of some transcendent value or principle. All of these researchers would maintain that growth is more than simply adjustment to the norms of our own particular culture, and consequently, most would argue for some sort of universalistic notion of what it means to mature. They trace their lineage, after all, through French structuralism to Kant and in a sense back to Plato. They are not mere relativists. There is more to the universe than what we alone make of it.

The objection is almost always raised in this regard that these are dangerous ideas, ethnocentric and elitist. While I've no desire to put that debate to rest, perhaps it helps to associate movement through stages with climbing along a ridge with a number of ascending peaks. Virtually everyone ascends the first few, but as the climb continues, more and more people remain along the way, choosing their own favored peak for its unique view. While it is true that later peaks may be higher and one can see more broadly from them, it is unwise to presume that the view from one is more pleasing or in any absolute sense "better" than another. I have climbed in the hills of Vermont and the Himals of Nepal; it would be plain silly to proclaim one "superior." It depends, after all, on what you want to see. Yet this is not to say that climbing is unimportant. For there is something within us that must grow and those among us who will ascend. We must honor that—in others and in ourselves.

A more prosaic way of putting it is simply to note that the "value" of a particular level of development depends on its context. Some environments and some people fit each other better than others; they are more appropriate to certain ways of seeing than others. Whether a given environment is "good" in an ethical sense is a philosophical matter, not a psychological one. Few would maintain a "value neutral" stance about Auschwitz, and yet out of that hell, Viktor Frankl, the psychoanalyst author of *Man's Search for Meaning,* emerged whole to write an inspiring testament to the value of his journey through despair. What enabled him to survive—and to help others survive—was his recognition that despite apparent hopelessness and radical loss of meaning, it was possible to emerge whole if one were willing to take responsibility for one's own sufferings, to weave of them a fabric of meaning. Frankl was not born with that capacity. At the very least, one might argue that richer development increases our ability to make sense where none appears. In a world of growing violence and frenetic change, that ability may be all we have between ourselves and despair.

Taken together, these ideas would suggest that growth can be understood as a series of transformations in our ways of making meaning. As infants, we are embedded in an environment that demands relatively little of us. Virtually our every need is cared for (if it is not, we let our environment know in no uncertain terms), and what we learn if our parenting is good is to trust. But as we grow, we place increasingly greater demands on our world, and it on us. In time, we find that we can no longer get what we want from our parents in the old ways, we can no longer continue to assimilate without doing some changing ourselves. And so we begin to accommodate our structures of thought to the shifting environment. Over several years, as Piaget has demonstrated, we form new, more adequate ways of organizing the world, of making sense out of it. And looking back, we wonder how we could ever have been so simpleminded. Thus we move through progressive transformations as our world grows more complex and as we see more from each standpoint: first our home, then friends, institutions, and humankind. Each new horizon demands that we form new, overarching ways to make sense of the diversity and conflict we see with increasing clarity around us. For each, we need to learn to think in whole new ways.

A friend, who learned to swim later than usual, once described the critical event. He had been out wading on the lakeshore when all of a sudden the bottom seemed to fall away; he apparently had stepped off an underwater cliff. He panicked and started kicking with his feet and pushing with his hands. Somehow that allowed him to keep his head above water and get turned around until he got his feet under him again and made it to shore. "I guess I didn't exactly learn to swim at that moment," he said, "but I got the idea. You can't move the same way when the water is over your head as you do when it isn't."

Indeed. In a certain sense, my friend accomplished a transformation, however brief, in the way he moved in the water. His environment suddenly changed drastically, and he accommodated; that is, he changed the way he moved to fit his new environment. The cost of failing to do so in this case was rather more drastic than the cost of passing up a developmental transformation, but the idea is the same. My friend didn't actually change once and for all at that moment, but he "got the idea." So it is, I think, with transformations. Some change in our world suddenly forces us to relate to it in a sharply different way, and though we may revert back once in "safer" waters, we have learned something enduring. The next time it happens, we will swim.

Recall how Sandy, who longed to be "a legitimate member of the world," described her transformation from a conventional self largely defined by her family toward greater independence and a mind of her own as she moved into deeper waters.

> I feel like that the way I guided myself through life was to go back to my family and say, "Tell me what to do. Am I OK?" . . . rather than seeing, looking, understanding how *I* operate and finding out how *I want* to think and how *I want* to deal with myself and how *I want* to treat other people from my own perspective and my own point of view.

Notice here the deep transformation, not in what she thinks about but in the very structure of how she sees what she thinks about. It is a shift of *perspective* from viewing herself through the eyes of others toward increasingly seeing through her own eyes: "from my own perspective and my own point of view." It's that fundamental shift of *stance* that we are looking for.

Similarly, Perry gives us the words of a student who is just in the process of discovering that the bottom of his lake has dropped away—a transformation from multiplistic to contextual thinking.

I know that, ah, there is more to me, and
more to the things about me than I knew before. I
won't say I understand them; I just know they're
there and that I may never fully understand or appreciate them. Before, I had ideas about where I
was going and what I was going to do. I had a plan.
I had a certain program about what I was going to
fulfill. . . .

Well, what I've appreciated is this: that I
may get something I wasn't planning on, and that
some of the things I'm planning on I may never
get. . . . What I'm saying is that I don't think I'm
in perfect control of myself and the world anymore. And I think I'm probably the better off for
it, because if something should come up, if the
bottom should be pulled out, I wouldn't have been
aware of the fact that this could happen [1968, pp.
118-119].

This sense of the "bottom pulled out" is common to descriptions of transformation. Buddhists refer to the sensation of
enlightenment as being akin to what happens when the bottom
falls out of a bucket of water. For some time it seems that more
has been lost than gained, yet beneath that lies a knowledge
that the exchange was immeasurably for the better. "At least,"
the student says later, "I've started to think now." As Perry
describes it, one begins thinking when one stops believing. The
shift into contextual relativism is "the point of critical division
between 'belief' and the possibility of faith. Belief requires no
investment by the person. To become faith, it must first be
doubted" (1968, p. 131). It is at that point that choice becomes
real and responsibility takes on a new meaning. The ground of
our being must shake and be sundered before we can take the
radical leap of faith that may carry us across the chasm.

It should be emphasized that what we hear from our students depends on what we have asked. These tectonic shifts
happen in various ways, along a range of different fault lines in
the same person. The shift Perry describes is different from the

one Kegan or Piaget might discern. And yet they are connected too, for contextualism would be impossible without formal operations, Kegan's interindividual balance unthinkable without contextualism. The important point is that growth in our species is an enormously complex matter, best observed through many lenses.

Dialectic—The Dynamic of Transformation

If growth means transformation and transformation means the yielding of old structures of meaning-making to new, then how does it take place? What actually goes on during the process of transformation?

Let us look again at the journey Perry describes. The pilgrim moves from dualism, in which one construes the choice to be absolute, outside of oneself, and a simple matter of *this* or *that*; to multiplicity, when the simple two-part frame is reconstructed; to contextualism in which the discovery is made that right and wrong are not particularly useful ideas except under certain circumstances. The choice is no longer external, no longer about absolute good or evil; choice has moved dramatically inward and is now understood to be about choice itself. Perry describes this journey in exquisite detail, giving us student-eye views of the lunging struggle to accept, then reject, then reconstrue the meaning of knowledge, authority, and truth in our lives. The three-part movement from old, simple meanings to loss of meaning to new meaning bears a keen resemblance to the "romantic descent" of nineteenth-century Romantic literature as well as to the mythic quest so powerfully captured by Joseph Campbell. At the nadir of his journey, the hero enters most deeply into the source of his fear as he confronts the formerly irreconcilable opposites of being and nonbeing, male and female, time and eternity, good and evil, light and darkness, hope and despair. Transformation demands at this point not that he choose one or the other but that he move *through* those contradictions and become whole, not again, but anew. It means synthesis, a placing together. It is what Campbell, deliberately punning "atonement," calls "at-one-ment." Not for nothing is it called the "moment of truth," for it is a new form of the self in which the old truths are radically revised and the old schisms not simply healed but obliterated. It's a whole new ball game.

The tendency to move from either-or choices to polarities is a common preparation for transformation. As the reader will have noticed, in describing their experience of growth, people often imply or even explicitly describe tensions between one or another polar opposite: an inner versus outer self, subjective versus objective, or the needs of others versus their own needs. These tensions are the stuff of growth; when they are going on, we know we are alive—though the pain at times may make us wish we weren't. But tensions, by their nature, cry out for resolution; at some point, we want the pain to stop. One way to do this is by landing on one end of the polarity and screaming to the gods, "This is it!" We can mount the bumper sticker on our car: STAMP OUT DOUBT. Another is to acknowledge the legitimacy of the tensions themselves, to escape the trap by naming it.

Consider the idea of *dialectic*. The term shares with the word *dialogue* its roots in the Greek, *dialektos,* to "speak across." As Plato used it, the term referred to a discussion aimed at discerning the truth about some philosophical matter or other, and Socrates stands as the acknowledged master of the art. Without entering into a discussion of Socrates' sometimes questionable rhetorical tactics, it is safe to say that the ostensible intent of a dialogue was that each party would put forth an observation for examination by the other. Out of the give and take of their discussion would emerge common agreement on Truth. "Dialectical thinking" thus refers to a process of thought that relies instrumentally on formal logic but, more importantly, on the relationship of one idea to another. It presumes change rather than a static notion of "reality." As each assertion is derived from the one before, truth is always emergent, never fixed; relative, not absolute.

Most simply, it can be diagrammed thus:

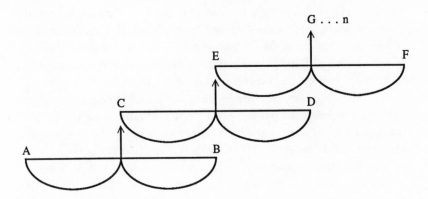

To begin, a "thesis" is stated or an assertion made (A). This is countered by a contradictory statement or "antithesis" (B). Out of the two positions emerges a "synthesis," which, in turn, becomes the thesis for a further dialogue, countered by a new antithesis, and so on. In theory, the process goes on forever; there is no resting point. Truth is where the disputants choose to take a break.

But a synthesis is not formed simply by merging thesis with antithesis in a kind of intellectual détente. *Synthesis is not compromise.* If I suggest that an object is black and you counter by calling it white, our synthesis is not that it is gray. Rather, to reach agreement, we must come up with a formulation that accounts for both positions, doing damage to neither. We do this by leaping to a higher abstraction, by distancing ourselves from it sufficiently that we can *see the whole process,* not just our own side of it. The object, we might agree, is both black and white, *depending on where one is standing.* We thus avoid the either-or trap, not by backing down but by moving through and above the problem to see it afresh. We come to recognize that our own version of the truth is conditioned by where we happen to be standing at the time. The only route out is through an understanding of the opposing position. This is why listening to positions different from our own is so important. In order to reach deeper similarities, we must acknowledge existing differences as fully as possible. The current struggle to define more humane gender roles for our rapidly changing culture is a case in point. As long as we fail to distinguish between equality and sameness, we will remain trapped in a gray androgyny as unappealing as a universally tan human race. The way out is to recognize the enduring differences between men and women, yet hold these in the broader context of our common humanity and the imperative of mutual compassion and equality.

For the paradox is that we best see ourselves in the mirror of the Other; we move forward by going sideways. Robert Frost, a notably contrary man, put it this way in his poem "West-running Brook":

> Speaking of contraries, see how the brook
> In that white wave runs counter to itself.
>
> . . . .
>
> The universal cataract of death
> That spends to nothingness—and unresisted,
> Save by some strange resistance in itself,
> Not just a swerving, but a throwing back,
> As if regret were in it and were sacred.
> It has this throwing backward on itself,
> So that the fall of most of it is always
> Raising up a little, sending up a little.
> Our life runs down in sending up the clock.
> The brook runs down in sending up our life.
> The sun runs down in sending up the brook.
> And there is something sending up the sun.
> It is this backward motion toward the source,
> Against the stream, that most we see ourselves in,
> The tribute of the current to the source.
> It is from this in nature we are from.
> It is most us [1949, pp. 328–329].

Speed skaters and sailors know this. In unsure waters or on slippery ice, the best offense often looks like a good defense as the skater thrusts her blade from side to side or the sailor tacks first one way, then the other to move into the teeth of the gale. We move by contraries. This is useful to remember, for when we seem to be swept away from all sense of purpose, when we fear we are heading in precisely the "wrong" direction, our movement may have purpose in a larger frame. Much of the fear we experience at such times is a consequence of our inability to see that larger frame, is rooted in our unwillingness to let go, to risk a transformation that at the moment may feel more like disintegration. At such times, we need experienced travelers to tell us that it is safe to go that way, to trust in our own contrary movement toward the source.

To understand transformation, then, it helps to see it as containing a tension between and subsequent resolution of contraries. Gregory Bateson, a man who saw the interconnectedness of all things to an extraordinary extent, notes that an English schoolboy trained to defer to authority may become an ideal model of what is expected of him or may reject it all and become a pariah, but the boy "cannot conceivably acquire irrelevant patterns." Bateson goes on:

> If we know that an individual is trained in overt expression of one half of one of these patterns, e.g., in dominance behavior, we can predict with certainty (though not in precise language) that the seeds of the other half—submission—are simultaneously sown in his personality. We have to think of an individual, in fact, as trained in dominance-submission, not in either dominance *or* submission [1972, p. 92].

Only when he recognizes this intrinsic ambivalence can the boy, himself, transcend his "training." History is dotted with situations in which an oppressed people overcome their masters only to become oppressors themselves. It's what anthropologists sometimes refer to as tacit enculturation and educators as incidental learning. Marshall McLuhan knew it when he coined the phrase "the medium is the message." We learn as much or more from the *way* we are taught as from the content itself. Put more succinctly, *forms instruct.*

Paulo Freire, the Brazilian educator who saw so clearly the intrinsic relationship between education and transformation, points out that real freedom can never emerge out of the un-examined struggle of the oppressed against the oppressor, for in that struggle are only the seeds of a new oppression. Rather, we must recognize that the problem lies with the nature of the struggle itself. In doing this, we circumscribe both combatants and name the problem from a perspective that includes the legitimate aspirations of both. Oppressed and oppressor must each come to see the trap they are in; they must see the whole wheel, not just their own spoke, and rename it. Says Freire,

> To exist, humanly, is to *name* the world, to change it. Once named, the world in its turn re-appears to the namers as a problem and requires of them a new *naming*. Men are not built in silence, but in a word, in work, in action/reflection [1970, p. 76].

The act of new naming reifies the unseen and draws us upward; at once it adds a new rung to the ladder and calls us to climb. From "I am right" to "you are right" to "we both have rights," the idea of justice allows us to break out of the trap.

So how does all of this relate to the idea of development? Recall the lifelong dialogue within ourselves between self and other that Kegan considers the central issue of our lives. On his map, we move from early inclusion in the family to increased separation during our school years to a new kind of fusion with others in our teen conformity to the formation of new bound-aries around the self during our early adult years and then back to a higher integration at the interindividual stage. Throughout, we move back and forth in saccadic fashion between self and other in ever-widening ripples as the boundaries of each "evolu-tionary truce" form and yield and form again.

Moreover, Kegan emphasizes that transformation requires resolution of old dichotomies within a frame that accepts both old and new. "It is important to bear in mind," he says, "the distinction between *abandoning* the old longing on behalf of the new, and *integrating* the new with the old, a distinction essentially between the dichotomous and the dialectical" (1982, p. 154).

The most intriguing aspect of Levinson's work as well lies in his recognition of the importance of dialectic. Here he has this to say:

> Every developmental transition presents the opportunity and the necessity of moving toward a new integration of each polarity. To the extent that a man does this, he creates a firmer basis for his life in the ensuing phase. To the extent that he fails, he forms inner contradictions that will be reflected in the flaws of our next life structure [1978, p. 198].

Thus, to move ahead into the next phase we need to attend to the tensions we have created by moving into this one. Those tensions are located along the four polarities he has described. Their resolution will be accomplished as we are able to name ourselves anew, manifesting fresh mixes of youth with age, femaleness with maleness, creativity with destructiveness, and attachment with separation.

Further, arguing that dialectical thinking actually represents a developmental advance beyond formal operations, Michael Basseches has recently published a book called *Dialectical Thinking and Adult Development* (1985) that offers the fullest treatment of the subject yet.

Consider Luke Skywalker's task in the *Star Wars* trilogy as he struggles with the conflicting urges to kill or yield to his father. At one point, while still in training, he rejects his mentor's advice to enter a forbidding cave unarmed (no defenses are allowed when we confront our destiny), taking with him his light saber. There in the darkness, he is met by a vision of Darth Vader. He strikes out at it, lopping off its head. When it rolls to his feet, he sees his own face in Vader's mask. He has failed the test, has fallen back from the terrible demand to remain at the center of the dilemma, and as a consequence, finds only himself. Fortunately, however, this is only a practice run arranged by his wily mentor (mentors are big on practice runs), and in the climactic scene, at the very heart of the Death Star, in the belly of the beast, he is finally able to cut the Gordian knot, not by killing or yielding but by fighting his father and at the point of victory, laying down his weapon and refusing to kill him. At once he is able to give his own love voice, to fulfill his destiny in a quite unexpected way, and to become a Jedi knight. The transformation is complete.

Although in a somewhat less dramatic and mythic fashion, Irma, a mother of four, underwent a similar transformation. At the age of forty-five, her last daughter safely graduated, she decided to return to school. I became her mentor. She had spoken several times about the difficulty she was having around the topic of evolution as taught in an anthropology class. This led to a series of conversations about the role of religious teachings in her life, about how these were conflicting with what she was now learning in college. In an attempt to resolve the tension between secular and sacred teachings, she took a class in ethics. One late fall afternoon we met in her home to talk about it.

"My God, even the spices are in alphabetical order!" I think, as Irma speaks carefully across the immaculate kitchen table about the abortion debate in her ethics class. Through the window, I see the wind picking up, the predicted storm slapping wet flakes against the pane. Inside there's not a whisper.

"Maybe the more you think about it, the less you're certain what your response in the situation would be because every situation would give you a different outcome."

A woman of strong, conventional religious belief, Irma has found the class's open attitude toward sexuality and particularly abortion to be both disturbing and fascinating. At the moment she is struggling with a paper on the topic. I ask her how she plans to deal with all this gray matter.

"I have what seem to be just disconnected thoughts that when I put them down don't jell," she replies. "I can see both sides, and I'm not sure which side has the better claim; I'm not sure which way I want to go. I've picked up so much material, and it's so hard to settle on a point of view."

This is clearly painful for her; she winces as she speaks, squints toward the spice shelf as if looking for help from all that order. Yet I've a clear sense that she is staying with it. It's almost as if her keen mind demands the challenge, leans into the struggle to make sense of the onslaught of new material, sorting, sifting, "carding through" her notes. She could, after all, simply close her eyes when the flashes grow too bright. That's a chief function of fundamentalistic thinking—to keep information manageable and reduce painful ambiguity. But Irma has clearly not done that, has instead risked learning more than is good for her.

"There were two conflicting points of view, and I could identify with both sides. But you can't take a position if you feel both sides strongly because again you're caught between the two. And I suppose that's been the story of my life these last couple of months: being caught between the pro and con of the subject matter of a paper, or between duties at home and family relationships versus the responsibilities of school and life."

"Is it worth getting educated?" I ask, curious about how she pulls it all together.

"Well," she replies, shaking her head back and forth, almost as if to settle something out, "I don't know whether I'd call it getting educated or not, but certainly I've taken in a tremendous amount of new material!"

"What's it done to your head?" I wonder aloud. She laughs a bit grimly.

"Sometimes it just rattles around in there and just bangs against everything else." Her laughter again masks the pain trapped in the metaphor. I ask her what it feels like, and she talks at length about the frustration of sorting so much diverse information. Somehow it used to be easier, though she says she can't imagine how that could have been. But now it is important to her to align her ethical views with her political position, her religious beliefs with everyday commitments. The boundaries of her world have exploded outward, she has seen the form of her own thought, and the effort to locate herself, to heal the frayed ends is exhausting. As we part, I find myself torn between a desire to help her pull those ends together and a sense that it is a task she can best do for herself. She seems to know that too, and though she appears to welcome my concrete suggestions, in the end she takes her own course.

Months later I talk with her again and learn that she has begun to sort all of those pieces and to feel an intensified need for commitment to something, to test the new fabric she has begun to weave. "I can't live with all these loose ends forever," she says with a laugh as we chat during her graduation reception.

And still later, we'll meet at her new place of employment—a volunteer agency providing alternatives to young women considering abortion. "I don't suppose I'm any more sure than I ever was," she will say. "Probably less. But this seems important work. And I need to do something I believe in."

Irma chose not to turn back. Somewhere in the darkness of that ethics classroom she summoned the courage to look the hard questions in the eye, slide down their haunches, and slip beneath their feet to the other side. She did not so much *answer* them as acknowledge their legitimacy. By truly hearing "the other side," by confronting her polarity, she was able to build firmer answers of her own—answers that she knows are not absolute but that she has woven strongly enough to hold her weight as she makes her way home. Her choice of work is thus a marvelous synthesis, allowing her to hold both positions without being paralyzed—a genuine transformation.

I have attempted in this chapter to show that significant learning and growth involve qualitative, developmental change in the way the world is viewed. We grow through a progression of transformations in our meaning-making apparatus, from relatively narrow and self-centered filters through increasingly inclusive, differentiated, and compassionate perspectives. I have also argued that dialectical movement is central to such qualitative change. What are the implications of these assertions for our teaching?

As teachers and counselors, it is valuable for us to be aware of the overall directions of growth, to consider our work in a larger frame. The idea of resolution of opposites, central to the dialectic, is a powerful one. It allows us to see that our students may be moving ahead when they appear to be retreating or going hopelessly astray. Knowing that forward movement may occur paradoxically by going backward or from side to

side, we can take a step back and watch our students more carefully than we might if we feared they were merely backsliding
or wandering.

In addition, a more subtle understanding of the dynamics of their development will allow us more effectively to help
our students to move. For they will make meaning of whatever
we do, and knowing this, we can understand better why it may
be of value to play devil's advocate, to ask them to argue conflicting sides of an issue, to explain a particular position through
another's eyes. By offering opposed and juxtaposed frames of
reference, we can help them to make meanings that are cor-
respondingly broadly based, that rest on a felt sense of the
legitimacy of the Other.

This is why it is so important for teachers to encourage
students to immerse themselves in differing perspectives. It is
why the traditional liberal studies well taught can be such
powerful transformative experiences. History calls us to see the
world as the medieval church did; literature offers a Raskolni-
kov; mathematics raises fundamental questions about how we
symbolize "reality"; art shows us human torment through the
eyes of a Picasso; philosophy asks us to leap from Hobbes to
Berkeley; and anthropology argues the internal logic of canni-
balism.

Yet as we offer our challenge, it is important that we also
support our students in their dismantling of old structures and
construction of new. As they begin to reassemble their worlds,
we can offer them the tools of our methodology; we can model
for them new ways of making meaning. At the same time, we
should recognize that things have changed, and we may need to
step back a bit. This is a time when students often begin to
move out on their own as they make their own connections
among ideas, see relatives and old friends in a fresh light, and
reach out for new friends. We are still needed, but in a different
way.

Chapter Six 🐌

Completing the Journey: Helping Adults Integrate New Insights

> The final belief is to believe in a fiction, which you
> know to be a fiction, there being nothing else. The
> exquisite truth is to know that it is a fiction and
> that you believe in it willingly.
> —*Wallace Stevens,* Opus Posthumous

The darkness met, it remains for the hero to return home bearing the prize. Enlightenment is not all there is. One must reconnect with the world, or the journey is not complete. Growth requires both separation and connection. For Odysseus, returning those long ten years from his great victory over Troy, the overriding metaphor is that of the weaver, the vision of his wife, Penelope, at the hearth. He is drawn homeward by a call to heal, weave again a fabric, regain a sense of the wholeness of his life. For the return home is a completion of what Joseph Campbell calls the "cosmogonic cycle," the universal round, the great helix on which we are all drawn in the upward coil of evolution.

In this chapter, we will consider how students heal, reconstruct their vision of "truth," name themselves anew. Several homeward-bound students will carry us along, describing in their own words how they managed to piece their worlds together again. And we will see also how their teachers helped—or failed to hinder them—as they traveled.

In our work with the developing student, it is important to know when to move in and when to step back, when to support and when to challenge. This is a time for building, and it is often valuable at this point for us to grant students more initiative than we might have at an earlier point in the journey. It is, after all, their own world under construction. A close understanding of what that process entails will help us to know better when the project will be furthered by hard questions, when by enthusiastic encouragement, or even when by our absence. It will also help us better sense when our words will be heard and when ignored. For our work is about timing, and timing is about sensing what is going on inside our students.

Because it is building time, students must attend to the "how" of things. This is the time that we can help students gain a sharper awareness of the *process* of their own development, to construct a platform from which they can see their own thought in a way they could not before. On an intellectual level, this means helping them to recognize how the form of their writing and the logic of their answers provide a new kind of "rightness" so they come to recognize that the *method* may be as important as the result. We can also help them to this realization by being more explicit now about our own assumptions and methodology so they will come to see that even *our* truth is relative to its context. More broadly, it means helping them to develop a new vision of themselves based on their own experience rather than images they have absorbed from others. For we do not simply hone minds, we help people to name their wholeness. The words *heal* and *whole* share a common root. This is a time for healing.

But it may not be as easy as it seems. There are obstacles. One might, for instance, refuse to return, wallowing like Odysseus with Calypso in the easy irresponsibility of one's new intellectual indulgence. Perry noted this attitude among some students, calling it "temporizing." It may simply be a recognition that "I'm not ready yet," or it may be prelude to a more entrenched form of inertia: "escape" into alienation. Said one student,

> "I just don't see any need to draw any conclusions towards it at the moment. I'm perfectly

satisfied with all of it in ways. Not to say that I
don't get depressed, but I'm sort of satisfied with
that too; it's very nice to be able to sit and think
and smoke and play pool" [Perry, 1968, 195-
196].

Or we may simply find it more comfortable where we
are. Our lives may call us to rest here or simply fail to provide
reason to move on. Developmentalist Jane Loevinger places the
"modal position in adult life" somewhere between conformity
and individuality, stages analogous to Kegan's interpersonal and
institutional balances. Many people, Loevinger says, seem to
have found a comfortable place to rest midway in their voyages
away from the tribe toward broader, more internal sources of
identity. There is an awareness of an inner self, separate from
the expectations of society, yet ideas about what is "right" or
"proper" are still quite stereotypical, and that secret self is not
yet free to go public; the distinction between public and private
selves is rather sharp, and the two need not have a great deal to
do with each other. Consequently, while the right to exercise
one's individuality is granted, it remains an aberration, a departure from the way one "should" act. The journey into one's
own "dark side" has been considered but not yet taken. We still
seek to eliminate rather than acknowledge the "negative" parts
of ourselves, believing the purpose of the journey to be the
attainment of perfection. We have yet to learn what we can
only know from the other side of the gulf—that wholeness is a
far more precious gift than perfection.

And the memory of lost innocence still pursues us,
threatening to draw us back into the warmth and security of the
unquestioned beliefs of our childhood. "Wouldn't it be nice,"
we think, "to believe in something solid again just once." That
was much of the feeling behind Ellen's tale of crossing the river,
the loss:

You know, when you get over here, you
leave something—you have to—and sometimes I
wish I was that person back there. But I can't be,

and I don't want to be. . . . I mean I can't ever be
that person again. Once you cross the river the innocence is gone.

Don't look back! is the imperative of this point in the
journey out of the underworld. Until we know in our bones
that Truth is relative to its context, commitment seems forever.
To turn around is to risk turning to stone. Is it possible, we ask,
to make a commitment to something without calcifying? What
was that difference again between faith and belief?

So there are no guarantees. There can't be. That, after all,
is what the transformation is all about. If it were a sure thing,
it wouldn't get you there.

Yet at the end of the journey lies a new identity. Traveled with integrity, the way home leads to a fuller and clearer
sense of who we are, a new and broader boundary between oneself and the world. The struggle to be something more than the
person others have made, to construct and then live up to a set
of *our own* expectations, is one of the most compelling struggles of our adult lives. When we left Sandy back in Chapter 3,
she had seen the struggle coming. Describing herself as "pulled
by a current" toward greater independence, she longed to become "a legitimate member of the world." What has happened
since then?

The contrast with my last visit to see Sandy could scarcely have been greater. In place of the brittle crust of the snowbank grew a swath of tousled grass; tiny clumps of chamomile
made their incongruous place between cracks in the sidewalk
where earlier the salt had failed in the bitter cold to thaw the
ice. A soft breeze drifted up the hillside from Lake Champlain,
and overhead the maple leaves rustled. Where before Sandy
had opened the door not a moment too soon, now I found myself almost wishing she had forgotten our appointment so I
could disappear in search of a soft patch of sunlight by the lake.
The old saw about Vermont's two seasons (winter and the
Fourth of July) makes days like this collectors' items.

But alas, the door was open when I arrived, and Sandy,
looking like the day, ushered me into the living room where we

sat and got caught up, the tape recorder nestling between us under a potted philodendron. As she spoke, I realized with a growing sense of awe that a good deal more than the weather had
changed since last December.

Recall that Sandy had followed an intensely personal
study of "family systems theory" with an effort to carry out a
more "academic" study of psychology, for she had come to
fear that she lacked the kind of detached, academic thinking
that she believed necessary for success in graduate school
should she go on and become a trained therapist. She also had
begun to feel, like many students in programs of this sort, that
she needed a general overview of the subject matter—the sort of
survey conventionally fed to freshmen. She was beginning to
feel a need to "enter the world" and to make it on her own. A
sense of independence was very important to her, and the language of movement in her speech was striking. But in December, the future had still been uncertain; she had felt something
less than confident of her ability to keep moving through the
darkness ahead and looked to her adviser with considerable reliance and not a little awe. "She's an extraordinarily rich person," she said of Grace, who seemed able to maintain her balance amidst conflict in a way Sandy admired, who possessed an
alluring sense of independence, who could listen so well, who
appeared to be very clearly on a journey of her own, and above
all who had been there before. "There's something, there's a
feeling that she's been through something, and it's been rocky,"
Sandy had said, "but there's something about her that seems
accepting. Whatever her situation is, she seems accepting of it."
These were, of course, the very characteristics Sandy sought for
herself; what she chose to see as Grace's strengths were those
that she projected at the end of her own journey and yet paradoxically without which she would be unable to complete the
journey itself. With all of this in mind, I turned on the tape recorder anticipating a headline story of mentor and student moving bravely together into the murk of ignorance and uncertainty.

But the study had not gone well at all. Grace had been
the wrong person for what she needed at the time, Sandy said.
She had needed someone who knew a lot about the general field

of psychology and who could give her the support and structure she needed. As an educator, Grace had an insufficient depth in psychology and furthermore had been overwhelmed with outside work and was thus unable to be there for Sandy when she needed her.

My stomach sank. I began to wonder what would happen if all my subjects turned out to have disastrous relationships. Research can only stand so much of this stuff. How do I write my book? Then, somewhat petulantly reminding myself that just because the drama didn't go according to my script didn't mean it had none, I moved ahead with the interview.

Although Sandy took pains to separate Grace the person from Grace the teacher, the study had been frustrating. Most of the time Sandy had felt adrift in a "huge ocean of psychology" with no one to give her the bearings she needed. Only toward the end did she begin to pull her ideas together, but by then it was too late. Her final paper left her vaguely dissatisfied, and the oral presentation to her fellow students was confused, scattered, and "very, very upsetting."

At one point, reading the work of a particularly difficult theorist, she had felt "just devastated" to think that she might be unable to find the right psychologist for her, the one she could "identify with" and whose work would guide her in her subsequent practice. The more she read, the more she saw that "different ones would pull me in for different reasons, and they'd all have their point of view and they would all be significant. And so it was more me realizing that I've got to have my own point of view and take from whomever." She laughs nervously as she says this, and I ask her if she can recall any moments when she knew "what had to happen."

"Let's see," she says, and leans back on the sofa, resting one arm along the back, gazing at the ceiling, tapping her lips pensively with the index finger of the other hand. Slowly she begins to reconstruct the previous term's work. The first part of the study had gone relatively well, but it soon became apparent that she was not satisfied with simply drifting where the currents led. That might have worked earlier, but not this time.

"I needed to define more what I was doing, and it was

hard being so general and I wasn't sure where I wanted to go next. And I realized too that some of my own issues in the study weren't being met. I think that was the big thing. And so that's when I decided that I had to find my own narrowed goal to finish the study; and there was a time in there where I was trying not to but feeling I needed to, and that was the most difficult time. And I wasn't hearing from Grace at that point either, so I was tearing my hair for a while." She laughs without a whole lot of conviction, and I ask her what that moment felt like.

"I felt like I was under the ocean, you know, just sort of somersaulting backwards [that laugh again] knowing that I would eventually come up but not knowing where or quite how to do it at that point, and still excited about where I had gone and just about the study. I was excited about the study even though it was very frustrating at times."

"What happened to get you through that?" I ask, hoping for some sign of Grace.

"Well, I had to come up very quickly," she replies, laughing uneasily again, "because I was getting to the end of the study, and that's when I realized that I wasn't going to get it from Grace, that I had to figure it out for myself."

She goes on to explain her fear that the study wasn't "legitimate," somehow it wasn't all right for her to be studying psychology. So, she says, "I wanted to see if I wasn't legitimate, why were other people legitimate? Why was it legitimate for Maslow to study psychology? . . . So I started reading their personal lives and that's what straightened it out for me. . . . I saw how much people's beginnings, their personal beginnings and their emotional lives led them right into the psychology they developed, and I was then able to see how my personal life tied into what I was trying to do."

And despite her misgivings about the study itself, in discussing it later with another faculty adviser who helped her gain some distance on it, she felt a "great relief" about the term's work: "I understood where my confusion was and why it wasn't only me that was making me confused, but it was the situation, the way the study was set up."

In effect, what seems to have happened is that the study worked at the outset because she could simply follow a set of initially prescribed readings. But when the time came to take more of her own direction, she felt lost because she was unable to ground the study in any kind of context that had meaning for her. In her more dualistic days, the authority of the instructor might have been enough to give the study meaning, but Grace was not providing that sort of authority; for Sandy's more multiplistic self, personal exploration would have done; but this time she needed more than that. This time, in order to make sense of what she was learning, she needed her ideas *to make connections*—with her own experience, with the "outside world," and with other ideas. Something in her knew that and drew her to the thought of studying the lives of the idea makers themselves. That was the breakthrough. For it allowed her to see how ideas are formed in the context of real lives, something she could grasp with her intuition. It thus bridged that intellect/ emotion gap that had been plaguing her. The gap crossed, she was then able to see ideas from *both* inside and outside. As she says, she understood "that the world doesn't only revolve around me, [but] that everyone comes from their own circumstances, and they have their own makeup . . . people come from their own perspectives, that one is not necessarily more right. People arrive at where they are because they come from their own circumstances, have gone through their own processes, and have arrived at something that works for them but doesn't necessarily work for everybody." In short, she was finally able to give the study meaning by placing it in the context of human lives, coming to understand not only how ideas emerge but seeing in a brand new way how she, too, was a product of her own history.

So despite a study that left her with mixed feelings, she was very clear that the term had resulted in growth for her. Last winter she had spoken with urgency and passion of her desire to be "a legitimate member of the world." But that goal had seemed still well off in the future; the tenses were markedly changed now. "The world is a lot bigger," she says, nodding to no one in particular. "I feel pretty confident about who I am, and especially about where I'm going. I'm not as afraid of the possible future as I was. I feel confident that I'm in a process and the process can only keep building; and earlier, when I last talked to you, I didn't have that confidence of knowing what was on the other side."

She seems to have crossed some sort of a barrier between herself and that elusive "other side." "I've never seen a way that I can fit into the world before," she says. "I've always felt like I'm on the outside and I don't fit in, that what I'm doing is a game; it's not legitimate. Someone else is supporting me."

Legitimacy is an important word for Sandy, a kind of gatekeeper between the two sides: home and world. It has about it a strong connotation of "belonging." Yet it is not the kind of belonging to be had in her old family world, or as a possession of her husband. Rather, to be "legitimate," she needs to feel that it is OK to be who she is, on her own terms. When she can do that, she will have earned her new membership in "the world."

In Kegan's terms, she seems to be suspended between the interpersonal and institutional stages, moving fast to the latter. At the same time, Perry's lens lets us see that she took an enormous step toward "legitimacy" when she saw that the ideas of her psychologists emerged from the contexts of their lives. As she became able to place herself in context as well, she could accept in a fresh and quite liberating way her own legitimacy. By reducing her fears about legitimacy, the study has allowed her to imagine much more realistically that she might, indeed, "make it" and become a therapist. And for her, this new skill will be the ticket for her emergence into the world as a fully contributing adult.

But something else seems to have happened, some other barrier crossed besides this. She speaks several times of a new ability to trust both others and herself—this despite a term with an adviser on whom she felt unable to rely. And out of this trust she describes a greater ability to teach herself. What's that about, I wonder?

She is speaking slowly, thoughtfully now, her voice almost a monotone but tinted with urgency.

"I know I'm much more comfortable with my intellectual abilities, and before I had this big question about whether I had any, and I really relied on my emotions to learn things and travel forward. Now I feel more how to balance those two things so they can go together." The travel metaphor appears several times as she talks, her voice trailing fire, picking up momentum.

"I'm starting to feel really excited about knowing that no matter what dimension I travel that it's me and there's something to it and it's all right and there's something to learn that helps the whole picture of who I am. And that's really exciting. That came a lot from reading James Hillman, you know, traveling into the black and not closing it off and running away from it but realizing that it's part of who you are and it's legitimate and it's OK and it's important."

There it is again, I think, and check. "Traveling into the black?"

"Well," she says, turning to me, instructing, "there's a negative side and a positive side, and you try to keep in the positive side so it keeps you from exploring the fears and the sorrows—instead of seeing that there's no such thing as negative and positive. . . . I have trouble with words like *wrong* and *truth*; for one thing, it ties in with what I was saying—that there's a positive experience in life and there's a negative. And what Hillman has encouraged me to think is that between the positive and the negative is one that goes straight down [that laugh again] and that includes positive *and* negative, and it dissolves truths and right and wrong; that it's more of an encompassing of all of who we are and seeing that all of who we are contributes to how we live our life."

I've no idea what expression is on my face as she says all of this, but it feels like watching a child being born. She goes on.

"And there's no such thing as wrong. I really believe that. And there's no such thing as right; there's no such thing as truth. It's more that there's a dropping down into something and broadening what we are that is unique and also universal— and understanding how we're universal and how we're unique is what I'm most interested in right now."

Later, as we talk about her relationship with Grace, the dialectic comes up again. When the study began, Sandy was "in awe of Grace" and "treated her like a guru a little bit." But now, she continues, "it's more in balance. . . . I think what I want in the end is to be friends with her and to feel like a peer; and I think I have to some degree."

In an earlier study, she explains, she had taken all the blame on her own shoulders when replies came late. She started to do that again this time, but being more willing to accept her own negative emotions, she acknowledged that "I was starting to feel annoyed and angry with Grace, frustrated with her that she wasn't doing it right, or that we both weren't, but it wasn't just her and it wasn't just me; and so that's when I started taking over more and just, you know, realizing *this is my study*. I wanted it to work for myself and began to feel just less that Grace was greater than me in all ways. And so I felt it started coming into balance because of that."

"What do you mean by 'balance'?"

"That we're out of the context of being student/teacher, that we're both human beings." What was Grace's part in helping this come about? According to Sandy, rather little. Grace had helped her to clarify her initial goals, had gotten her started with her reading, but as far as the content of the study went, that was about it. From there on, Grace simply (!) served as a reader for what Sandy was writing, encouraging her, and providing superficial proofreading. The result of this benign neglect was that "it made me realize that *I* was making the study work. I was putting all that in and . . . that she wasn't going to teach me. It was more that I was reflecting off of her."

Sandy sees advisers as guides now rather than teachers, adding that "I think there's more of an exchange than I'd realized before. I think *they're also* on a journey, and in a sense I'm a guide for them. I think I see it more that way now. It can't be completely one-sided." Later, when I ask her what she feels is the most important thing she learned from her relationship with Grace, she pauses a moment, brushes aside the content, and replies, "that I have to, in a way I have to guide myself first before I get guidance from someone else."

When I leave the house a short time afterward, I have

completely forgotten the weather. My mind is spinning. Here I
am writing a book about teaching, yet Sandy's enormous learning emerged from what seems almost no intervention on Grace's
part at all. How will Grace see it? I wonder, and head for our
appointment at her office in the state department of education.

As it turns out, Grace is in remarkable accord with
Sandy's account. She shared Sandy's dismay over the material
outcome of the study and seemed relieved to learn that Sandy
looked upon the study in such a positive light. Had she deliberately refrained from providing more structure, I ask.

"It was somewhat deliberate," Grace says. She prefers to
work in a style that encourages students to take the initiative
for themselves, adding that she felt strongly that even if she had
provided more direction, Sandy would have resisted it. "There
was always some resistance when I suggested she could do such
and such; she was never very happy with it."

It would be easy to conclude from this particular case
that Sandy made her way in spite of Grace, and there is certainly some truth to this. But I think it is important not to confuse invisibility with absence. Grace's profile, however low, hov-
ered significantly in the study's background. Sandy saw her as
an independent person and knew that her own movement
toward that stance would be compromised if she allowed Grace
too much space in her life. She seems to have held Grace as a
transparent image rather than a concrete presence, shaping herself in response to Grace's outlines rather than in conformity to
her wishes. Grace had the wisdom to see that and to respect
Sandy's need for autonomy while acknowledging her concurrent wish for support. How did Grace do this? How did she respond to Sandy's appeals for structure?

"Well, we talked about what structure would mean, and
we talked about what she was looking for in the class that she
took and then dropped at the university—about why that
hadn't been successful. Most of what we discussed was why it
was that she wanted the structure."

Thus, rather than focusing directly on what might have
been Sandy's "failure" and trying to "fix" it, Grace raised the
discussion to an analysis of the broader context—to Sandy's

need for structure. This enabled Sandy to stay out of the old dialectical trap about whether she was "legitimate" or not and brought Sandy's attention directly onto the developmental issue facing her—her own growing strength, her increased willingness to care for herself and stand on her own. This is the evolution that Carol Gilligan considers the hallmark of maturity, a step that "dissipates the tension between selfishness and responsibility through a new understanding of the interconnection between self and other" (1982, p. 74). In effect, Sandy came to rename her work not as selfishness but as an act of care for herself. Seeing it thus, Sandy was more able to construct a new perspective on herself, a platform between and above the horns of her former dilemma.

And when Sandy eventually came up with the breakthrough idea of studying the lives of the psychologists, Grace was quick to support her. She knew that what Sandy was finally looking for was permission, and she readily gave it, recognizing that here was an important opportunity for Sandy to break out of her "rigid perception" of what it meant to be "academic and scholarly." Evidently as things turned out, it was.

Toward the end of the interview, as I did with everyone, I read a short statement and asked Grace to comment on it. It went like this:

> In my search for truth, I kept looking for someone who had the answers. But now I realize that no one has the answers to the important questions of life. The best we can do is construct our own answers from the evidence we have and act on them even though we might be wrong. It seems that on the journey to truth, we can never come home to stay.

And as usual, I asked what "home" meant to her. Here is Grace's reply:

> Well, it means the place I was when I was about thirteen and beginning to think about the is-

sues and knew for certain what they were, what my
opinions were, what the truth was . . . certainty.
[And you can't come home again now?]
No. I guess if home is comforting, it is the
relativeness of everything. It's somewhat comforting to know that a lot depends on circumstance,
the relationship of one thing to another, on some
confluence that's as important as any absolute.
There may be an absolute, but just as important
are the ways in which certain forces or activities or
circumstances or whatever, sort of come together
at any particular point—which doesn't mean that
there isn't any good or bad. I think there are, I
mean for me there are some things that are bad and
some things that are good, so it is not totally
amoral. It's like *you can be held as securely in a big
net off the ground if the connections are good as
you can on a solid rock* [italics added].

The question was designed to get at contextual relativism,
and clearly it worked in this case. For it is just the kind of epistemology that Grace describes here that we value as an end
product of a liberal education. If the journey metaphor as we're
using it here has any usefulness for understanding intellectual
development, then surely "home" of this sort must lie at the
end of the journey—not the home from which we are all banned
from the day of our departure, the home of which Thomas
Wolfe's novel speaks so eloquently, but the new home that we
forge for ourselves, the home we attain on the other side of the
journey through the dark. For if the first half of the journey is
characterized by a downward slide into dissolution and disillusionment, the second is the story not of reillusionment (at least
not in a conventional sense) but of acceptance. It is necessarily
through acceptance of the darkness, not its obliteration, that
we can transcend it. It is only from the gift of multiplicity and
"meaninglessness" that we can construct a new meaning, that
we can, in fact, come home.

Because the mythology and, indeed, a number of case histories seem to emphasize the Sturm und Drang of transformation, it is easy to imagine that the passage must necessarily be a painful one. But it need not be so. For some students, the release from all-encompassing Authority brings a refreshing freedom. One student, relaxing into the interview, described her feeling of almost voluptuous delight in all that freedom to learn.

> I love to learn. I read voraciously. I'm always looking things up. They asked me what I wanted for a wedding present, and I got a set of *Encyclopaedia Britannica* because there's always things I want to know I can't get my hands on. Umm. Which I love. You know, it's my favorite. I take them to bed, you know, and just . . .

It was with this sort of multiplistic worldview that Emily returned to school. Bob, her mentor, suggested she study some literature along with her practical education courses, and she did. Her shift to contextual thinking was relatively smooth as she found her new voice and came to see herself as a product of her history rather than an imposed stereotype.

Thinking Something Makes It Real

While in teachers college during World War II, Emily met a wounded veteran, dropped out of school, and married him. Over the years that followed, she raised five children, one of whom was severely ill much of the time. It was not until they were out of the nest that she felt she could complete her formal education. "That's why I'm pushing sixty and still striving to become a teacher," she explained with a wiry grin. Even though she acknowledged that it was mostly for her own "self-satisfaction," she was taking education courses to augment her experience as a substitute teacher in the hope that it would lead eventually to certification.

Emily was enjoying her studies thus far, but if she read two books with different views on the same topic she found it hard because

> when I read one book I can kind of agree with their theory, and then when I read the next book I agree with that. So then I have to go back and see what basically I believe and then put my belief against those two books and then take what I really believe. I'm not going to take what somebody else believes and adapt it for my own. I'm willing to read it, but I'm going to put my own beliefs in practice in judging which I would prefer. Or maybe neither. Maybe my own.

A practicing Catholic, she prided herself on her tolerance of other faiths. "They say the Catholic church is the true religion, but what religion doesn't? As long as a person is sincere and loves their neighbor, I don't think God cares what religion you are."

As a student, Emily believed that it was imperative for her to respect and listen to her teachers, especially her mentor. Yet she felt free to disagree if need be, and even though she "was scared to death of him" when they first met, she had come to admire him for his ability to get along with people. She felt equal to him "as a person," and her opinions were equal to his. What separated them was his greater knowledge, and she looked to him to guide her toward gaining more knowledge for herself.

Bob, her mentor, a "radical seminarian" in the late 1950s, had moved north and worked in public education, eventually becoming an elementary school principal. Forty-five at the time of our interview, he was the father of two children just entering school.

His greatest pleasure came, he said, from watching students "take off," especially those who had worked for years to care for others and who now were turning to education as a gift to themselves. He loved to help people "see the possibilities in themselves and the world around them."

Emily, whom he had known as teacher, adviser, and employer, was such a person. He admired her for her candor, compassion, curiosity, and particularly for her "openness to learning." He hoped he could be a "beacon" for her, letting her see that "there are other points on the compass" and other people from whom she could be learning, for he was somewhat uneasy about her tendency to put him on a pedestal; it was a role he resisted. She needed to take some of the confidence she placed in him for herself, he said.

Being cast as an authority made Bob uncomfortable. Helping people to become more self-reliant was of central importance to him. "I don't think I've ever wanted to be God," he said. "I feel increasingly at ease with ignorance—my own as well as others'," he added with a wry grin. "I am very uneasy with individuals who have The Answer to the problems that have been asked through the ages." If he had a bête noire, it was narrow-mindedness and dogmatism. The ideal student was always finding new questions to ask, and he hoped "that Emily will be asking the questions eventually if she isn't asking them now. Maybe there will be two of us asking the same questions."

A year later, Emily is looking forward to graduation. It has been a good year, and she has grown "intellectually and spiritually." She feels she can converse more readily with people now, she feels "more adequate, better equipped," and she knows she has done it herself. "I'm making myself a bigger person," she declares.

"I have learned the power of words. Don't you find me talking more powerfully than I did last year?" she asks rhetorically, and goes on to explain that she is much more able now to express her feelings rather than "just doing and hoping people understood." It was hard for her at first to speak up in classes. She was afraid of being laughed at, but over time—and it helped that Bob was her teacher in several courses—she came to feel that "I'm enough of a person so I can state what I think and if they don't want to go along with that, they don't have to."

Along with her greater loquacity, however, has come a decrease
in her earlier tendency "just to blurt out" her opinions. "I think
longer before I speak," she says. "Now I really sit and think
things out."

She seems to have found a new distance from her work,
an ability to distinguish between who she is and what she does
that allows her to take criticism not only more graciously but
perhaps more productively as well. At one point, a writing
teacher criticized one of her poems, saying it would look good
in a seed catalogue.

> A couple of years ago that would have devas-
> tated me because I would feel I had done my best.
> . . . I might have thought, "I'll go right back in and
> never show anybody my poem again." . . . But real-
> ly if you look at it, it's humorous. I wrote a poem
> and there's no substance to it, but it would look
> good in a Burpee's Seed Catalogue. On the other
> hand, that's *her* opinion. Maybe I like the poem.

A year earlier she described herself as others saw her: a
"flexible, tough cookie." Now, asked the same question, she
offers a detailed description in terms of her own history.

> I am what I am because of what has hap-
> pened to me in my lifetime. I am a product of the
> Depression, I'm a product of the Second World
> War, of the Korean War, the Vietnam War, and
> my viewpoint is going to be much different than
> those students [I teach] who are probably fifteen,
> sixteen, seventeen years old. . . . What I am is a
> combination of the things I learned from my par-
> ents, what I learned as an adult, as a single adult
> and as a married adult, and what I learned as a
> waitress for many years.

And commenting on an affair between two married neigh-
bors, she notes that she would earlier have simply seen it as

wrong; now she thinks it is not wrong so much as foolish because the man, who is much older, is only going to be hurt in
the long run, and "it seems such a foolish waste."

Does she feel that she has made any gain in the "knowledge gap" she described in her first interview? She still feels un-
equal to Bob in that regard, "but I'm catching up." And although she has added to her knowledge, she points out that she
can now "put it to better use. . . . It's the use you put knowledge to that is beneficial. It's not keeping it in your head."

Of Bob, she has little to say aside from her affection for
him. She saw relatively little of him after the Bible as Literature
course she took with him a semester earlier and does not seem
to need him for much any longer. But she remembers how he
had asked each student to bring a Bible along. She was surprised to discover that everyone brought one that was somewhat different. "I think the most important thing was learning
how to cope with other people's beliefs that are different than
yours. I think that's the most important thing I learned from
Bob, ever." She goes on to explain that not only do others have
a right to their opinions, but those opinions are "real" in an important sense. "Thinking something makes it real," she says,
echoing Hamlet.

Bob tells with enthusiasm about how he encouraged
Emily to undertake a local history study that allowed her to
combine her knowledge of the area with her love of storytelling
and her own inquisitiveness. The study taught her to ask good
questions and to sift among many answers for the best (not the
"right") one, he says, adding "if she could leave from my influence with a seeking mind, then I would have accomplished
something. And in some ways I think that happened. I think
that took place."

Yet while he is pleased with his influence, "in some way
you don't want to question 'why' too much because there may
not be any answers . . . to know there has been some influence,
that's satisfying enough in itself." And he is quick to point out
that ofttimes students will grow "in spite of you." Emily did it
by herself in the end, he says, and that is as it should be.

Although the relationship, as he describes it, was not a

particularly intense one, it was characterized by warmth, trust, mutual concern, and "a growing friendship along the way." He knows the religion course had an important influence, as did his ongoing encouragement. But he feels that the local history study was a fitting culmination because it led Emily to examine disparate data and seek to make connections. And although he stops short of saying that she is a full-grown intellectual, she has clearly begun the process of "intellectual growth" as he defines it here.

> Intellectual growth . . . is to maintain that sense of inquisitiveness and the ability to be able to see connections; and in seeing those particular connections to be able to arrive at a synthesis of how things fit together, how things are integrated, how the world and the universe are a whole. But also to realize that you as a part of that whole don't necessarily understand it totally . . . there are exceptions, gaps in our understanding.

Bob is quick to agree that love plays an important part in his work. By this he means a sense of concern and caring that he feels matters if a mentor-student relationship is to work at its best. It is important, he says, because it allows him to see the student as a "total human being" rather than simply a mind to be trained. It lets the mentor acknowledge the reality of the student's "problems or concerns in that particular phase." "But," he adds, "you also have to be able to care enough to let them go." His relationship with Emily "will probably taper off" shortly after her graduation, and that will be fine. He offers a kind of benediction:

> In some ways it's almost like the parent-child relationship, knowing that you have had an impact on some individual and gone beyond just setting up a program. But within that particular program and that particular relationship things have happened. [And when it is done you can say]

Now you're on your own. There are other people
that are going to come along in your life who are
going to be helpful, who are going to grow with
you, who are going to fall in love with you, who
are going to be concerned about you. And I thank
God that I've had the opportunity to be a part of
that whole process with you.

Such benedictions, which mentors often provide, serve
as little graduation ceremonies to mark the change in the terrain. They are especially important if the relationship is to continue on a new plane or terminate cleanly. Without some acknowledgment of the change, one or the other partner may feel
cheated or hurt, a feeling that often turns to anger, a convenient if inappropriate way to end.

Although mentors often leave as the traveler crosses the
threshold back into the world of light, some remain to aid in
the transition. For the time of coming home can be one of considerable turmoil. In its way it is analogous to the dilemma of
the returning Peace Corps volunteer or Vietnam veteran—travelers reshaped by the demands of a distant world, no longer able
or even willing to fit comfortably into the old slots. (Said one
returned Peace Corps volunteer, "I tried and tried to readjust,
but it didn't work. Finally I gave up and adjusted to being un-
adjusted." Click!) After an experience of transformation, Campbell reminds us, "the first problem of the returning hero is to
accept as real . . . the passing joys and sorrows, banalities and
noisy obscenities of life. Why reenter such a world?" (1949, p.
218).

The question is especially poignant as we teeter on the
brink of commitment, that point where we decide to move
ahead and begin walking on that "big net off the ground" that
Grace was willing to call reality. It is easier if in the course of
uprooting our notions of right and wrong, of teaching us that
we construct our own realities, the transformation has also
displaced our sense of what is "normal." For the returning
traveler is always just a little crazy in the eyes of old acquain-
tances.

Living on the Border

It is May. Ella and I have driven off along the threads of dirt road that brush the border with Canada to the edge of a small lake. We talk quietly, she standing randomly on the tiny beach looking across the flat water, I sitting on a half-submerged boulder. Warblers flit among the alders, listening and commenting erratically.

"Back when you first started all this," I ask her, "what did you think you'd be like when you finished?"

"I dunno. Maybe freer than I am. Solve more things maybe. Thought it would prove something." She talks in a low, almost sullen way. She's angry, I think.

"What was it going to prove?"

"I thought it would just shut up that stupid nagging that was always after me to do something. I thought it would be like, 'OK, you get your degree, it's over, and then you can get on with other things.' That's what I thought. But the only thing it proved was how far I've got to go. Opened up another whole can of worms." She looks back at me, hostile and pleading at once.

"So you're not what you thought you'd be?" I ask, smiling to glaze the obvious.

She snorts, enjoying the irony, then looks away, across the lake. "I'm a lot more than I had any idea I could be—as far as being a person goes." Then she turns back, releasing the sarcasm slowly, like her breath. "I always thought that with a little knowledge you could make the 'right' decisions. You could tell right from wrong and you could go around telling everybody that 'You're right, you're wrong; this is good, this is bad.' " And she shakes her head with a short laugh, almost as if she is trying to get something unstuck. "I sort of thought it was hooked with education somehow, and you learned *that* somehow through books." She is silent for a moment, eyes somewhere at the edge of the shore and water. Then she adds, mostly to herself, "You lose."

Grappling for balance between my delight at her struggle and compassion for her disillusionment, I try to help her come out.

"And it didn't turn out that way," I say, muting the question.

"Nope. Now the only thing you do is say, 'Well, you could be right and then again, you could be wrong, and it might be good for you but it certainly wouldn't be good for me.' It just colored the whole world gray."

"So the world is different?"

"No," she replies, clear this time. "It's not the world. It's me."

The certainty in her tone provokes me to follow it. Who, I wonder, is this "me"? Commitment is the issue for her now; she needs to be thinking about that new person, a person who can come into being only as she begins to act in her new world. I ask her if she feels more or less certain than she used to.

"I know for sure I'll take care of myself!" she replies with a broad grin. "I never knew that before. I never thought I could. But" and her voice fades again; she looks down at the sand: "it's the whole thing about endings and beginnings. I used to dread having anything end. Or begin. And instead of getting it cut off now, it just keeps going in circles. There aren't any beginnings; there aren't any endings." She looks back up. "But I don't fear either one anymore."

Recalling our earlier conversation on the way here in the car, a conversation in which she had talked about a recurrent dream of herself sitting by the water fearing to go in, I smile and say to the far shore, "Sounds like you better get into that water next time you have that dream."

"Why?" she asks with a laugh, knowing.

"It sounds like you're ready to swim," I reply. She tries a last maneuver.

"Maybe I'd choose not to."

"You don't have any choice until you get in," I respond, and she agrees. We both fall silent.

Later, heading back, I talk about my notion that for many people the degree is a kind of grail that once attained will transform them. What they don't realize, at least until later, is that it's not the degree, it's the education that transforms, not the goal but the journey.

"Yeah," she says. "I've been rereading a lot of the papers

I did for different courses. I keep thinking, 'I wonder who did that?' There's like, no connection with me. If I had them to do again, I could never do them like that. Same person couldn't do them." She pauses and gazes out the window at the manure pile trailing from the tip of a crippled conveyer belt as we bump past. "Same person doesn't exist anymore."

"What would the new person do now?"

"Probably be a whole bunch more wishy-washy about the whole thing. Everything is so damned definite in those papers."

"Is the new person definite about anything?" I ask, curious about her slipperiness.

"I dunno. Don't know. Hope not." The irony is back.

"But you said that you were surer that you could do things now. That there was a confidence there."

"Well, there's a confidence which is . . ." She searches a moment for the sense, "which is like a core I never had."

"What's in that core?"

"I guess that's what I'm looking for," she replies and falls silent again. Then, "Maybe I don't want to know. Maybe it consists of nothing," and she turns to me. I feel her eyes against my temple as I drive, boring in. "You create your own reality. I really believe that. You *do*. As long as I know that, I can take care of myself; let's leave it at that. Don't tear it apart [another pause] 'cause maybe it's not there."

Perhaps it had nothing to do with her return to education, but Ella's relationship with her husband went into severe fibrillation after that. She had already begun to lose friends, a condition she wryly referred to as "leaving friends on the tracks." It was hard for her to tell whether the choice had been hers or theirs. She would tell herself that she wasn't really any different, but she knew better. It was a good thing she was no longer as ready to define herself through their eyes as she used to be. They thought she was crazy.

At the same time, she became friends with a new range of people, "people so different from the ones I knew before. It's like having a whole lot of doors open." She found she valued her sons' dawning adolescence in a whole new way. She could welcome what lay ahead rather than regret the loss of their childhood. Swimming, as she was, as we all do, through a sea of friendships, she was learning to let go of some in order to dive but learning also that she could reach out in whole new ways to others as she became a more graceful swimmer.

I was an important part of Ella's new world, but our friendship grew slowly. Recalling her first impression, she said,

> He breezed into the room and was so casual and everything was fine. And I thought "Oh my God, no!" There was this air of confidence about him: "Everybody's gonna get through this and there's no doubt in my mind," and I was thinking, "Ha, I'm not at all convinced." I was very, very much in awe of him for a long time.

For my part, I had, quite simply, never seen anyone with an intellect like hers. She had put together a self-assessment portfolio for her community college degree entirely without help, and it was the best I'd seen. I was impressed. Needless to say, I encouraged her to continue her studies as my student.

Over time, we came to see each other increasingly as human beings, less as mentor and student. But for a long while Ella felt the more vulnerable of the two of us. She was the one, after all, putting her work out there for criticism; all I did was lean back and make comments. She wanted to know me as a human being more than I her. Yet as the months passed I was able to let her know that I didn't have all the answers, and she, for her part, grew less interested in getting them—from me at least. I was able, as well, to talk more about my own feelings, about what was going on in the life I kept at home, away from work. This was hard for me, partly perhaps because of who I am but partly too because like most men, I separated more sharply than many women do, my home life from my work life. "What," I would find myself asking no one in particular, "do my children have to do with how I conduct my work?" But for Ella the answer seemed to be "a lot!" "Where are you inside that shell?" she would ask in a hundred ways. "Who are you in there?" And as I struggled to answer, she was able to reach out to other people as well. I was, in a certain sense, someone safe with whom she could practice her own swimming lessons. For that matter, she wasn't such a bad teacher herself. More than any other student, Ella taught me that I could share more of myself too.

Self-disclosure from the mentor seems to play a crucial part in the full evolution of a mentorship from hierarchy toward symmetry. Often flayed and vulnerable, the student needs to know that he can trust his teacher. In the early stages of development, authority is enough, but as the student grows, his willingness to trust an authoritative mask without knowing what lies behind it dims. He comes increasingly to ask, "Who are you? What lies behind that facade? Can I really trust you?" And if the reply is inappropriately muted, if the mentor is unable or unwilling to doff the mask and attempt to answer the question, things begin to die. The relationship grows hard and eventually will crack.

Listening to protégés talk about the early development of their relationships, that pressure from beneath rings out again and again: "I just wanted to know *who* she was. I wanted her to let me see her as a person!" Describing his own particularly powerful association with his business instructor/mentor, one student told me this:

> After our initial contact, we would talk after
> class a lot and it was pretty clear that he liked me
> as a student, but nothing really changed a lot be-
> yond that. I mean it was a warm relationship, but
> somehow it just wasn't special. But one afternoon I
> had a meeting scheduled with him and stuff at
> work had been going badly and my wife was get-
> ting on my case, and I just felt shitty. I hadn't
> done the assignment and called him to let him
> know I wanted to cancel. He said, "C'mon over
> anyway," and so I did. We got talking, and for
> some reason, I just decided to spill out how I was
> feeling. I mean I never did that before with another
> man. But he was listening and really seemed to care

what was going on with me. I really felt better
after that, and the next time we met, he started
talking about his own life a little. I mean not a
whole lot, not like I spilled on him, but he told me
some stuff about his own life, about troubles with
his work and with his kids, that really made me
say, "Hey, this guy is really a human being after
all," you know?

With only a little reflection, it is apparent why it has to
be this way. Continued development for the student mandates
a decrease in the power of authority, a greater need to see
through appearances, a new sense of the value and importance
of an inner, personal, emotional self. Clearly, the kind of relationships that will both appeal to and sustain a person moving
in those directions must be those that are capable of penetrating and discarding masks. But it works the other way as well. To
the extent that the mentor is able to become human, the student is empowered to see more deeply. Mentor becomes a practice ground for seeing all human beings with richer insight; she
or he prepares a safe plot for intellectual and emotional growth.
In the next scene, we will catch a glimpse of the power of intimacy to enrich learning. While mentorships of such intensity
are rare, they do suggest the remarkable connection that can
occur between an open heart and an open mind.

Robin and Alison worked together for six months largely
by mail, in contact directly only at the beginning of the study
for several days, and again at the end, for the conclusion. Yet
they developed a relationship of extraordinary intensity and
power. In her mid twenties, it is obvious from the outset that
Alison is a contextual thinker. She was not drawn to the relationship out of any kind of awe for the authority of her mentor. Likewise, Robin's attraction to Alison was less that of an
authority toward a willing pupil than of an older person who
saw in a younger something very precious, something she valued in herself as much as in Alison, twenty years her junior.
Here, they talk about their study together.
When Robin first saw Alison, she thought, "Boy, this is

a really sharp woman." But because Robin was a teacher of
mathematics and Alison an artist, she didn't imagine that they
would work together. As it turned out, however, Alison had
studied math and was more than competent in the field. She
attended one of Robin's classes and decided to study with her.
She saw in Robin, "a certain warmth, balanced by enthusiasm
. . . a very direct person, a very sincere person, and sincerely
interested in what she was doing." At the same time, "she was
still serious; she demanded a certain standard; she was knowledgeable about her material." For Alison, respect was important.

> I felt a respect for her. She was able to give
> me ideas about things I was unfamiliar with. She
> inspired in me a sense that she does know what
> she's talking about, and that was important to me.
> It seemed so natural at the time, but I think that if
> there hadn't been the respect, that I wouldn't have
> considered her for the study—if I hadn't just natu-
> rally respected her. I respect her ways of thinking,
> a certain sharpness of mind, a quick mind. I like
> someone who in a conversation can sit down and
> grasp your way of thinking and go along with
> the idea. It requires a certain balance so their mind
> is working and they can take in certain patterns of
> thought too.

Robin shared her student's respect. At first, she was uneasy with what she saw as Alison's "speed-thinking," a characteristic she viewed in herself with mixed feelings.

> But I felt very early on that she was very
> solid, that she really knew a great deal and had a
> real depth inside of her, and I could identify with
> that [quickness] because I'm a very speedy person
> too . . . we run on a very similar kind of basic
> energy. . . . I have enormous respect for her mind
> and intelligence and integrity and ability to go to

the sources and to find things for herself; and one
of the things that impressed me right off is her intellectual honesty. . . . I just was so comfortable
with that with Alison right from the start. She
would always say what she didn't understand, and
I found that so refreshing, so good to work with.

As the study progresses, Robin felt "really overwhelmed"
by both the depth and breadth of Alison's work. It was graduate work, very abstract and of high quality. For her part, Alison
reveled in the work, giving her curiosity free rein, yet not hesitating to move deeply into problems she herself would often
pose. She felt that Robin was helpful to her in just the right
ways, assisting Alison to "pull out important questions," pointing out interesting new directions, encouraging reflection on
"what it meant that the study was developing that way." Robin
was "accessible"; she was encouraging. Yet if she disagreed or
felt Alison was unclear, she would say so directly.

We would share on a very honest level. That
kind of directness with each other made the bond
strong, and I never felt frightened to be honest
with her, to share with her the fact that I had forgotten all my geometry or something very basic
like that; and the humor in our relationship was
nice. She could kid me about something that I
didn't know, and I felt very good about that. At
the same time, I respect her in a way that I would
not really kid her, but we could share humorous
things. I think respect is extremely important. She
respected me and could always criticize me, but
it was always in a very respectful way . . . a mutual-
ly respectful attitude.

Although their association began with a high degree of
mutuality, as it grew, it became richer on many different levels.
Alison felt it was particularly important that Robin was willing
to share her personal opinions and some aspects of her inner life

during their correspondence. Knowing that she was dealing with a whole human being rather than a disembodied mind allowed her to understand *how* Robin thought, not simply *what*. Conversely, in that personal sharing, Robin would come to understand *how* Alison put together her ideas. For Alison, the context of ideas was essential, and it could be experienced more richly in a personal relationship than through a disembodied and abstract one.

> Some very personal opinions came up because we both were explaining ourselves to the other; we came to be able to hold [a different] opinion and yet share it with the other; and I respect somebody who can have an opinion but who's not arrogant in that opinion and is willing to share it and explain it and defend it in light of your opinion . . . you maintain respect by being there to share what you have. If you always keep this incredible distance, I lose my respect for someone because I feel they're hiding something.

The dialogue of learning is of special importance to Alison as well, and she distinguishes between "a follower of someone" who simply absorbs the ideas of an authority "at face value" and a true "student/mentor relationship" in which there is an "exchange of ideas *and feelings.*" Clearly, a sense of mutuality and equality in the relationship is important to her—not simply because it feels right, but because it makes for better learning as well.

> I felt very connected to Robin in a most positive way, as somebody I was growing with. Interesting, I say "growing with." I did feel we were growing together, but there's still a sense that we are both developing something together. Again, it's not the sense of "I'm way above you," but there's communal growth, and sometimes just a growth in our own dialogue . . . a sense that we were sharing

and growing in our communication. Anything, no
matter how deep your idea is, I think you gain in
perspective when you share it. I think our relationship is stronger because of the constant dialogue.

As we talk about the study in her office, Robin describes
a deep sadness as the tutorial came to an end.

"What do you most want to give her?" I ask.

"Just self-confidence, you know, and just a good life—
whatever that means. A good life." She laughs, a short, birdlike
warble. "She's so worthwhile, and she's been through so much
pain, like so many people have." She laughs again, but it seems
more a release than an expression of delight. She is letting something go, I think. Robin goes on.

"She's just so . . . she has so much to give the world with
herself, and she really doesn't, hasn't quite learned, I think.
She's learning, but I mean how to fully nourish herself is what
she hasn't quite mastered." Robin laughs again in that almost
sobbing way. It is clear that Alison has touched something deep.

"Is part of her in yourself?" I ask.

She replies that in some ways they are very different.
Then adds, "But there's a part of her that's very much me right
now because she loves mathematics as I love mathematics, and
she sees its wonderful connection with the world and with life
in ways very few people see." Her eyes have grown red as she
speaks, and the tears come. I wait, feeling awkward. I'm less
comfortable with pain than many people and less able than
Robin to let it have its way.

"What's responding in you now?" I ask, as gently as I
can. "What is that?" She laughs again. After a long pause, she
replies, slowly, haltingly.

"It's so many things. It's hard to articulate or to try to
get it into a linear thing. . . . It's not just mathematics, although
a big part of it is. But I mean there's a kind of commitment. . . .
It's kind of hard to talk about. It's embarrassing because, you
know, to be in that position, to feel that you know someone
else is kind of looking to you for something, and you feel inade-
quate and unable to give . . . and at the same time, not com-

pletely." She pauses a long while, then speaks again, more stead-
ily this time.

"There's just a lot of fullness connected to it, and a particular sadness too. Tremendous pleasure, tremendous joy that
one could have shared so much in common with someone else
and that one could be so privileged to think one is actually contributing to the real intellectual and full awakening of another
human being . . . it's very moving."

At just that moment the phone rings. She dabs up the
rest of her tears, answers it, and a few moments later it is time
to leave. As I stand in the doorway, she says, "I just hate to call
it love; love is so many things, and the word has lost its power.
But I just care tremendously. We had such a powerful connection, such a really powerful connection."

Students like Alison are the ones we usually call "bright"
and delight in teaching. They are self-directed, ask excellent
questions, grasp ideas and their implications quickly, and
though unafraid to disagree with us are usually savvy enough to
do so carefully. Indeed, there is a demonstrable correlation between high grades and contextual thinking. We like these students. They may not agree with us, but we think alike.

Looking back on my own shift into contextualism, it is
sometimes difficult to see a single moment clearly. But as a student in American history and literature at the time, I do know
that I was spurred on by a *range of diverse content*. My teachers demanded that I integrate it around central questions. I still
have those papers today: "Lewis and Clark's Journals: A Study
in the Making of an Empire," "A Theory of Art in *The Marble
Faun*," "The Role of Women in Works of Henry Adams." Each
of these and others forced me to integrate my reading with my
historical knowledge, with art, with ideas from other material as
well as in relation to the outside world.

Here, as I write, is a paper comparing Plutarch's with
Shakespeare's version of *Coriolanus*, and there a piece of "original
research" on local dialect in New Hampshire. I was being asked to
consider original sources, discovering in the process that what we
view as "historical truth" is inevitably constructed through human observers conditioned by their own times and purposes.

On top of them all, yellowed and fading, rests a major paper I wrote for Fred Rudolph, a mentor to this day. "Humanity, Identity, and the American Negro," I called it, pulling together around the issue of identity such authors as Genet, Tocqueville, Douglass, Booker T. Washington, and W. E. B. DuBois to make what emerged as a personal *statement of commitment* to the emerging civil rights struggle in the South. How could he have known that as a senior in college I was reaching out for a new *identity*, that I sought a *dream* to capture my *youthful idealism*, that I needed to move toward *making commitments* as a basis for the future work now looming so close? How astonishing, I think, that Fred could have known me so well to have placed that needle in precisely the right place at just the right time!

Rudolph was, of course, working intuitively, as many great teachers have. But intuition and magic need not be entirely mysterious. To look more deeply at what helps students move into contextualism, let's return to the principles that surfaced at the end of Chapter 4 and see how they might apply now that the student's job is no longer to dismantle old structures but rather to construct new ones.

To engender trust is central to any strong, nurturant relationship. But while the trust that characterizes an early relationship owes much of its strength to the ascribed authority of the teacher, a more mature trust is sustained increasingly by the shared commitment of each partner. It must be constantly recreated. Like any living thing, trust wants tending. To keep it alive requires a small, but steady stream of risk—the will to drop the screen that protects our eyes from the full glare of another's presence. This is especially true as a relationship matures and the growing student asks more of the teacher's humanity. In the strength of a maturing trust, the partners are freer to challenge each other's ideas, knowing they are held by the mutual commitment. Conversely, with a diminishing need to protect a mask, each can afford to hear the other more fully and can learn more deeply. Thus the relationship becomes the caring context for the dialectic, the culture out of which a transforming synthesis can spring.

Watching now to *see the student's movement,* the mentor

looks for signs of rebuilding. The student is now capable of re-
moving herself from immediate identification with ideas; she
can talk about them as existing in some measure apart from herself; she can attend to their form, asking about the logic and
flow of an argument, checking for use of evidence to support a
position, considering how the historical setting and evolution
of a phenomenon has conditioned it, conscious of underlying
assumptions. This will be a time to note a growing sense of
voice as the student increasingly clarifies the new boundary between herself and others, broadening it to include more, honing
it to discriminate better.

Now is the time to *encourage the student's own voice* as
he moves away from echoing outside authorities, and away also
from simple self-absorption. The contextual learner can understand differing perspectives but is not overwhelmed by them,
and has developed sufficient internal power to use the ideas of
others but can do so in support of his own voice. The teacher's
job at this point is to help the student complete the dialogue:
from "They think," through "I think," to "Given that . . . it
seems . . . " complete with evidence. This is what moves thinking out into the world where it can stand or fall on its own.

Whereas the earlier purpose of *introducing conflict* was
to aid in the breakup of calcified thought, now the value is that
students can come to see that the power of one idea over another rests in how well it incorporates diverse information, how
well it is constructed, how elegant its form. Moreover, by giving
several different interpretations of an event, whether the results
of a physics experiment, the outcome of labor negotiations, or
the meaning of Van Gogh's last painting, we encourage students
to form their own theories, to marshall their own evidence, and
ultimately to express their own emerging selves through their
ideas.

As before, we encourage a sense of progress by *emphasizing positive movement*. Growth is seldom steady; it inevitably
moves in fits, starts, and contraries. But by watching for and reinforcing those moments when the student performs at her best,
by restating and underlining language that seems to construct an
image of forward movement, we can help the student develop,

even if the words' full meanings may yet lie ahead. By position-ing herself just in front of her charge, the effective mentor thus acts as a magnet, drawing the student forward.

And finally, with *one eye on the relationship,* we can help it to grow deeper and more balanced. We need not develop the intimacy of a Robin and Alison. Indeed, no one could sus-tain many mentorships of that intensity. But we can sustain an appropriate sense of balance as the time approaches to let go and watch our students fly on their own. And while at depar-ture, we are rarely equals in terms of the subject matter, like Socrates, we owe it to our students to remind them that finally it is only by recognizing our profound ignorance that we can grow toward something like wisdom.

Chapter Seven 🐦

Barriers and Incentives to Learning and Growth

> In the beginning is relation.
> —*Martin Buber*, I and Thou

In the search for a more workable understanding of human growth, it seems only logical to focus on the part most obviously "growing"—the individual. For that reason, most of the research thus far has followed people's trails as they become older and sometimes wiser. But clearly, human beings do not develop in isolation any more than tadpoles evolve without a pond. In recent years, developmentalists have paid increasing attention to the nature of the environment in which development occurs, or stalls. Without a fuller vision of the ecology of development, we are sharply limited in our understanding of the role that other people, particularly teachers, mentors, or advisers, play in the growth of adult learners. To understand what mentors do, we must understand how they influence the environments that "hold" students as they grow, how they help to orchestrate the transformative dance between the self and its shimmering, changing world.

We begin with a brief introduction to three basic ideas from general systems theory, moving next to a more detailed discussion of how environments interact with evolving individuals, specifically in light of Robert Kegan's thought. The principles that emerge from that discussion then light up a conversation with Anne, a thirty-five-year-old mother of three who is fighting for her balance amidst a whirlwind of family and cultural forces. A detailed analysis of how these forces work for and against her development concludes the chapter.

General Systems Theory

General systems theory, an idea originally constructed by naturalists as a way of comprehending growth and change in nature, brings fruitful explanatory power to the study of human beings as well. Rather than resting simply on the most obviously "changing" objects in a field of possibilities, the eye of the general systems theorist looks at the *relationships* among those objects; it seeks the invisible threads of influence within which any action inevitably occurs. Systems theory thus allows us to see not only how individuals behave but how individuals and environments interact. It reminds us that we must look to complex sets of "contingencies" that affect the developing person in a variety of ways.

We teachers sometimes speak of "pushing" our students to "higher" stages of development. We want the best for them, after all, and we need to know that we have made a difference in their lives, an important difference. Yet this seems a risky way to think about helping people. Not only does "push" have an unsavory whiff of coercion about it, but it probably isn't the way things actually happen anyway. To push a person to change is about as effective in the long run as trying to push a chain uphill. People best develop under their own power. As teachers, we have a lot to say about the conditions under which our students may find that power, but we must remember that the power itself is theirs. That realization may come as a disappointment at first, but it is finally a gift, for if we believe we have such power and do not, we are caught in a foolish delusion, and if we really do have that power, pity the poor student. Better to recognize that we are only a part—however important—of a whole set of forces affecting the growth of our students. A systems perspective provides a valuable inoculation against the illusions of omnipotence endemic to our trade.

But there is more. Environments do not simply stay put;

they too change—in response to external factors, to their own inner dynamics, and to changes in the behavior of the particular organism in question. Everything, as Gregory Bateson points out, is in motion.

> . . . the evolution of the horse from *Eohip-*
> *pus* was not a one-sided adjustment to life on the
> grassy plains. Surely the grassy plains were evolved
> *pari passu* with the evolution of the teeth and
> hooves of the horses and other ungulates. Turf was
> the evolving response of the vegetation to the evo-
> lution of the horse. It is the *context* which evolves
> [1972, p. 155].

Environments respond to us just as surely as we to them. In the interplay of individual and environment, we can hear a kind of dialogue between the two, each responding to the response of the other. Movement, evolution, proceeds from the silences, from the gaps in the conversation. This is an essential point, as we shall see in a moment, for in a "perfect fit" between self and world, there is no movement, any more than there is learning in a conversation where neither partner hears the other.

A third insight from systems theory is the idea of sub-systems. Any system can be seen as being at once a part of a larger system and as having smaller systems within it. The analogy is similar to that of focus in vision. We see different "realities" depending on whether we focus our eyes on a cluster of grapes, a vine, or a vineyard. What we see depends on where we look. That seems obvious enough. What is often forgotten, however, is that where we look generally depends on where we are standing. It is much easier to insist that what we see is what any reasonable person would see; we *want* our truths to be universal. But universality is more a matter of vision than of determination. If Walt Whitman could see something universal in a leaf of grass, and Martin Buber in a human relationship, it is because of the depth of their insight, not the force of their will.

In any case, it seems apparent that the transformations

we are concerned with can be understood as having something
to do with a radical change in vision, with perception shifts
from smaller to larger systems, a metaphor echoed in Robert
Novak's notion of growth from "horizon to horizon" as we
ascend (1971). Thus, when we speak of the environment in
which mentors and students work, we are speaking of a *perceived environment,* one that includes the student's view of parents, spouse, children, "significant others," and the mentor—as
well as ideas, memories, dreams, values, external events, old
patterns, and new information.

Because no two people ever see exactly alike, we are all
bound to live in somewhat different worlds. It is this difference
that makes for both horse races and human growth, for there is
always a somewhat ragged fit between what we and others consider real. This misfit can be especially apparent during times of
change—our own, the environment's, or both—and it is at such
times that we may lean especially hard into the wind to restore
meaning, to make sense of what seems to be shredded by the
gale. This leaning outward has been labeled "cognitive dissonance," the gap between what we believe should be the case and
what appears "in reality" to be true. As a vacuum, we abhor it
and are drawn out in the effort to close the gap, to restore coherence. Fortunately for most of us, the gaps are relatively
minor parts of our total world. Most days the sun rises as we
expect, and we are able to keep our balance in the breeze. But
some people live in stormier spots, while others are more sensitive to change. Every gardener knows that the climate has everything to do with what can and cannot grow. Should it be any
different with human beings?

The Holding Environment

In a book with the unlikely title *Maturational Processes
and the Facilitating Environment,* D. W. Winnicott, a British
child psychologist whose work is particularly germane to family
systems theory, describes what he calls the *holding environment.* Deriving the term from the physical activity of holding
an infant, he uses it to refer to the parents' psychological pres-

ence within which the child can gain a sense of the "continuity of being" necessary for successful separation from the mother (1965).

Since one important part of being a baby is to move, however haltingly, toward a new kind of independence, the environment must be neither so supportive that there is no motivation to leave it nor so harsh that if the child does, she wishes she hadn't. To provide a "good enough" environment, Winnicott says, parents must be neither negligent nor perfect. For a child to develop a sense of self, she must be able to make some sort of association between what she does and what she gets, between action and consequences. If, as in the case of poor parenting, her actions are met with random punishment, she learns that she is no good; if met with indifference, that she is unimportant. In either case she feels powerless. Conversely, if all of her needs are met before she even knows she has them, she fails to learn that her actions will make a difference: that wailing with hunger will bring food. The value of hunger is that if both she and her environment respond appropriately, she learns that she can make a difference in the world. In crying, she takes a first tiny step to defining who "she" is. She begins to trace a boundary between herself and her environment. Identity is born, and will be born again and again with every new tracing for the rest of her life.

A "good enough" holding environment helps us carve that boundary in a way that will allow us to consolidate each new sense of self so that we can maintain meaning and coherence in the world and yet remain open to a lifetime of fresh wonders. As any parent who has held a crying child knows, it's all in the balance. There is a time to hold and a time to let go. In that knowing, says Winnicott, in our sensitivity to our children's needs for being held and being free lies our gift to their growth.

Robert Kegan has extended Winnicott's insights across the whole life span. In *The Evolving Self,* he describes how we move through a procession of holding environments, or "cultures of embeddedness." Each holds us for a time in equilibrium, supporting and releasing as we grow. Although he describes these cultures as discrete entities, it is probably more accurate to think of each as blending almost imperceptibly into the next, like the view through a microscope as we change focus. With each new turn of the knob, a fresh perspective emerges even though the object under examination remains the same.

The first environment, which Kegan calls the "Mothering Culture," is in harmony with the earliest developmental stage, the "incorporative" self. It is characterized by both physical holding and a certain failure to meet the child's every need. (Most parents know how easy it is to "fail" that way; it's nice to know that perfect parents aren't perfect.)

The next, or "impulsive," stage is accompanied by the "Parenting Culture" in which the child's needs for fantasy and intense attachments are met but in which the child is encouraged to leave the immediate warmth of the family for brief periods, is encouraged to be responsible for his or her own feelings and to experience qualified independence.

As the child moves into the school years, a third environment, the "Role Recognizing Culture," swims into focus, supporting the emergence of the "Imperial" self. Here, the child's budding independence and self-sufficiency are encouraged more actively, yet at the same time, the culture demands that the child acknowledge mutuality in his or her relationships, emphasizing the importance of trust among friends.

With the onset of the teen years, the importance of interpersonal relationships intensifies in the "Culture of Mutuality," which ushers in, and is enhanced by, the growth of the "Interpersonal" self. Subjective feelings are more fully acknowledged, and collaborative self-sacrifice takes on a greater value. Yet while supporting these qualities, the culture demands that the adolescent assume individual responsibility amidst the wash of mutual friendships, asserting the concurrent importance of independence from the group.

If conditions are right, this environment yields yet again in later years to the "Culture of Self-Authorship" as the "Institutional" self emerges. Authority becomes something we possess rather than defer to; a career rather than simply a job, a life partner rather than a helpmate fill our sights. We find ourselves among friends who value our uniqueness, and we lean toward those who see beyond our external, social masks. Institutions that emphasize competence and achievement hold for us more appeal than those offering simply a sense of belonging or status.

And yet for some, this is not enough. As with all holding environments, this culture too hosts the worm of its own destruction. We begin to question the value of so separate a self; we yearn for work that offers a deeper meaning, friends who speak to our vulnerability, a spirituality that asks new and more profound questions. We are propelled toward the "Interindividual" balance in which a "Culture of Intimacy" holds us as we grow in our capacity for mature love, interdependence, and a new kind of self-surrender.

Kegan's sense of the evolving interplay of self and environment is exquisite. We both create and are created by our environment as we move along, and if our movement is relatively smooth, we remain always open to that critical discontinuity that makes an environment neither too harsh nor too perfect but just "good enough." As Winnicott first suggested, always the "good enough" environment both meets and contradicts our needs for growth and, in so doing, calls forth an essential developmental dialogue, an internal conversation through which we struggle to make sense of the conflicting messages coming from a changing world (Basseches, 1985).

It is this evolving set of contraries within successive holding environments that gives Kegan a framework for suggesting a common form for each culture of embeddedness. Environments, he tells us, do three things: they provide *confirmation, contradiction,* and *continuity.*

When we look at the confirming aspects of an environment, we see those parts that essentially conform to the shape of the individual. When a father holds a crying child, he holds him close until the sobbing begins to subside. In that act, he communicates that he can acknowledge his son's pain and yet not be drawn into it. As teachers, when we confirm we let our students know that we understand their ideas though we may not agree, their fears though we are not afraid, their pain though we are not hurt.

Environments contradict by raising questions about the adequacy of confirmation. Contradiction is the antithesis to confirmation in the developmental dialogue; it is the gap between person and world, things as they "might" be and things as they "are." As the child's sobbing slows, the father can release his son to reenter an uncertain world. The time for holding has passed. Good mentors let their students know that authority has its uses but is limited, and the task of reentering the world includes taking one's own authority along.

In the idea of continuity lies the synthesis, the bridge from one developmental balance to the next. The adequate environment, says Kegan, "sticks around," like good parents when their twelve-year-old decides to "run away." Such bridging between old and new worlds allows the broad movement to take place and helps those in transition to know that there is some meaning and coherence in what can seem fragmented and senseless. Just knowing there is a connection between worlds, that there will be someone ahead when we arrive yet still there should we turn back, can be the extra encouragement we need to swing out over the brink. This is why mentors are ambivalent figures; they must represent both old and new worlds at once. Not only by "being there" and listening, but by their mere existence as experienced travelers, mentors provide continuity. Beyond that, by offering a map (by including discussions of personal evolution in literature, history, or art courses, for instance), a teacher can oftentimes make that sense of continuity still more concrete for her student.

With all of this in mind, let us turn now to meet Anne, a thirty-five-year-old student in an external degree program that links term-long correspondence study with two-week periods of campus residence. Her purpose in returning to college is "to become educated." Listening in on our conversation, consider how Anne is moving; note her attitude toward authority, her view of knowledge, her sense of a growing edge. But consider also the forces in her life: her friends, relatives, and culture, her goals, aspirations, economic situation, and values. How does each contribute to the swirl of support and challenge that holds and releases her as she grows?

Two years ago at the encouragement of her husband, Anne decided to return to college. It was an enormous step, for not only did she have two children in school but her family was stationed in Saudi Arabia half a world away from where she was to spend her two-week "residencies" twice a year.

The first residency was particularly difficult, for she had married directly out of high school and had never been separated from her family for more than a few days. She was homesick and found many of the other students difficult. The strong feminist orientation of the program disturbed her. "I just wasn't ready for it," she explained. But she managed to stick it out, completing a study in women's literature with an outspoken feminist mentor—a study about which she is curiously silent.

The second time around might have gone more smoothly as she studied art, a field in which she felt more confident. In this case, however, her male adviser "came too close. He didn't seem to care whether I was married or not." When she rejected his advances, she felt he took it out on her artwork, calling it conventional and too inhibited.

But again, she prevailed, and returned for a third term. This time, she wanted to study philosophy to sharpen her "critical thinking." "I feel all the time put down by men," she told me. "And I guess I want to learn how to argue back, how to think like them," she added. "But it's difficult for me to be critical. I really get excited by new ideas, but every time I learn something that I think sounds right, I hear another idea and then I think that one is right, and then they just all sound right so I find it hard to pick any of them apart."

We talked a while longer about her experiences thus far in the program, and it became increasingly apparent that she felt adrift. "I came into this program pretty sure I knew what I believed, but now, with all these different ideas, I'm not so sure anymore. . . . I just don't know what I believe in."

I agreed to work with her, and we put together a study around the idea of virtue—how do you know something is good? Since she wanted to work with "philosophical ideas," we made up a lengthy reading list of Greek philosophers, adding a world history text, books on critical thinking and problem solving, and materials to help her apply all of this to the Saudi and American cultures of which she was a part. She was to write a sequence of papers first describing Greek ideas of virtue, next exploring the genesis of Christian definitions, and finally reflecting in light of her reading upon the values she grew up with and those surrounding her in the Middle East. Then, off she went.

Six months later she returns a week early to discuss an extension for the study. It has not gone well. Although the quality of what I received was fine, there was little of it. Her few letters spoke darkly of "difficulties with my family." We find a quiet corner of the student lounge, and I ask her about it. Outside, the late April sun has thawed winter to a few scabs of snow tucked in the shadows. The grass is a tentative green.

"Well, what's been most important about the study hasn't been the actual learning," she begins, flashing me an apologetic comic pout. "It's been overcoming my feelings about the study itself. It was a study where my mind would seem to turn off; it turned against me. I'd get distracted."

That had been obvious. Since shortly after she left in October I had been kicking myself for having apparently miscalculated her capacity. And yet it didn't make sense. From all I could tell six months ago, she certainly had the brains to handle the material. Needing something concrete, I ask her if she can think of a time when she felt particularly "distracted."

"Yes," she replies. "It was in December. I was overwhelmed with getting ready for the holidays, and on top of that I wasn't feeling very good about myself anyway." She pauses a moment, looks around the room as if for an escape, and then plunges on.

"Well, my father-in-law came to spend the month with us. He's a Christian minister with a really good education, and so naturally he was interested in what I was studying. I told him, 'philosophy.' Well, the first thing he said, even before we even tried to talk about Socrates or any of the other philosophers was the fact that he wanted to make sure I knew that ... " She stops, gropes for the thought again, "that ... he wanted to make sure that I didn't get led astray by philosophy

because unless I had someone to lead me correctly, I would
jump to conclusions that weren't valid. And I think he was also
afraid—and I think that I probably reinforced his fear—that I
would come to some conclusions that were not necessarily bib-
lical."

She adds the footnote with a mischievous wince. The
theme is growing familiar, but I'm not yet sure how central it is
to her tale. As she goes on I begin to get nervous.

"So we started to talk about it. And for every point I
tried to bring up, he had another point. And for every point,
he had questions, things I hadn't thought about. I can't even
recall right now because I got so intimidated. And the fact that
whenever I would say something, or would express an opinion,
he'd say, 'Well, you know, I've studied at Harvard, and I've
taken four years of Latin,' and he just gave me the impression
that I didn't know what I was talking about. And because I
didn't have enough knowledge to back it up, I became very frustrated."

As she speaks, my disquietude gives way to dismay. What
has this man been doing to her? "Frustrated"? Is that all? I lean
forward, watching every word.

"At one point, we were talking about philosophy, and he
said, 'Well, I have a friend who studied every imaginable philosophy and after years of work, he came to the conclusion that
the Bible is the only book in which forty different authors came
to the same conclusion.' And I said, 'Well, if I had the time, I
could find forty different people who could come to the same
conclusion as Socrates did and some of the other people having
one perspective and that's to find the ultimate truth. I mean
Christians aren't the only ones seeking the truth!' And he was
really upset with me for that. Besides, just because forty people
agree doesn't make it true!"

I'm not sure where she is taking us, but her defiance is
clear enough. I nod visibly and smile my approval. She goes on.

"And later, I was telling him about certain diaries I had
read in which a woman described her perceptions of the Civil
War that were quite different from the usual descriptions, and
he said, 'You really should be careful about what you read be-

cause I can see it is leading you in the wrong direction, because if you want to learn about history, read authentic history books where men are scholars and have studied this.' And I said, 'Well, everybody's perception is different. This is just their view, what's in *their* hearts.' And he said, 'You can't believe that stuff.' And I said, 'Why not? The books are just somebody's perception of what happened.' And he said, 'No. Men who are scholarly and did research are the people that you should listen to.' And I said, 'Do you mean that you're telling me that what these women have written is not valid? And he said, 'Yes.'

"At that point I said, 'That's absolutely ridiculous! People can have different perceptions of the same thing. For instance, there can be one problem and one person can come around from the right and be able to solve it, and one person can come around from the left and approach it in this way. And they both come to the same solution to the problem in different ways. Are you trying to say there's only one way?' And he said, 'Yes.'

"And then my husband came in and asked him to go out for a walk. And as he was leaving, I said, 'Yes, and white bread is always better than brown bread!' But the whole thing made me feel very uncomfortable, because in times like that you don't have enough knowledge to back it up, and so I feel very intimidated."

By this time, I'm a jumble of emotions—appalled and angry at the self-centered destructiveness of this fatuous Polonius, pained at Anne's understated anguish, and excited too at the potential in her tale, with her sheer guts in standing up to his pomposity. But for some reason, in the search for an appropriate response, the detached analyst in me gets the upper hand. I decide to bring the event into the present and see what we can learn from it.

"What would you need in order to be able to battle more successfully?" I ask her, trying to give her a weapon.

"Probably to know more about the subject matter itself and to understand it in a better way. And probably just practice in learning how to debate that kind of thing."

From our previous work together and from several things

she has just said, it is clear that she sees knowledge as cumulative. Her father-in-law derives his power from *the amount* of knowledge he possesses. Her shortcoming is that she doesn't have *enough* of the stuff. At the same time, she has significantly added a qualitative dimension. I decide to pick up on this leading edge in her thinking.

"How might you understand it in a better way?"

"Well, maybe like to see how it's connected to other things. Maybe to see how one perspective has evidence that supports it better from other parts of life, I guess. I'm not sure."

She shakes her head slowly. "But I don't know." She looks down at her hands and pauses a long moment. "I don't know. Maybe it just isn't worth the fight. I mean with people like that."

She has picked up the battle metaphor, and I am left with several choices. I can continue with that, I can go with her leading edge about making connections, or I can respond to her obvious emotional distress. The despair in her voice leads me to the last. As it turns out, the decision to go with her feelings takes us into a whole new area.

"Yes," I say softly. "But it doesn't do your ego any good."

She laughs, brushing away the emotion. "Well, you know, as they were leaving, he came to me and he said, 'Mom and I have been talking, and we seriously think you should take up interior decorating.' "

"Oh my God," I think, the anger rising again. But I let it go and begin to look for supports.

"Where is your husband in all this?"

"Well," she replies, "he's kind of in the middle. He tries to explain to me that I have to consider the source and that Dad's from a different generation and . . . I guess I can sort of see that, but it doesn't make me feel much better. And I think my husband feels that I'm making him choose in a situation like that. And he doesn't think I should even discuss it. But I can't put my books away. I can't get further behind!"

Her voice is tinged with desperation, but this time I decide to continue to work with her strength.

"How did you end up handling it?"

Her face and voice brighten again. Despite her fragile and conventionally pretty appearance, she possesses an awesome resilience.

"Well, I felt pretty good after I made that comment about white bread. And just after, I was talking with my daughter, who had been having real trouble while Grandpa was here, and she just wanted to stay away from the house as much as she could. And my mother-in-law came in and said she had heard part of the conversation. It was interesting because we were talking about different ways of seeing, and she hadn't heard the part about how there was 'only one truth.' So we were talking about it and we got into some of the things she had read. Well, she's really been growing a lot. She's seventy, and it's really neat. So we were having a conversation and I was talking about two ways of seeing things, and she said, 'Isn't that just wonderful? You should ask Dad about that.' And I said, 'I *did*.' And she said, 'What did he say?' And I said, 'He said there was only one way.' But you know, he had put himself in a corner by saying there was only one way. And he's in education and we know there's more than one way."

By this time I have cooled off again, and my fascination with this whole extraordinary tale bubbles forth. I decide to share it with her.

"Well, one of the things that intrigues and pains me as well is that as people are beginning to grow, they get out of whack with their environment. And here's Anne, struggling to find her own truth in this environment in which she is growing, and here comes Grandpa who really threatens to hold her back."

She breaks in, still steaming along. "I feel I have a lot of forces working against me. In that situation I felt like I won one battle, but I feel like that it left me feeling very inferior because I was struggling at that time to read this book, working so hard to try to figure out how to pronounce some of these words, and I'd ask my husband, and Grandpa would come along and pronounce the word, and it just seemed like he knew everything. I'd feel so stupid that I couldn't figure it out for myself. It was so easy for him and so hard for me, and in this environment,

your ego is being damaged on a daily basis. You're constantly
being reminded that you're only a woman, that you're inferior."

I ask her what she means about "this environment," and
she talks at length about the difficulty of being a woman, not
only in the Saudi culture but in the American compound as
well. She is allowed to make no business transactions without
her husband's approval, she can never venture out alone or with
other women, and even among Americans she rarely feels understood. Being a student sets her apart. Though a few women support her, when she tells people what she is studying, most are
indifferent. Men challenge her, and she feels like she's being
tested. "It's scary to me," she says. "So I find myself not saying
what I'm doing. Or just letting them take over the conversation."

As our talk winds down, we turn, rather unsuccessfully,
to a discussion of how she can set up a network at home of people who might be supportive. "They're all wrapped up in their
own worlds," she says. "I feel pretty much alone."

Clearly, woven through this vignette there are conversations within conversations within conversations. At one level we
hear the authoritarian, "dualistic" voice of Grandpa thundering
its certainty against Anne's quavering but courageous "multiplicity" as she struggles to affirm her own different voice, not
simply to oppose his but to legitimize her own. She argues not
that she is "right" but that her way of seeing is more adequate.
Yet because her balance is still unsure, she feels helpless, drawn
back by assumptions she has still to reject.

At another level, there is the conversation between Anne
and me. It was not a carefully constructed clinical interview; it
was simply one of a number of meetings I held with her in the
course of our work together. I was not trying to push her any-
where, to "make her develop." Yet powerful developmental
forces were at work, and I sought to help her understand those
forces in a way that she could feel less overwhelmed by them.

At this point, however, I want us to consider what Anne's
story has to say about the influence of the environment in the
life of adult learners. She herself picks up on the language of
systems when she says, "I feel I have a lot of forces working

against me." Just what are those forces? How do they work against her? And what is the interplay of other, more positive forces in her life?

In thinking about those questions, we must first establish what systems we are talking about. Consider the Anne whom she views as her "self" and the Anne I see to be one system. This "Anne system" is embedded in another system we shall call her environment—what both she and I consider her "outside world" of people, information, and significant events. For purposes of the exercise, these are our main two systems: one a subpart of the other. In defining them this way, it should be emphasized that we are constructing our problem from our perceptions, not from any "objective reality." All of our "data" come from what Anne told me on tape in response to my questions about her interpretation of an event. We are not seeking "the facts" in Sergeant Friday's sense. Rather, it is the *way Anne makes meaning* of all of this that we are after.

A second task is to decide what the goal of the system is. Although both individuals and environments are in motion and could thus be said to have goals, to keep things in bounds, we will consider only Anne's goals for now. Her purpose in returning to school is to "become educated."

When I asked Anne what education meant for her, she replied that it would help her to "feel I was doing something with my life," and she went on to explain that she wanted to learn more so that she could feel more equal to other people, "especially men who are always putting me down." How could she do that? By learning more and arguing better. When she compared herself with those in her home environment, she tended to describe them as "having so much knowledge" whereas what she admired about her fellow students was that they seemed to be so worldly and "critical." Thus, she saw home through the eyes of an earlier developmental stage, school through a later one; and she looked to her study with me to move her from the first way of seeing (represented by home) to the second (being in the world).

Not surprisingly, my own goals for Anne were informed by much of the developmental thinking we have discussed previously. While I generally find it difficult to peg a person in any single stage, it was apparent to me that Anne was working with a view of knowledge and authority that Perry terms multiplis- tic. That is, she saw knowledge as concrete but quite diverse; she clearly agreed with the classic multiplistic assertion that "everyone has a right to his or her own opinion," and she felt, conversely, quite isolated in her quest for truth. After all, if there is no ultimate truth, if the world is entirely subjective, then we are hopelessly sentenced, as Tennessee Williams had it, to "solitary confinement inside our own skins."

Part of this sense of isolation derives from Anne's stance toward authority—fiercely opposed to Grandpa's effort to exer- cise it over her, but still strongly swayed by it. Authority still rested in lots of knowledge and a Harvard education. She seemed caught between a thesis that "Truth is objective and supported by sheer weight of facts" and an antithesis that it is personal and subjective. Since the thesis seemed still to hold more weight, she looked there for an escape. Knowledge, for her, was still "out there," found rather than constructed, and to become her own authority, she needed more facts. Yet another part of her believed that the way led toward becoming more "critical"—toward seeing how things are connected, how to sup- port assertions with evidence, how to argue more effectively. This, after all, was the style she saw around her when she was on campus.

It was in an effort to address these two parts of her that we designed her study around both Greek philosophy and criti- cal thinking skills. I hoped that by acknowledging and building around her desire to accumulate knowledge, I could help her to see that in its use rather than its quantity lay her strength.

But Anne's growth was more than just intellectual. She was struggling to transform her role from "only wife and moth- er" to include responsibility to herself and to those beyond her immediate world. In Kegan's terms, Anne seemed on her way from an interpersonal orientation toward an institutional stance. Her ambivalence toward the feminism of her fellow students attested to her dilemma: how to remain a "good wife and moth- er" on the one hand yet acknowledge the view of herself that was materializing with increasing clarity as she emerged from the protection of the earlier stage. Still firmly connected to an interpersonal self—a self in which loyalty is primarily to those we know face-to-face—she was hearing ever more loudly the call of women she did not know but whose plight moved her as she grew increasingly willing to acknowledge and care for her own pain. Again, the way through the dilemma, the transformative questions, "How can I have both my family and my self?" "How am I connected with women I don't know face-to-face?" still lay ahead. Those were questions demanding the formation of, and trust in, an abstraction for which she was not quite ready. Her movement was clear enough, though. Desperately in search of her own voice from among the cacophony of male voices around her, she felt the pain sharply as her voice was drowned out again and again and again.

Given the systems we have defined and the goals we have seen, what are the "forces" working against Anne? In this particular drama, Grandpa clearly moves downstage center. It is quite plain to Anne, without knowing a thing about Perry's research, that her father-in-law is "against" her—not because he disagrees, but because he sees the world in a way that she thinks too simple. (Remember that we are talking about a Grandpa whom Anne has constructed. It is impossible, and probably irrelevant, to know whether he is "in fact" dualistic.) But she is caught in a bind because she also gives him considerable authority. She is not yet able to dismiss his perspective and thus defuse his power—or perhaps more accurately, she is too emotionally embroiled to separate the way he thinks from who he is for her, a stance her husband is urging on her. In effect, she *gives* him his power by virtue of her own worldview, not yet sufficiently distanced from his to free her from its power. So when he makes that crack about "interior decorating," he strikes at the very heart of her aspiration to grow out of her "interpersonal" world, for interior decorators are seen by neither Anne nor Grandpa as career professionals with an integrity of their own. Rather, they mean for both, a way to keep her in her place, a glorified housewife.

One can scarcely imagine a society less supportive of

Anne's aspirations than the Saudi one where she finds herself. Yet her own culture is small comfort. She sees few others who understand her or who can share with her the experience of returning to school. The highly conventional world of an overseas compound can brook little deviance from what it views as propriety. The men, especially, seem to be career-oriented expatriates with little of the sort of caring sensibilities that Anne needs, especially from those to whom she still gives too much power. Caught as he is between his concern for her and his obligations as son and businessman, her husband plays a mediating role. But he seems unable to give her the emotional support she wants, to acknowledge to her that he knows how important the conflict with his father is. Rather, he chooses to separate the two and downplay the entire scene.

In addition to her relatives and the surrounding cultures, Anne's role as wife and mother—as she construes them—come constantly into conflict with her job as student. The holiday preparations were only a glimpse of the dozens of daily demands from her family that would drift like a huge, indifferent iceberg between Anne and her study. The desperation she feels ("I *can't* put my books away; I *can't* get further behind!") is endemic to women like Anne, trying to be mother, wife, and student, to resolve the conflicting demands of the old and the new selves.

The material of her study also seemed to get in the way as much as it helped. Some of it was difficult; the words unpronounceable. Because of her view of the nature of knowledge, she felt she had to read each book, cover to cover, understanding each page before going on. To skim for important ideas (which ideas were more important anyway?) seemed like cheating to her. She carried an almost moralistic set of convictions about "proper" study that is characteristic of many students in her position: one must read and understand all assignments and not speak until the right answer is known; papers should be complete and perfect before they are read (soliciting help on drafts is dishonest); to use an index for a particular reference without reading the entire work is cheating. "I never feel I can talk about a subject until I know it well," she tells me. "I can't talk about it in bits and pieces." And authors? People who write books always know what they're talking about. If you can't understand them, it's your fault, never theirs.

Undergirding all these inhibiting "forces" is her own limited worldview. Because we are talking always about a *perceived* environment, the problem ultimately circles back to the way Anne sees the world, makes meaning of her experience. None of the forces that seem so inimical needs to be so intrinsically. But the particular set of lenses she is wearing mandate that it will be so. It is to help Anne change those lenses, enabling her to see all her emperors in the flesh, that is at the heart of educational transformation. But before we get to that, let's consider some other forces in Anne's environment. Which ones can help her through? What factors support her growing edge?

Despite feeling at times a misfit among her fellow students, Anne made close friends and listened earnestly to their "more radical" views. Although she thought them often "too critical," she felt the power of their thinking and was drawn toward the people around her who seemed so much more self-contained than she. Somehow they knew something that she needed to learn. What was it?

Anne's husband seems at different times both helpful and unhelpful. It was he, after all, who encouraged her to get into all of this in the first place. That it may cost him his wife must have occurred to him, but she still sees him as generally supportive. "He does more of the housework now than he used to," she says approvingly. And his mediation in family conflict is more than a neutral activity, for it relieves her of at least some of the guilt for her part in the initial stress.

It is noteworthy that immediately following the argument with Grandpa, Anne turns to her daughter to share their mutual feelings toward him. As women, they have in common the experience of subordination, and Anne is increasingly finding a voice in which to express her mixed feelings about men. Next, enter Mother-in-law. All three women continue the discussion, this time in a much more mutual and caring way. Later in our own conversation, discussing differences between men and women, Anne said this:

> If a woman finds out [about my study],
> she's either not interested or says "that sounds ter-
> rific!" And then she'll start saying something like,
> "Isn't it hard? Don't you have trouble?" Real per-
> sonal questions about it. They kind of make you
> feel better because you start saying, "Oh," and you
> start remembering things you have read. She comes
> on to you as a . . . almost a "I wish I could do that.
> Tell me about it." And you start saying, "Oh, you
> could do it." And then I start remembering things
> when I'm in that situation . . . with a woman it al-
> ways comes out on a personal level, about how we
> deal with a subject. . . . It stimulates a lot of per-
> sonal feelings.

It is clear that in other women Anne finds the support
she needs—not simply to heal wounds but to make herself still
more vulnerable, to talk about what she is learning, to hear herself speaking at last in her own voice. Unlike most of the male
world around her, she knows that in her vulnerability lies her
strength. The tragedy is that there seem to be so few women to
whom she can turn.

Although some of her assignments turned out to be more
inhibiting than helpful, this was not always true. Anne found
the several problem-solving books to be quite enjoyable. They
answered her own need for practice in an area where she felt
weak, and they were calibrated in a way that allowed her to
grasp most of the problems and feel a much-needed sense of
accomplishment. Further, through them she could learn more
effective ways of approaching problems; they helped her toward
constructing a methodology for making sense out of former
confusion and thus for pulling the pieces of her multiplistic
world into a new coherence, an essential step in her expansion
toward contextual thinking. Although she found much of the
reading in philosophy difficult, our correspondence helped, she
said, to clarify much of what was going on in *Symposium* or the
Crito. More important was her feeling of accomplishment at
having worked her way through some of these works. For this

was full-fledged adult literature, and in knowing that she had read and understood them, she was able to make a very important statement to herself about her role in the larger world outside of her home. Finally, because the history text we used was arranged thematically rather than chronologically, Anne was able in her writing to draw effectively on both historical and cultural data to support her speculations about what finally emerged as our culminating question: "What makes a virtuous woman—in the eyes of the Greeks, the early Christians, contemporary American culture, and Anne Guildhall?" In writing her final paper, she was able to view a common topic of obvious personal concern to her from several perspectives while at the same time drawing on these perspectives to begin formulating a statement of her own personal philosophy. In that act, she also spoke for the new self she was becoming.

But beyond these factors, it seems to me that the single most important aid in Anne's odyssey was her own courage. It allowed her to stand her ground against her father-in-law's pomposity and come out with a victory, however Pyrrhic. It gave her what she needed to remain in her residencies despite feeling a misfit and thus to make friends, converse long hours, and absorb bits of powerful and transformative knowledge. And ultimately Anne's courage enabled her to open her eyes just that extra crack, letting her see what previously she dared not. Once inside, such information inevitably does its work, for it demands a place. Thus we create for ourselves each new world.

Perhaps because she lived in so isolated an environment, the conversation with Anne allowed me to see more clearly than ever before the wonderful intricacy of our work. Neither Anne nor I nor anyone else in the drama was untouched by the others. Grandpa was responding to a study that Anne had developed with my help, yet his response affected Anne, who in turn provoked a new response from me. And that was only one interchange among three characters! Clearly we were all moving in a *complex, interactive dance with the environment.*

Then, too, I began to see more clearly how that environment would in some ways *confirm,* in some ways *contradict,* and in some ways *provide continuity* for Anne's movement. I could see how valuable it could be for us to see the whole lives of our students as much as possible in order that we could better know when to move ourselves. Part of the job, it seemed, was to acknowledge my part as one of the forces in Anne's life and to work in the ways suggested in the previous chapter.

But another part was to help Anne to see the forces impinging on her life, including myself as one of them. For *mentors are both a part of and "meta" to the environment*; at best they do more than simply add to the environmental forces at work on the learner. They also help the traveler see more clearly where she is headed so that if she can't avoid the pitfalls, at least she can know better when she is in one—and thus take fuller advantage of the unique opportunities that most pitfalls offer. It is because of this special quality that I have wanted to discuss separately what mentors do. It seems that the time has now arrived.

Chapter Eight 🐚

Strategies for Guiding Adults Through Difficult Transitions

> I must only warn you of one thing. You have become a different person in the course of these years. For this is what the art of archery means: a profound and far-reaching contest of the archer with himself. Perhaps you have hardly noticed it yet, but you will feel it very strongly when you meet your friends and acquaintances again in your own country: things will no longer harmonize as before. You will see with other eyes and measure with other measures. It has happened to me too, and it happens to all who are touched by the spirit of this art.
>
> —*Herrigel,* Zen in the Art of Archery

> Unlearn, unlearn!
> —*Yoda, in* The Empire Strikes Back

A green, gnomelike creature small in stature and great in wisdom, Yoda appears midway through the *Star Wars* trilogy to provide Luke, the hero, with the knowledge he will need to save the galaxy from the lowering power of Evil. For the last eight hundred of his nine hundred years, Yoda has been training the Jedi knighthood to serve as agents of virtue in the struggle between the light and the dark side of the Force. He is a mentor's mentor. Along with his former protégé, Obi-Wan Kenobi, he guides Luke through his transition into adulthood, confirming his importance, challenging his ability, and reminding him of his destiny—to meet and resolve his conflict with his father, avatar of darkness.

The primary theme of the trilogy is that of a young man coming of age, making his own place in the galaxy while acknowledging his debt to his father. Five thousand years ago, *The Odyssey* told a similar tale about Telemakhos. Mentors figure prominently in both, for as long as young people are faced with growing up into the world, so long will mentors be needed to help them.

But while mentors are surely stars in the drama, the part they play varies in important ways according to the particular transition faced by the protagonist. Since most of us make a number of changes throughout our lives, it is not surprising that on reflection, we may recall a number of mentors. Some remain for years, some for only a few months; sometimes the relationship is intense, sometimes purely instrumental; and though perhaps mentors seem more plentiful in our earlier years, often they appear in less conventional form later on. Yet always, if we are to call them mentor, they helped us through a transition of some sort. And if the relationship has been positive, we have grown from it in some way, for the idea of growth is inextricable from the idea of mentor.

Recall that Levinson suggests that mentors are characteristically a half-generation older than protégés—just the right age to mediate between parents and children. This makes good sense and is a useful guideline for calling someone a mentor rather than friend, or even teacher. Yet it seems too restrictive to account for the numerous mentorlike relationships that people report when they begin talking about their lives. Perhaps it would be more useful to let the quality and power of particular relationships help us define mentor rather than this arbitrary, though clearly helpful, age criterion. If we simply think of a mentor as someone we feel drawn to who seems to know things about life that we need to learn, it may help us to recognize that mentors can appear throughout our lives, whenever we encounter a new transition. As the nature of the transitional task changes, so do our mentors. It seems more than coincidental, for instance, that as a young man seeking validation of my own dream, I found most of my mentors in men who seemed the personification of what I wanted to believe possible for myself —especially in the world of work. Yet at midlife, my mentors are more often women, some older but some younger than my-self. For what I have now to learn has less to do with becoming a functioning part of the working world or with resolving pa-rental issues than with the kind of inner realignment that Levin-son describes—a redressing of earlier imbalances between mascu-line and feminine, attachment and separateness, young and old.

But mentors are more than simply isolated individuals who enter our lives, "intervene," and depart. Rather, they are creations that emerge out of particular demands our lives make on us. When they do their work well, they help us to see not only the tasks before us but also the broader context that gives those tasks meaning. With Yoda, they remind us of our destiny.

Thus, mentors are both part of and apart from the envi-ronments of their protégés. They are in the world but not of it. Viewed from one stance, they are simply another of a number of forces working for or against the traveler's evolution. But from a different angle, they can be seen rising above the flood, sending down messages to the beleaguered voyagers, helping them to "see" what they cannot, warning them of looming gales or lurking shoals. From there, they can help their charges to understand from a greater perspective the forces affecting them, thus enabling them to change direction.

In Anne's case, just the act of listening to her story, of giving her an opportunity to speak about her struggle and to name it, helped her to bring it under a new kind of control. Lis-tening, as a friend once observed, is a powerful intervention, perhaps the most powerful we have as mentors. It is not a pas-sive process, for the good listener is always alert for things of special significance in a tale and acts, however subtly, on what he hears. Thus, when Anne began her story, she knew by my in-terest that here was something important. I leaned forward; I nodded at certain times and not others; I cheered some acts, ignored others; I asked questions, focusing attention on particular people in her drama, asking how she felt about this or what she meant by that. And at one point, I sketched a model of how I was interpreting the story, one that gave her some new language and a more detached way of understanding her dilemma. Throughout, I was attempting to let her know that her inner life was important but that reflection upon it was important too. Thus, I was *selecting* particular elements of her story, reinforcing some, letting others slide unnoticed. In this way, I became a mirror in which to see herself anew. How much credence she gave to the new image was a reflection of the power she chose to give me as a part of her transformation.

In the remainder of this chapter, we will look more closely at some of the ways that mentors tilt the mirror they hold up to their students. I will suggest that mentors seem to do three fairly distinct types of things. They *support,* they *challenge,* and they *provide vision.* As through much of this book, I have used the term *mentor* and focused on that role primarily because that is the work I do. But I hope it is fully apparent that the functions and activities described in the following pages are by no means restricted to that particular work. They are drawn from a wide range of sources, experiential, literary, and theoretical. At bottom they are principles offered to anyone concerned with guiding development, be they teachers, physicians, advisers, administrators, counselors, civic leaders, pastors, rabbis, or other mentors.

Similar to what Winnicott means by "holding," the notion of *support* refers to those acts through which the mentor affirms the validity of the student's present experience. She lets him know through her empathy with his feelings or her comprehension of his words that he is "understood." In systems language, she attempts to bring her boundaries into congruence with his. The analogy to physical holding is a good one, for in a sense of being supported, cared about and for, lies the ability to trust. And trust, as Erikson has eloquently reminded us, flows at the source of the entire developmental process. It is the well from which we draw the courage to let go of what we no longer need and to receive what we do. Without a reasonably well-established sense of basic trust, it is difficult to move ahead. Courage and trust are sister and brother.

While the function of support is to bring boundaries together, *challenge* peels them apart. The mentor may assign mysterious tasks, introduce contradictory ideas, question tacit assumptions, or even risk damage to the relationship by refusing to answer questions. The function of challenge is to open a gap between student and environment, a gap that creates tension in the student, calling out for closure.

But there is a larger context. Simply to provide support and challenge leaves unanswered the question "toward what?" And although ultimately the leap must always be made into the dark (Shunryu Suzuki notes that to attain enlightenment we must know it is impossible; Tillich says the same in a Christian context), mentors do offer a kind of light. This third function I call *providing vision*. It is similar to Kegan's idea of the "confirming" function. Mentors "hang around" through transitions, a foot on either side of the gulf; they offer a hand to help us swing across. By their very existence, mentors provide proof that the journey can be made, the leap taken. And in helping their charges look ahead, to form a dream, to sketch their own maps, mentors offer "a fair chance of winning through," as the Old Man said to Telemakhos. Always this is done in the service of what Nevitt Sanford calls self-reflection. That is, unless we are able at some level to name the change, to see it explicitly in a new way, the transformation is not complete, for as a generation of psychoanalysis would confirm, it is only by bringing our changes into conscious awareness that we can be assured that they will stay put. "No amount of situation or behavior changing will lead to personality development in adults," says Sanford, "unless accompanied by self-reflection" (1980, p. 65). Mentors can help us do that. "Welcome," they say in a thousand languages, "to the new world."

It should be apparent that any interchange with a student will involve a mix of support and challenge, both going on at once. Though useful, to separate these two functions is arbitrary, for what is support for one person may be challenge to another. In a fascinating experiment some years ago, researchers delineated those supports and challenges that were most appropriate for "dualistic" students on the one hand and "relativistic" students on the other. Dualistic students felt support in a high degree of structure and were challenged by diversity. Relativistic students, on the other hand, found support in diversity and challenge in the necessity to make commitments amid uncertainty (Knefelkamp, Widick, and Parker, 1978). The researchers then designed classes to "fit" developmental needs with appropriate environment. Their work remains among the best efforts yet to apply developmental principles to the classroom.

Here is one way to visualize the effects of support and challenge on development.

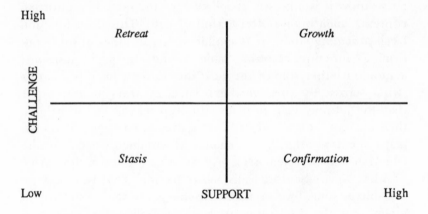

When both support and challenge are low, little is likely to happen. Things stay pretty much as they are. When support is enhanced, however, the potential for some sort of growth increases, but it is likely to emerge from the inner needs of the learner rather than from any stress imposed by the environment. The learner is "confirmed" and may feel good about himself but may also lack the capacity to engage productively with the outside world as well as he might if he were encouraged to communicate more actively with it. The risk that some highly "student-centered" college programs run is that in encouraging primarily "self-expression," they fail to help their students to acknowledge the legitimacy of a world different from their own and thus miss the crucial leap into contextualism.

Too much challenge in the absence of appropriate support, on the other hand, can drive the insecure student into "retreat," forcing a rigid epistemology to replace the promise of a more fluid and complex worldview. It is no coincidence that many of the converts to new "radical" religious groups have dropped out of college after a year or so. Overstrained by the diversity they encounter there and undersupported in what can be a tragically cold and uncaring environment, they fall back to a more secure adolescent conformity, safely embraced by authoritarian simplicities. It is reassuring to know that in time most recover enough to leave their sanctuaries, but the costs in the meantime can be considerable (Levine, 1984).

Finally, in an appropriate mix, development can occur. Just what that is, of course, depends on the particular needs of the student and style of the mentor. And clearly not every teacher will work for every student. But if we are to believe that good mentorship can be learned, at least in part, then it is in our interest to expand our capacities and deepen our sensitivity. To that end, let's look at some of the things that good mentors seem to do.

Support

Support is the activity of holding, of providing a place where the student can contact her need for fundamental trust, the basis of growth. It means moving to confirm the student's sense of worth and helping her to see that she is both OK where she is and capable of moving ahead when she chooses. In the next several pages, we will consider several supportive functions. The list is not exhaustive, yet perhaps it identifies the primary elements of mentorship.

Listening. While it is obvious that mentors must literally hear what their students are saying, the term *listening* goes beyond merely hearing. It means actively engaging with the student's world and attempting to experience it from the inside. What does it *feel* like to be this person? How does she see the world, make sense of diversity and complexity? What are the forces holding and propelling her life?

It is remarkable to listen to a good mentor talk about her

students. Joanna, who interviewed Martin back in Chapter 4, can tell you the ages and names of her students' children, how things are with their spouses, how they are feeling about their work, and what they want from their educations—usually on the basis of a single conversation! It is not that she pries into their lives so much as that she simply evokes the kind of trust that calls her students' stories out. And as they tell, she listens.

Mentors often have a good sense of their charges' inner lives as well. Again, this knowledge seems to arise less from probing than simply staying alert to what their people are telling them both explicitly and implicitly. They tend to accept the concerns and fears of their students rather than hastening to assure them that they "shouldn't get so upset" or that what concerns them is inconsequential. Describing first impressions of mentors, protégés often say things like "I felt that he *saw* me more clearly than anyone had before" or "It was so powerful to have someone you respect see you so well, know you so well." That sense of being "seen clear through" comes from the willingness of the mentor to accept where the student is and to acknowledge the legitimacy of that stance rather than to see the student as someone in need of modification. In many cases it also comes from the student's need to be seen this way. Particularly at early stages, we *want* our teachers to be omniscient.

This is not always easy to handle. For some mentors, to be given the kind of power that many students proffer at the outset of the journey can be disconcerting. That is probably just as well, for students' need to give authority to their mentors is best understood as a transitional need, one we ought to help them outgrow. Yet to reject that need outright can be injurious to the potential learning. Part of the art of the job is to accept without clinging to the authority we are given; the other part is to let it go when it no longer serves its purpose.

An important way in which some mentors establish a trusting bond is through mirroring the language and even the movements of their students. A close analysis of the dialogues in this book will reveal a number of such cases. Bandler and Grinder (1975) developed their entire theory of "neuro-linguistic programming" out of such uses of language in its many forms.

In most cases such mirroring is intuitive on the part of the mentor. Yet intuitions can be sharpened, and while there is a clear danger of manipulation inherent in NLP, an increased awareness of how we listen and respond on many levels can improve both advising and teaching.

Providing Structure. Some years ago I helped to develop a "learner-centered" curriculum for adults. Most of the prospective students had no more than a high school education completed years before. They were anxious about returning to school, and their study skills were rusty. Yet still aflame with our own countercultural ideology, we rejected such traditional trappings as clear course sequences, class syllabi, and even reading lists. Indeed, the very word *curriculum* carried for us a smarmy connotation. Why should we lay such a heavy trip on our students? They were adults, weren't they? They could make up their own curriculum as they went along. Needless to say, we learned—slowly I must admit—that our students needed more than that.

Although it makes sense intuitively, there is also ample evidence supporting the contention that anxious students need considerable structure and guidance, especially when they have been away from study for years. For such students, close personal attention, clear expectations, specific assignments, short and achievable tasks, and predigested material (textbooks rather than source material) are important. Summarizing research on the effects of anxiety on learning, Peterson and Snow conclude that "high anxiety" students who are low in ability do very poorly without close guidance (McKeachie, 1980). This does not necessarily mean, however, that they need a teacher hovering over their shoulder. Related research suggests that such students do well with programmed instruction materials. Lectures, often considered anathema for adults, may in fact be quite appropriate in their time if they are carefully designed.

Paradoxically, close support can often provide the best setting for the kind of creative play that results in effective problem solving. As long as the support is open-ended, allowing a sense of safety for the student without at the same time constricting, it can be an effective setting for the sort of "loose qualitative analysis" that seems to be an important first step for skilled problem solvers (McKeachie, 1980).

The important point here is that for the majority of adult students just easing their way back into higher education, a high degree of structure may be supportive at first. Those who have left their need for dualistic thinking behind will quickly enough make it clear that they have minds of their own. As teachers and mentors, we ought to resist the quite understandable temptation to thrust all students into the cold at once simply because some have profited from that treatment. On the contrary, we would do better to start inside until it is clear they are ready. Then we need only open the door.

Expressing Positive Expectations. In a detailed and practical study of the skills possessed by effective teachers and mentors in adult programs, Carol Schneider and her colleagues found that having positive expectations of students is one of the most important aspects of effective advising. Good mentors and teachers believe that average students are competent, they identify and affirm others' capabilities, they express the view that students are capable of change, and they accept student suggestions for changes in learning plans when they are "consistent with the student's learning objectives" (Schneider, Klemp, and Kastendiek, 1981).

Describing what their mentors did that was most helpful, students in my own research replied that they "gave me confidence in myself," "kept pushing me and telling me I could do it," and "had faith in me even when I didn't." Effective mentors seem to wield much of their power through the vision of the possible they hold for their students. Thus, they balance both a present sense of where their students are and a dream of what they can become—without allowing either to eclipse the other. It is almost as though they hold both present and future, actuality and possibility in tension, offering it for their students to accept.

But the stunt is not always easy. As teachers we are bound to be confronted at times (sometimes far too many!) when a student's work falls short. Balancing the imperative of providing "honest feedback" with the equally compelling need to let them know that they "can do it" is enough to strain the best of us. Those who manage it often do so by nesting their criticisms within a positive frame. Said one mentor, "I can always find something good to say, and I usually lead with that." He went on to describe how he tries to help his students see the problem in terms of their own best performance and highest expectations (standards he helps them construct) so that they are measuring themselves in their own terms rather than his. "I reminded her about an excellent paper she had written before," he said, describing a student in a sociology class. "I said, 'I know you can do it because you did it then,' and she had to agree." Thus, by holding her to her own terms, he was able to reflect back a clear image—one she could recognize but with which she was not wholly familiar. She had to stretch to accommodate it.

Piaget's concept of décalage is useful here. Recall that no one is ever "wholly" in one stage or another. Thus, although we function most of the time in a given stance, we carry both past and future capacities as well. Under stress, we tend to slip back; we tighten our grip on what feels most secure. When we feel safe, on the other hand, we can relax and reach out. That's why a supportive tone to the relationship is so important. It lets the student move to her leading edge. Knowing this, mentors will sometimes reinforce that growing fringe of a student's thought by listening for it and naming it, as I did when Monique toyed tentatively with the word *tolerance*. By giving it my "blessing," I endowed the term with special power—a power that, incidentally, endured for some time. I met her on the street two years later, and one of the first stories she told was about how much more tolerant she was than her coworkers.

Serving as Advocate. Campbell (1949) reminds us that mentors are often seen as "powerful allies" on the journey. They intercede with the powers, they translate arcane runes, they protect the pilgrim from assault. This aspect of concrete, instrumental help is one of the most frequently cited functions of mentors studied in the business world. They literally give their charges a boost up the corporate ladder, putting in a good word for them at key meetings, suggesting their names for promotion. Similarly, academic mentors sometimes sit on committees reviewing their students' work and as such may be called on to explain or defend it.

Knowing this, students understandably feel anxious, for the system itself grants mentors considerable power. As students would hand me their study plans, I would often need to reassure them against feared decimation at the hands of a faceless and distant review board. The fear was real and legitimate. For some, any show of uncertainty on my part would trigger escalations of anxiety. The power they would give me seemed to grow in direct proportion to the threat they felt.

Similarly, as guides we often provide support simply because we have been there before and appear to know where the journey leads—be it through the tangled mysteries of distribution requirements or the terrors and delights of multiple truths. Whether conducting an independent study or a full class, the mentor is seen to possess knowledge, skills, or wisdom that lies ahead for the student. Given such power, it is not surprising that our support can be so delicious, our criticism so devastating.

Sharing Ourselves. "I wish I could just know him better as a *person*" is a common sentiment among protégés. As long as the relationship is relatively complementary in form, the student is bound to feel the more vulnerable. Initially, especially for students at fairly early developmental positions, the distance is usually acceptable. Indeed, so strong is the need for authority in early positions that one would be unlikely to hear such a student wishing to see his mentor's clay feet. As things progress, however, the pressure increases for the teacher to reveal himself as human, not god. Conversely, as he does so, the protégé finds it increasingly easy to project himself into the mind and spirit of the mentor, thus speeding the breakdown of a constructed ideal and inappropriate authority. How and when this occurs varies greatly, but a healthy relationship, like a healthy individual, needs to grow in the capacity to share inner concerns more freely. Timing, as usual, is paramount. Given too soon, the receiver may ignore it or perhaps actively reject it. Given too late, it may simply be scorned. But with the proper care, the gift of self-disclosure can lead to a valuable deepening of the relationship for both partners.

Making It Special. One of the most compelling qualities of the relationship is that it feels so special. The student feels uniquely "seen" by the mentor, and when the mentor is endowed with particularly desirable qualities or unusual power in the world, the effect can be a potent tonic. Here, a protégé speaks of his first encounter with his mentor,

> It was like I was so awed by him, I was so impressed with his brilliance, with his history, with his personableness, with his profound sense of me. It was like he saw *me* in ways that I couldn't even see me. Like he valued me in ways that I did not value me. It felt like he loved me in ways that I did not love me. And I was so awed by that [Zucker, 1982, p. 120].

This sense of specialness can be both a support and a challenge, of course, for however much one might try to remove expectations, they are inevitably a part of the gift. The question is not whether they exist but how they affect one and how powerfully they are mediated by a sense of one's own given value. To the extent that the mentor knows and values the student as a unique person—and that the student senses this—the relationship will maintain a reasonable balance.

Additionally, this specialness creates a kind of two-person hothouse. Within its walls, the student can reveal herself in ways that she would not to others, for there is an understood quality of trust about it. The relationship becomes a special culture in which certain kinds of growth are encouraged and others discouraged. To an extent, the outside world is sealed off, as it must be if this "inside world" is to offer special opportunities not available under ordinary circumstances. Because the experience of being closely listened to is so rare for many people, it can also be just the needed catalyst for the cautious emergence of a new sense of self. By listening, the mentor can give that new self an audience, often for the first time, an ear to hear the first tentative affirmations of a position the student knows to be on her leading edge, ideas too risky to entertain outside the safety of this space, a still tender voice speaking itself into being.

Mentors do a lot of supporting, and it should come as no surprise that this particular activity seems to come more easily to female than male mentors. For if mentoring is an androgynous act, then support is to challenge what female is to male. Indeed, the male conditioning in me shies away from the whole idea of support as somehow "soft" and indulgent, whereas many female mentors seem reluctant to challenge, to impose their own values, or otherwise to do what they feel would be violence to the integrity of their students. Rather, they tend, like Grace and Dolores, to provide a less intrusive environment —one that leaves the student more freedom for exploration. They seem as well to draw the line less sharply between themselves and their students. Perhaps this grows out of a conviction that the quality of the relationship is fundamental to effective mentoring and a fear that to separate themselves too much from their students would endanger that relationship. It is noteworthy that when I asked the mentors and students what their most important duty was to each other, the women overwhelmingly named honesty and openness as central. Asked why, they explained sometimes with a hint of exasperation that obviously you can't have a nurturant relationship in which there is no trust. Dolores put it this way.

> Without honesty there is no relationship . . . there could be no trust without honesty. [And why is trust important?] I don't feel that I would follow anyone down any path if I didn't trust them, and I would not trust somebody if I did not feel that they, within their conscious effort, were being honest. And I would not expect anybody else to follow me if I was not honest with them and they could not trust me.

The men placed less value on honesty, more on activities

like providing guidance and fostering independence. It was as though they focused primarily on themselves or the student while the women were looking at the space in between. It is a fascinating distinction and seems to bear out the speculation about the female need for connection, the male's for separation. But for now perhaps it is enough to note it and to observe that some of us are better at providing support and others at offering challenge. Both, finally, must be given a voice in the developmental dialogue between self and other, separation and attachment, letting go and reaching out.

Challenge

Just as support calls the mentor to conform his boundaries to those of the student, challenge peels them apart. It means opening a distance in the relationship, drawing the student outward to fill the gap, straining him to move, to accommodate his inner structures to the new environment created by his mentor's distancing. In social science language, it means creating a cognitive dissonance, a gap between one's perceptions and expectations: I think I should be *there,* but I see myself *here.* Leon Festinger (1957), who invented the term *cognitive dissonance,* maintains that there is an intrinsic human need to close such a dissonance, to harmonize it again with our own inner selves. That, he says, is what learning is about. We move to close gaps. Likewise, it seems to be at least part of what teaching is about: to open gaps. Mentors toss little bits of disturbing information in their students' paths, little facts and observations, insights and perceptions, theories and interpretations—cow plops on the road to truth—that raise questions about their students' current worldviews and invite them to entertain alternatives, to close the dissonance, accommodate their structures, *think* afresh.

Here are some of the ways they do it.

Setting Tasks. Most commonly, and most visibly, mentors set tasks for their charges. The tasks may be obvious—memorizing sacred texts, doing homework, writing papers—or they may appear nonsensical. Herrigel's archery master told him he must stop trying to hit the target, Hank told Richard to argue against himself, Virgil directed Dante downward on his upward journey. Sometimes the tasks are incomprehensible because the teacher is holding a perspective the student has yet to develop. Still living in a tacit world, Richard found it difficult to suspend judgment. Virgil knew Dante could never see the light until he had plumbed the darkness. And sometimes, as Mr. Miyagi, the teacher in *The Karate Kid,* knew, a "mindless task" is just what we need to teach us about our minds. The current fascination with behavioral objectives is often polished with claims that students ought always to know where they're going before they set out. But while the competency-based movement has righted a good many educational wrongs in its brief life span, its supporters would do well to remember that there are times when our minds can be our own worst enemy, when a good dose of confusion is exactly what a student may need. There are places on the map that disappear when we look at them, and sometimes the only way to get there is to go somewhere else.

In addition to setting the exercises, mentors often ask for some kind of analysis of the tasks, reflection on the meaning of the job. This may come in conversation or it may come in a more formal assignment such as a paper, a project, or a test. The value of this is, of course, that it encourages the student to create a context for the activity and see it in a broader way than simply as the task alone. In addition, it allows for generalization of the principles so that the student can apply the learning in other settings than the immediate one. In a larger sense, it encourages the student to think about her own thought, a skill essential to the strengthening of formal reasoning.

Throughout, the mentor is there, encouraging, cajoling, threatening, but always selectively reinforcing this behavior over that, casting light on one aspect of accomplishment rather than another, and thus bringing the learner to "see" a different world than she might otherwise have seen. Through this close interaction in which the student's energies are bent toward accomplishing the task, the teacher's standards and expectations become internalized in the student. In effect, the student comes to incorporate the mentor within herself. This growth of an inner teacher can effectively complement the other dimensions of internal enrichment as the "institutional" self that Kegan describes continues to take form. Ultimately, the student becomes her own guide—a blend of her own shape and that of her mentor.

Thus, the mentor's challenge to reflection encourages the protégé to speak out increasingly in her own voice. This often comes slowly, especially when the student is struggling with the straps of dualistic authoritarianism. "Who me?" says Betty. "I don't know anything worth talking about." Surrounded by an overwhelming world of authorities, she feels quite incapable of peering over the wall for herself. Several students in an educational philosophy class I once taught were perplexed when I asked them to criticize some of the readings. "Why would you assign us to read these experts," asked one student, "and then turn around and ask us to criticize them?" It simply did not make sense given what she believed to be the purpose of education.

This is the time when plagiarism can be less a crime than a sad misunderstanding. "Why should I put it in my own words when the textbook puts it so much better?" "Who knows the facts better than the author?" That the teacher might prefer a student's own thought to an expert's knowledge seems barely conceivable. Education, after all, is about getting knowledge from authority. That one might use one's own capacity to ask questions and organize thought while still using the ideas of others has not yet come clear. The synthesis between self and other that allows each its legitimate function still lies ahead. But calling the student's voice to emerge is of central importance, for clearly we do not learn to speak unless encouraged to do so, nor think without practice.

Engaging in Discussion. Summarizing current research findings of value to college teachers, Wilbert McKeachie emphasizes that college learning involves the construction of new frames of meaning. To help our students in that endeavor, he notes, "we need to carry on discussions in which students have an opportunity to express their problems and progress" (1980, p. 90). As must be apparent by now, one of the most enjoyable aspects of the mentor's work is the sort of "developmental dialogue" that appears in the vignettes. Talk. Talk is of elemental importance in development at all but perhaps the highest levels. It is central to the mentor's role. A primary purpose of such dialogues is to help the student to engage with different perspectives, different ways of viewing a problem or a phenomenon. In the trusting and privileged relationship between a caring teacher and a student, the risk of exploring new ideas is minimized, and the student is encouraged to experiment in ways she might not otherwise try. Such discussions, it should be emphasized, are most effective when the mentor considers her task not to instruct but rather to understand her student's thought and perhaps to raise questions about it.

In a classroom, for instance, it can be effective to ask an outspoken student if he has understood a position just expressed by another student. Indeed, for discussions of controversial matters, some instructors insist that speakers may not express an opinion until they have outlined the previous speaker's point of view satisfactorily. Even where the subject under discussion is not overtly controversial—describing how a Native American saw the coming Europeans or how a minority client views the world—it can be important to encourage students to take perspectives that differ from their own. In his slim and elegant treatise on "a spirituality of education," Parker Palmer suggests that "to teach is to create a space in which obedience to truth is practiced." Such a space, he says, is one in which differing views are given respect, yet in which each person comes to hear his or her own voice more clearly and honestly (Palmer, 1983, p. 69).

If class discussion is not possible, written papers or well-wrought examination questions may accomplish the purpose. But the act of getting outside of one's own world and seeing it through the eyes of another is of profound developmental significance. For it demands that in some small way we cross the boundary between ourselves and another person or idea or sensation, and in so doing, that boundary becomes just a bit more permeable to new ideas and fresh views. In time, we come to recognize that the ability to travel is as valuable as the ability to live well at home.

Heating Up Dichotomies. One effect of this encouragement to take differing or opposite perspectives is that the exercise heats up the dichotomies and creates a greater pressure for resolution. The process can be painful at times as we hem and haw between the pro and con of a political debate, our inner or outer selves, or the demands of our family. Yet the inner dialogue is important, for it is through that saccadic movement that we slowly build a platform on which to stand and from which we can look down to construct a synthesis that holds both parts. It is important, at the same time, that the student be helped to recognize the *legitimacy* of that other stance. It is common enough for students after a while to acknowledge that theirs is not the only way, yet it takes time for them to recognize and know in their bones that those other ways are in some sense equally legitimate to their own. "If I could only get them to see that the Kulungi Rai are *full human beings* struggling to make sense of their world as we do of ours," said a colleague, "instead of just thinking they were quaint." That's a deeper understanding, calling on the development of contextual thought. And it takes time. It's a long journey from "Our ways are right, theirs are wrong" to "Our ways are sensible, theirs are quaint" to "Our ways make sense to us, theirs to them; we differ because our worlds differ." Yet it is only on the basis of this last viewpoint that we can begin to construct a reasonably compassionate world in which to resolve our differences without violence. The mentor can help that come about by challenging us to consider each side, to give each its due before we take a stand.

Constructing Hypotheses. A particularly interesting part of the shift from a conventional, culture-bound stance into contextual thinking is the development of what Piaget called hypothetico-deductive reasoning. This is the ability to spin off a chain of reasoned implications from a consciously constructed hypothesis. While this can be accomplished by precontextual thinkers, it becomes a regular mode of operating when we shift from seeing "the possible" as simply a subset of reality to recognizing "the real" as only a portion of the possible. At this point, thinking takes off and we begin to develop the capacity to imagine a world better (or worse) than the one in which we now live. With the development of self-conscious, assumptive thought, we can give that utopia its own legitimacy, a *real possibility*. A variation on this is the "as if" game. "Let's assume," it begins, and goes on to construct an elaborate argument based on that hypothetical assumption. Interestingly, the financial planning programs and simulation games currently available for computers would seem promising opportunities to help students develop that capacity. They allow the elaboration of any number of theoretical possibilities based on explicit premises.

Thus, this ability to let air under our assumptions seems a necessary precursor to contextual thought. That is, in order to see how ideas different from ours exist in their own legitimate framework, it is necessary to leap out from our shell of absolute certainty and construct a whole new world based on some other person's ideas of "reality," other assumptions of "truth." People practicing this form of reasoning may begin sentences with "Given . . . ," "Assuming . . . ," or "What if . . . ?" It is this sort of reasoning, this ability to cast a net of possibility out ahead of one's footsteps, that finally enables us to cross over the yawning gap that separates belief from faith and to leave behind our need for the bedrock certainty of absolutes. For once we finally realize that even our former absolutes are relative to some context, rest on some assumptions, we are at last free to risk movement out of the cave. This is why Plato's allegory of the cave makes such a marvelous teaching device for raising questions about students' givens. It forces them to consider, sometimes for the first time in their lives, that what they take for "reality" may be an illusion. Can there be any question why it is so important for people of all ages to exercise their imaginations? Only if we have practiced soaring above "reality" and living in imaginary worlds can we risk the flight over the existential abyss when its time comes. The ability to reason rests paradoxically on the willingness to suspend it. So it should come as no surprise that certain highly authoritarian groups and cultures struggle to limit their children's opportunities for fantasy. At some level, they seem to realize that in our imagination is the power to transcend our need for absolutes, that in our dreams rest the seeds of freedom.

Setting High Standards. One of the most persistent findings in studies of teacher effectiveness is that good teachers set high expectations for their students (National Institute of Education, 1984). They help their students construct positive self-fulfilling prophesies for themselves. Speaking of his goals for Emily at a time when she seemed still wandering in a forest of specifics, Bob hoped she would come to see how things are intertwined: "instead of having separate notes in a melody, she will have a whole piece of music that makes sense," and he encouraged her to study in ways that would help her do that. When Hank challenged the adequacy of Richard's second paper, he made it clear that he expected "serious thought," but he went on to describe for his student what he meant by that. The expectations were high but not incomprehensible; he took pains to couch them in terms that Richard would understand. Indeed, Hank routinely required students to rewrite their work regardless of how good it was. It taught them, he said, to reflect on their thinking, to see themselves through others' eyes—a central developmental accomplishment.

One of the dilemmas in teaching is that teachers generally both give tests and grade them. They thus retain dictatorial power. The paradox is that the ultimate goal is to free students from this power—in Ken's terms, to "help them fly." Thus, while good teachers set high standards, they work at the same time to help their students construct their own inner teachers, their own sets of expectations for themselves. They do this in part by making explicit both their expectations and their reasons for them.

Good teaching ought to help students learn not simply to answer questions but to ask better ones themselves. Students' growth ultimately depends on their developing the ability to look dispassionately at their own performance, their own answers to their own questions, and decide for themselves how they've done. What teachers need to teach above all is how to learn, not how to be taught. A major task of the mentor in this regard, then, is to challenge students to challenge themselves.

Vision

In the Castaneda books, one of Don Juan's main purposes is to teach Carlos to "see." By this, he means not simply the ability to perceive a different world but actually to apprehend "reality" in a fuller, more comprehensive way. The mentor is using vision as a metaphor for greater understanding.

Vision, in its broadest sense, is the field on which the dialectical game between the old self and the new can be played; it is the context that hosts both support and challenge in the service of transformation. By providing vision, mentors "hang around" while the protégé takes the leap. Notice that Athena appears as Mentor at the beginning and end of *The Odyssey*, for instance, but takes other forms in between. The enduring quality of this sort of guidance is captured mythically in numerous tales as mentors reappear to their protégés after death in the form of spirit guides. For even in their absence, mentors set a climate of expectations and provide a sense of continuity.

Modeling. Mentors most obviously provide vision by modeling the person whom the protégé wants to become. The model may be quite literal at early stages of development. A child, for instance, thinking concretely, may express a wish to become a lawyer like Mom or a teacher like Dad. Later on, the attachment is likely to be around general attributes rather than to a particular role: a mentor is attractive because, like Ken for Betty, he was so "knowledgeable" and spoke so distinctly, or because, as Jean said of Dolores, "She's got it all together, and I definitely haven't." Later still, the appeal may be integrated with a conscious awareness of what the student herself needs at that time. Alison, for instance, knew that she needed "a certain standard," yet also sought someone who was both passionate about her field and willing to work with her on her own terms. She describes Robin's appeal in richly interpersonal terms with a clear sense of how she needs to be held.

As with lovers, mentors and protégés seem most strongly drawn together when each seems to fill a need in the other. But as with lovers also, if one partner grows while the other remains the same, the affair may fall apart. Students who return to higher education in quest of more job opportunities or higher social status, for example, may look to their mentor initially as one who has what they want for themselves. Henry Higgins and Eliza Doolittle are the classic case here. He would teach her how to speak "correctly" and how to appear in "public." The phenomenon is common in programs for adults, especially since so many adult students are the first of their family to complete college. For them, a college education may represent a sharp shift in social class. As the film *Educating Rita* poignantly demonstrates, however, if the education seeps in, such superficialities are soon enough seen for what they are, and if the mentor is unable to transcend appearances, the relationship is likely to crash. For as the protégé changes, so also will her need for a model. This may be quite appropriate, of course. For unlike romantic love, there is no imperative that the pair remain eternally intertwined. And the mentor's task may very well be completed when the student leaves for good.

In other cases, the attraction may come from a protégé's desire to master a subject or develop a particular skill. This form of attraction is particularly common in the arts and among sports figures: Degas for Mary Cassatt, Haydn for Mozart, or Willy Mays for O. J. Simpson. But though we may be drawn to mentors for such immediate purposes, as we grow, we come to realize that their gift is not the opportunity to become *like* them but the challenge to become more fully ourselves *through* them. They call forth the best we have. They invite us to transcend ourselves. They personify our highest aspirations.

Keeping Tradition. Yoda was nine hundred years old. Part of the reason for portraying mentors as aged is that as guarantors of continuity they pass on tradition to the next generation. Regardless of our ideological stripes, teaching, as Neil Postman points out, is a conserving activity (1979). We have a stake in fostering, if not such values as free inquiry, responsible scholarship, and moral decision making, at least a committed iconoclasm. And while we may not be interested in watering the ivy on the walls, most of us would agree that something that goes on behind those walls is of enduring value. Said one student, "The master may be wrong, but not the faith." To that we owe our allegiance, both as mentors and students, and it is that which we seek to help our students come to discover.

The danger in this case, of course, is that we confuse the dancer with the dance. This is why the Zen master urges aspirants to "kill the Buddha," and why Sufis remind students that the master is the one who destroys the idol you make of him. Although our students may take a while to recognize it, what is important about our minds—or so our minds would have it—is not what is in them but how they operate. What we model for our students is not our knowledge but our curiosity, the journey, not the destination. As teachers, we recognize that we are channels through which information flows, configuring itself into certain patterns they may name "knowledge." However, the tradition we keep is not the knowledge itself but the capacity to generate it. When the time comes, we must have the wisdom to release our hold on both the knowledge and our students.

Offering a Map. In a sense, just by being who she is, the mentor is a map for her student. But the process can be much more than this. One of the adviser's earliest pieces of business is to listen at some length to a new student's story—her travels and her dreams. The experience of being listened to closely, much less of being asked such questions as "Why are you coming back to school?" "What do you want for yourself?" or "What would you really like to learn?" can be of great importance in helping a person begin to formulate her own plans more clearly. The decision to make major changes in one's life is often made intuitively, as is perhaps appropriate; but to think about the meaning of that decision in the larger context of one's life is crucial if one is to integrate such a decision well and construct of it a foundation for further growth. Mentors have an important part in making that happen through the interest they express in their questions about the whole lives of their students. Out of these questions students can then begin to construct their own maps in their own terms.

At the same time, I have found it useful to offer to students some of the developmental maps that appear here in earlier chapters. In one of my more successful seminars, I provided a core of common readings in developmental literature and then assigned special project reports on particular theorists in accord with what I felt to be key issues for each student: Levinson for a young man in transition, Fowler for a woman of deep religious commitment, Gilligan for a mother entangled in the demands of work and family. Because each knew I had selected that work for him or her, they each took special interest in that particular map and drew unique value from it.

Naturally, it is not necessary to require such a course for all students. But familiarity with several developmental schemes offers the adviser important tools for helping students to see their own journeys more clearly and thus take increased responsibility for their academic lives. As Winston puts it, "Advisers . . . can help students form comprehensive pictures of their present lives and articulate and plan for accomplishment of reasonable and attainable life goals" (Winston and others, 1984, p. 540).

Suggesting New Language. The words we use and the way we use them are powerful indicators of how we see, of our particular vision of reality. A glance at the "scoring manual" of any given developmental scheme will make this obvious. In Perry, for example, early dualistic writing is characterized by short, simple sentence structures, frequent use of absolutes (*never, completely, right/wrong*) and little use of *I.* Later, multiplistic writers tend to use language in highly personal ways, frequently referring to themselves at considerable length. They tend to make long lists of attributes linked poorly if at all. At more contextual levels, qualifiers proliferate. Terms like *it depends* or *assuming* set language up off the ground; sentence structure is more varied; there are fewer clichés, more qualifiers. And there may be a sense of motion in the language as though the speaker sees herself in a fluid world, moving somewhere rather than frozen in some absolute syntactic soup. Mentors can learn much from the way their students use language.

According to James Fowler, mentors' primary function is to "nurture us into new metaphors." They give us new ways to think about the world. The good teacher helps students not so much solve problems as see them anew. Mentors can give us new language, "magic words" in which are contained whole different frames of reference. Thus, language can be a catalyst for change as well as an indicator of it. Among some Hindu sects, for instance, the first act of the guru is to give the aspirant a sacred syllable or phrase to repeat during meditation. This mantra serves as a connection between the student and the source of "higher consciousness." In this way, language can *evoke* intimations of new meaning.

Teaching a course once, using the journey as a metaphor for growth, I found that students took readily to it, using it to see their lives' movement in a new way. I encouraged students to work with the metaphor both in journals and aloud, interviewing one another and sharing their stories. Many found that for the first time in their lives they had both a rich metaphor in which to frame the experience of their growth and attentive listeners for whom to construct it. The combination was memorable for all of us. In this light, Jung's comment that mentors are people who ask us *who we are* and *where we are going* shines for the crystal insight it is.

Providing a Mirror. One of the more important aspects of the special mirror that mentors hold up to their students is its capacity to extend the student's self-awareness. To see oneself in new ways, from a range of different vantage points, is the chief way we distill what we are learning from the challenges and supports of our world. In an expanded view of the self, one might almost say, lies the definition of development itself, for it is only when we are able to place ourselves in the context that we create for everyone else that we become fully relativistic in our own worldview.

One way of doing this is by providing feedback to students about their own learning styles. Citing research describing several different styles, McKeachie suggests that teachers can help students to "identify their own most effective learning strategies" and to "use a larger repertoire of methods of learning" (1980, p. 89). In effect, the mirror can both show students their best side and suggest new ways to see the world.

Socrates used the mirror to bring his students to see more broadly the ramifications of their particular perspectives. Drawing out his victims on a string of "if/thens" he would lead them inexorably to discover the logical implications of their givens and thus to see themselves in an expanded context. Teachers often find themselves doing this, working with students to help them comb their ideas, to see that if they are to be consistent with a given set of assumptions or beliefs, then logic may demand that they alter some of their conclusions. As a result, students come increasingly to see their own thought, to recognize it as a phenomenon in itself.

This works well, of course, when the student is engaged and willing to listen to a logical train of thought or entertain new information. In some cases, this may not be possible. Faced with conclusions she was unwilling to accept, for instance, Betty preferred to seal out the disturbing information her mentor offered. Richard, on the other hand, was drawn in by his own adulation for his mentor and evidently felt safe enough to risk realigning some of his assumptions and conclusions to make a more coherent and consistent whole. The result, of course, was a new level of self-awareness on Richard's part and a new capacity to see himself as capable of change. Hank's efforts to help his student form that new image seem, in part at least, to have been vindicated. When there is trust in the relationship, the student feels it is safe to leave his epistemological "home" and enter another for a while. This is important not because that one is "better" but because in each departure comes the ability to release old knowledge, in each arrival the will to accept new information. It is the traveling that most we learn from travel.

Chapter Nine 🙢

Teaching as Care: Achieving Quality Education for Adults

> Those having torches will pass them on to others.
> —*Plato,* The Republic

The proper aim of education is to promote significant learning. Significant learning entails development. Development means successively asking broader and deeper questions of the relationship between oneself and the world. This is as true for first graders as graduate students, for fledgling artists as graying accountants.

Education should promote development. A good education ought to help people to become both more receptive to and more discriminating about the world: seeing, feeling, and understanding more, yet sorting the pertinent from the irrelevant with ever finer touch, increasingly able to integrate what they see and to make meaning of it in ways that enhance their ability to go on growing. To imagine otherwise, to act as though learning were simply a matter of stacking facts on top of one another makes as much sense as thinking one can learn a language by memorizing a dictionary. Ideas, as Whitehead observed years ago, only come to life when they root in the mind of a learner.

This is not as simple as it seems, and is not without risk. For we develop by progressively taking apart and putting together the structures that give our lives meaning. And although the stage on which we are standing may grow daily less ade-

236

quate, it can be frightening to think of dismantling it, for we imagine it to be all we have. To build fresh structures, we must reach out ahead of ourselves, and we fear the chasm below. Viewed thus, success at the educational venture is less a function of brains than of balance and courage. It means being willing to doubt when it would be safer to believe, and believing when we would rather doubt. Like walking, it invokes a deliberate forward thrust, throwing us off center, demanding compensation. Each step in its own way threatens us with annihilation.

What allows us, finally, to take the risk is the faith that we will survive. At the heart of development is trust, a willingness to let go, to listen to voices we too often struggle to shut out, to receive clear-eyed what the world has to offer. Such trust rarely happens in a vacuum. We need other people with whom to practice that trust: parents, friends, children, teachers. For in a trusting relationship we can drop back and find the fear, heal what we come again and again to name our "self."

It follows that when we no longer consider learning to be primarily the acquisition of knowledge, we can no longer view teaching as the bestowal of it. If learning is about growth and growth requires trust, then teaching is about engendering trust, about nurturance—caring for growth. Teaching is thus pre-eminently an act of care. We must be concerned not simply with how much knowledge our students have acquired but also with how they are making meaning of that knowledge and how it is affecting their capacity to go on learning, framing the world in ever more inclusive and comprehensive ways. As teachers, we share responsibility for that process. Like guides, we walk at times ahead of our students, at times beside them, and at times we follow their lead. In sensing where to walk lies our art. For as we support our students in their struggle, challenge them toward their best, and cast light on the path ahead, we do so in the name of our respect for their potential and our care for their growth. As Dante's Virgil knew, to teach is to point the way through the fire.

In itself, there is nothing new here. College catalogues have long sung these hymns, and good teachers have always voiced the importance of caring for and about their students. What is new, however, is that current developmental theory has given us a far better idea of what those high-sounding words actually mean, and in doing so it has handed us maps of great promise, charting territory we have barely begun to traverse. In writing this book I have tried to piece together the shards of conversations and fill in spaces on the maps in a way that will prove useful to others scouting through this new and exciting terrain.

It should be quite clear by now that the book aspires to no final answers. There are problems to the approach suggested here, and I do not wish to make light of them. What right have we to foist our values on our students? Isn't this just therapy in disguise? How practical is this for large classes? This may be fine for the humanities but what about the sciences or professional education? And what is the place of subject matter in all of this?

Taken to extremes, these questions raise legitimate problems. To attempt a full discussion is beyond us here, but the skeptical reader is asked to consider that regarding the question of values, teaching is fundamentally a moral act. We can no more escape from our values than from gravity. Like it or not, we will teach what we believe. But we need not teach *only* what we believe. And when we do affirm our convictions, we owe it to our students to do so in light of the higher principle of their right to differ, their obligation to choose for themselves. Good teachers, as Amos Bronson Alcott said, have no disciples.

To those concerned about overstepping a boundary between counseling and teaching, I would suggest that there is a difference between caring and therapy. Teachers are not and should not be trained for the latter; clearly we need to know when we are out of our depth. But to share our common humanity with another person is a gift of birth, not training. The capacity to care for and about our students is available to all of us.

As for practicality, to teach from a developmental stance does not require radical individualization of the curriculum. It is richly textured rather than finely tuned teaching that allows the most room for growth. And while perhaps some subjects offer more promise than others, all knowledge exists in some context. The developmentally conscious teacher strives to make that context explicit so that students will recognize the place occupied by the human mind in the generation and meaning of "facts." Even the engineering professor recognizes that the genius of a Leonardo sprang from his ability to transcend his "context" and look beyond the given "facts" of his age. What we judge as "practical" is conditioned by our intentions. Is there a message here for our teaching?

Finally, despite the obvious importance of subject matter in any teaching, good education has always been concerned at a deeper level with the intellectual growth of the student, not simply with knowledge acquisition. To emphasize development is in no way to deny the importance of subject matter. It is simply to remind us that there is no such thing as "content" apart from the way in which it is understood. Given the clear evidence that modes of understanding evolve in human beings, it is important to recognize which particular modes are being practiced by which of our students. Even those who prefer to concentrate on the transmission of subject matter will recognize that a decent respect for the mind of the student can inform them of the best way to offer their pearls.

So, reservations, questions, and nearly completed book in hand, let us consider how a summary of the main themes of the book can help us to begin our own fresh journey toward more effective mentorship.

1. *We can begin listening to our students' stories.*

We can ask our students to reflect on the place of education in their lives, to engage with the idea of the journey, seeing themselves in motion, confronting and addressing obstacles, swinging back and touching home, moving ahead, getting stuck, crossing rivers, entering the forest, finding helpers, confronting images of themselves, making discoveries, gaining partners, seeing in the light, returning homeward. This question alone ("Where are you going?") can be all it takes to begin the venture.

Listening, we can be alert for the ways in which our students use language and think about thought. Do they talk in absolutes or pepper their speech with qualifiers? How do they use the words *right* and *wrong*? How do they resolve conflicting claims to "the truth"? Can they clearly express a point of view that conflicts with their own? How do they know when they are right about something? Are they concerned with being "respectable and proper" or with expressing their own minds? Where is their leading edge?

And we can set aside several days, changing our priorities if necessary, to sit down and talk with each of our students individually for at least ten minutes, asking them what is important to them and why. This may be as casual as handing out an appointment sheet in class or as elaborate as visiting them in their homes. But to take the time and to let them know that they matter in this universe is a gift we can offer. There has to be time for that.

2. *We can view ourselves as guides.*

Given that we and our students are on a journey together, we can work to engender trust as we go, we can watch for clues about our students' movement, we can encourage our students to speak in their own voices, we can challenge them to hear other voices, and we can emphasize their positive movement, helping them to feed their growing edge. Our best stance is one of a carefully tended mixture of support as they risk new territory, challenge as they bog down, and light as they seek to move toward or sometimes change their destinations. We can acknowledge the power of our presence in our students' lives and accept the responsibility for providing them with the vision they may lack. But we can also recognize that we are only a single force among many and that our ultimate task is to help them to understand those forces so they can better travel ahead on their own.

And we can examine our metaphors, watch our own language. Do we talk of "covering" certain topics? "Giving" certain information? "Building" skills? "Pushing" students to think? "Shaping" behavior? Do we think of students as vessels to be filled or inert objects to be molded? Perhaps there are less mechanistic metaphors available, metaphors that respect the organic quality of growth in our students, metaphors taken from our experience with human relationships rather than objects: dancing, encouraging, playing, holding, affirming, singing, nurturing, touching, accompanying, guiding, caring.

3. *We can plan our meetings and classes to promote development.*

We can experiment in our own classes, trying out new components to encourage development; or we can try designing whole new courses using multiple disciplines and perspectives. What kind of environment will provide appropriate mixes of support and challenge? How can we find ways to encourage students to apply their developing insights to the real-life issues they face at home?

In advising, we can take time initially to hear how students make meaning in the world, asking them to describe how they view themselves, how they decide among conflicting ideas, what they look for in a good teacher, and what they want education to do for them. On the basis of this, we can help them plan learning experiences that will move them both practically and developmentally.

We can consider designing special courses for returning adult learners to help them adjust to the new rigors of school life—to give them practice in the skills of test taking, paper writing, analytical thinking, and problem solving that we value and that contribute to success. We can provide opportunities for group discussion and common sharing of problems around readings in adult development and learning.

In career planning courses, we can build in sections for discussion of current findings in adult development research and theory; consider how the phases and stages of our students' lives fit with their particular desires for jobs or careers; encourage them to look at their own developmental positions in light of career expectations; help them to see how their work does or does not address their developmental directions.

If we are in a position to do so, we can consider incorporating adult development study more fully throughout the curriculum, using it as a catalyst to stimulate faculty in all fields to apply some of the principles suggested here.

And in all of our classes, we can attend again to the quality of the atmosphere, asking ourselves whether our students feel respected there, whether our teaching encourages an interchange of ideas that genuinely furthers our common search for more adequate ways of understanding, and whether we are helping our students to "re-cognize," to know again the truth as they evolve.

4. *We can turn to and bring together others who share our concerns.*

When we need help, we can find others who agree with us. At departmental meetings, we can share readings; work to establish a common language with which to discuss particular students; present "case studies" for discussion; share teaching, testing, evaluation strategies in the context of developmental principles; and support one another.

We can undertake our own research on student development; design ways to determine where our students are in their journeys at the outset of our courses, then test again at the end; make this work explicit and share it with our students and colleagues as we go along. Moreover, we can invite our students themselves into the investigation, seeing them as coresearchers, encouraging their participation as colleagues.

5. *We can recognize that in part our own growth depends on our students.*

We *need* to teach. We are, says Erikson, "the teaching species." We teach not just for our students but for ourselves as well. The drive toward generativity is an essential antidote to the midlife threat of stagnation. Without the affirmation born of extending ourselves beyond self-preservation, without the impulse to further this whisp of life in a dark universe, the questions that might enable us to move on toward something like wisdom would go unasked. We need our students as much as they need us.

So we can recognize our own movement, learning to see our students more clearly, understanding our own needs for separateness and connection more fully, listening more closely for what is special about each of our fellow travelers, encouraging them, casting light for them, holding them, seeking to understand them in their own terms, their own lives.

When I set out on this particular venture some ten years ago, I knew only that there had to be some better ways to understand what was happening with my students and what my part in their lives might be. Since then I've learned a great deal— from students, from reading, and from my life.

There is a reason why the metaphor of life as journey is so ubiquitous. Hackneyed though it is, it works. It allows both teachers and students to see their lives in motion; it provides an accessible and effective way of viewing educational change. It reminds us that our lives do have direction, that there is purpose somewhere beneath it all.

The idea of teacher as guide works too. It can change our notion of how we teach. For though we may have great knowledge and may know the territory intimately, our knowledge has special meaning with a traveler along. It is that special meaning that distinguishes teaching from telling. I have found the maps provided by current developmental research to be invaluable in helping both me and my students to understand more clearly where we have come from and where we might be headed. Those maps have made the journey more than just a vague metaphor.

When I first began to think seriously of writing down some of these things, I recall struggling to balance the intensity I felt for my own experience with the detachment I knew was important for a sense of perspective. I was aware of the shortcomings of too personal a pursuit of knowledge, yet I knew also that my greatest source of strength lay within me, in my own insight and passion. I remembered Robert Pirsig's remark that if you want to paint a perfect picture, you must first "make yourself perfect and then just paint naturally" (1974, pp. 324-325). And it seemed to me that my path led that way. "Best concentrate on the work," I told myself, "then write about it."

For the most part I have tried to do that. It should be obvious that I am a good distance yet from perfection, and I have long since rejected it as an attainable or even desirable goal. But still there is a lesson there. For good teaching rests neither in accumulating a shelfful of knowledge nor in developing a repertoire of skills. In the end, good teaching lies in a willingness to attend and care for what happens in our students, ourselves, and the space between us. Good teaching is a certain kind of stance, I think. It is a stance of receptivity, of attunement, of listening.

But this should not be confused with passivity. We are not *simply* nodding and smiling, holding and comforting. Receptivity is hard, active work. And we *do* demand. As educators, we do have a responsibility to "maintain standards" and hold high expectations for our students. Education is legitimately a social as well as an individual affair, and fairness is fully a part of our business. Yet fairness is not all there is to the game. There are times when justice for all must be tempered by compassion for one. Human *being* is both hard and soft. Care is both just and loving.

Because neither students nor teachers are inert objects, because we are growing beings responsive to our own ontology, because for all of us the world is emergent, teaching and learning are finally about relationship. In the dialogue between mentor and student lie most of the educational questions worth asking. "Give me a log hut, with only a simple bench; Mark Hopkins on one end and I on the other," said President Garfield of his former mentor, "and you may have all the buildings, apparatus, and libraries without him." While most of us might trade the hut and bench for a book or two, there is a certain truth in this wistful rhetoric. For more than any other factor, it is the partnership of teacher and student that finally determines the value of an education. In the nurture of that partnership lies the mentor's art.

References

Adorno, T. W., and others. *The Authoritarian Personality.* New York: Harper & Row, 1950.

Aslanian, C. B., and Brickell, H. M. *Americans in Transition: Life Changes as Reasons for Adult Learning.* New York: Future Directions for a Learning Society, College Board, 1980.

Bakan, D. *The Duality of Human Existence.* Boston: Beacon Press, 1966.

Baker-Miller, J. *Toward a New Psychology of Women.* Boston: Beacon Press, 1976.

Bandler, R., and Grinder, J. *The Structure of Magic.* Palo Alto, Calif.: Science and Behavior Books, 1975.

Baruch, G., Barnett, R., and Rivers, C. *Lifeprints: New Patterns of Love and Work for Today's Women.* New York: McGraw-Hill, 1983.

Basseches, M. *Dialectical Thinking and Adult Development.* Norwood, N.J.: Ablex, 1985.

Bateson, G. *Steps to an Ecology of Mind.* New York: Ballantine, 1972.

Belenky, M., Clinchy, B., Goldberger, N., and Tarule, J. "Connected Education for Women." *Boston University Journal of Education.* Boston, Mass.: Fall 1985, pp. 28-45.

Belenky, M., Clinchy, B., Goldberger, N., and Tarule, J. *Women's Ways of Knowing: The Development of Self, Mind, and Voice.* New York: Basic Books, 1986.

Barnard, J. "Women's Educational Needs." In A. W. Chickering and Associates, *The Modern American College: Responding to the New Realities of Diverse Students and a Changing Society.* San Francisco: Jossey-Bass, 1981.

Bettelheim, B. *The Uses of Enchantment: The Meaning and Importance of Fairy Tales.* New York: Vintage Books, 1975.

Bridges, W. *Transitions.* Reading, Mass.: Addison-Wesley, 1980.

Brown, R. D., and DeCoster, D. A. (eds.). *Mentoring-Transcript Systems for Promoting Student Growth.* New Directions for Student Services, no. 19. San Francisco: Jossey-Bass, 1982.

Buber, M. *I and Thou.* New York: Scribners, 1958.

Campbell, J. *The Hero with a Thousand Faces.* Princeton, N.J.: Princeton University Press, 1949.

Chickering, A. *Education and Identity.* San Francisco: Jossey-Bass, 1969.

Chickering, A. W., and Associates. *The Modern American College: Responding to the New Realities of Diverse Students and a Changing Society.* San Francisco: Jossey-Bass, 1981.

Choderow, N. *The Reproduction of Mothering.* Berkeley: University of California Press, 1978.

Christ, C. P. *Diving Deep and Surfacing: Women Writers on Spiritual Quest.* Boston: Beacon Press, 1980.

Cranse, R. "More Basic Than Basic." Unpublished manuscript, Community College of Vermont. Special Services Project, 1982.

Cross, K. P. *Beyond the Open Door: New Students to Higher Education.* San Francisco: Jossey-Bass, 1971.

Cross, K. P. *Adults as Learners: Increasing Participation and Facilitating Learning.* San Francisco: Jossey-Bass, 1981.

Daloz, L. A. *When the Thunder Comes: A Developmental Study of Adult Learners in Vermont.* Final Report to the Fund for the Improvement of Postsecondary Education. Montpelier, Vt.: Office of External Programs, 1981.

Dante (Alighieri). *The Divine Comedy.* (J. D. Sinclair, trans.) New York: Oxford University Press, 1961.

Dewey, J. *Democracy and Education.* New York: Macmillan, 1916.

Dinnerstein, D. *The Mermaid and the Minotaur: Sexual Arrangements and Human Malaise.* New York: Harper & Row, 1976.

Erikson, E. H. *Childhood and Society.* New York: Norton, 1950.

Erikson, E. H. *Insight and Responsibility.* New York: Norton, 1964.

Erkut, S., and Mokros, J. "Professors as Models and Mentors for College Students." Working Paper no. 65. Wellesley, Mass.: Wellesley College Center for Research on Women, 1981.

Evans, N. J. (ed.). *Facilitating the Development of Women.* New Directions for Student Services, no. 29. San Francisco: Jossey-Bass, 1985.

Festinger, L. *A Theory of Cognitive Dissonance.* Stanford, Calif.: Stanford University Press, 1957.

Fowler, J. W. *Stages of Faith: The Psychology of Human Development and the Quest for Meaning.* New York: Harper & Row, 1981.

Fowler, J. W. *Becoming Adult, Becoming Christian: Adult Development and Christian Faith.* New York: Harper & Row, 1984.

Fowler, J. W., and Keen, S. *Life Maps: Conversations on the Journey of Faith.* Waco, Tex.: Word Books, 1978.

Freire, P. *Pedagogy of the Oppressed.* New York: Herder & Herder, 1970.

Frost, R. *Complete Poems of Robert Frost.* New York: Holt, 1949.

Gamson, Z. *Liberating Education.* San Francisco: Jossey-Bass, 1984.

Gibbs, J. C., and Schnell, S. V. "Moral Development 'Versus' Socialization: A Critique." *American Psychologist,* Oct. 1985, pp. 1071-1080.

Gilligan, C. "In a Different Voice: Women's Conception of the Self and of Morality." *Harvard Educational Review,* 1977, *47,* 481-517.

Gilligan, C. *In a Different Voice: Psychological Theory and Women's Development.* Cambridge, Mass.: Harvard University Press, 1982.

Golding, W. *Lord of the Flies.* New York: Putnam, 1954.

Hall, R., and Sandler, B. "Academic Mentoring for Women Students and Faculty: A New Look at an Old Way to Get Ahead." Project on the Status of Women. Washington, D.C.: Association of American Colleges, 1983.

Hennig, M., and Jardim, A. *The Managerial Woman*. New York: Doubleday, 1977.

Herrigel, E. *Zen in the Art of Archery*. New York: Pantheon, 1953.

Homer. *The Odyssey*. (R. Fitzgerald, trans.) New York: Doubleday, 1961.

Inhelder, B., and Piaget, J. *The Growth of Logical Thinking from Childhood to Adolescence*. New York: Basic Books, 1958.

Jung, C. J. *Psyche and Symbol*. New York: Doubleday, 1958.

Keen, S. *The Passionate Life: Stages of Loving*. New York: Harper & Row, 1983.

Kegan, R. *The Evolving Self: Problem and Process in Human Development*. Cambridge, Mass.: Harvard University Press, 1982.

Kierkegaard, S. *Fear and Trembling*. Garden City, N.Y.: Doubleday, 1954.

Klein, C. *Mothers and Sons*. Boston: Hall, 1985.

Knefelkamp, L., Widick, C., and Parker, C. (eds.). *Applying New Developmental Findings*. New Directions for Student Services, no. 4. San Francisco: Jossey-Bass, 1978.

Knowles, M. S. *The Modern Practice of Adult Education: Andragogy Versus Pedagogy*. New York: Association Press, 1970.

Knox, A. B. *Adult Development and Learning: A Handbook on Individual Growth and Competence in the Adult Years for Education and the Helping Professions*. San Francisco: Jossey-Bass, 1977.

Kohlberg, L. *The Philosophy of Moral Development*. New York: Harper & Row, 1981.

Levine, S. V. *Radical Departures: Desperate Detours to Growing Up*. San Diego, Calif.: Harcourt Brace Jovanovich, 1984.

Levinson, D. J., and others. *The Seasons of a Man's Life*. New York: Knopf, 1978.

Loevinger, J. *Ego Development: Conceptions and Theories*. San Francisco: Jossey-Bass, 1980.

McKeachie, W. J. (ed.). *Learning, Cognition, and College Teaching*. New Directions for Teaching and Learning, no. 2. San Francisco: Jossey-Bass, 1980.

Merriam, S. S. "Mentors and Protégés: A Critical Review of the Literature." *Adult Education Quarterly,* Spring 1983, pp. 161–173.

Merriam, S. S. *Themes of Adulthood Through Literature.* New York: Teachers College Press, 1984.

Mezirow, J. "Perspective Transformation." *Adult Education,* Feb. 1978, pp. 100–110.

Missirian, A. K. *The Corporate Connection: Why Executive Women Need Mentors to Reach the Top.* Englewood Cliffs, N.J.: Prentice-Hall, 1982.

National Institute of Education. *Involvement in Learning: Realizing the Potential of American Higher Education.* Study Group on the Conditions of Excellence in American Higher Education. Washington, D.C.: National Institute of Education, 1984.

Novak, R. *Ascent of the Mountain, Flight of the Dove: An Invitation to Religious Studies.* New York: Harper & Row, 1971.

Palmer, P. *To Know as We Are Known: A Spirituality of Education.* San Francisco: Harper & Row, 1983.

Parks, S. *The Critical Years: The Young Adult Search for a Faith to Live By.* San Francisco: Harper & Row, 1986.

Perry, W. G. *Forms of Intellectual and Ethical Development in the College Years: A Scheme.* New York: Holt, Rinehart & Winston, 1968.

Perry, W. G. "Examsmanship and the Liberal Arts." In H. Hayford and H. P. Vincent, *Reader and Writer.* (3rd ed.) Boston: Houghton Mifflin, 1969.

Phillips-Jones, L. *Mentors and Protégés.* New York: Arbor House, 1982.

Pirsig, R. M. *Zen and the Art of Motorcycle Maintenance: An Inquiry into Values.* New York: Morrow, 1974.

Postman, N. *Teaching as a Conserving Activity.* New York: Delacorte, 1979.

Roche, G. "Much Ado About Mentors." *Harvard Business Review,* 1979, *20,* 14–28.

Rubin, L. B. *Intimate Strangers: Men and Women Together.* New York: Harper & Row, 1983.

Sanford, N. *Learning After College,* (C. Comstock ed.). Orinda, Calif.: Montaigne, 1980.

Schneider, C., Klemp, G. O., and Kastendiek, S. *The Balancing Act: Competencies of Effective Teachers and Mentors in Degree Programs for Adults.* Chicago: Center for Continuing Education, University of Chicago, 1981.

Sheehy, G. *Passages: Predictable Crises of Adult Life.* New York: E. P. Dutton, 1976.

Speizer, J. J. "Role Models, Mentors, and Sponsors: The Elusive Concepts." *Signs: Journal of Women in Culture and Society,* 1981, *6,* 4.

Stevens, W. *Opus Posthumous,* (S. F. Morse, ed.). New York: Random House, 1957.

Thomas, R., Murrell, P., and Chickering, A. "Theoretical Bases and Feasibility Issues for Mentoring and Developmental Transcripts." In R. D. Brown and D. A. DeCoster (eds.), *Mentoring-Transcript Systems for Promoting Student Growth.* New Directions for Student Services, no. 19. San Francisco: Jossey-Bass, 1982.

Tolkien, J. R. R. *The Return of the King.* New York: Ballantine, 1965.

Weathersby, R. P. "Ego Development." In A. W. Chickering and Associates, *The Modern American College: Responding to the New Realities of Diverse Students and a Changing Society.* San Francisco: Jossey-Bass, 1981.

Winnicott, D. W. *The Maturational Processes and the Facilitating Environment.* New York: International University Press, 1965.

Winston, R. B., and others. *Developmental Academic Advising: Addressing Students' Educational, Career, and Personal Needs.* San Francisco: Jossey-Bass, 1984.

Zucker, D. S. "The Mentor/Protégé Relationship: A Phenomenological Inquiry." Unpublished doctoral dissertation, Professional School for Humanistic Studies, 1982.

ð   ð   ð

Appendix

Much of the work with adult learners described in this book was made possible by the Fund for Improvement of Postsecondary Education (FIPSE), a discretionary fund associated with the federal Department of Education.

My own experience with developmental research comes in three layers. The first involved my participation in a collaborative network to explore the applications of current developmental research to postsecondary adult education. Under the guidance of Rita Weathersby and Jill Mattuck Tarule, representatives from Mary Baldwin College, Clark University, Loretto Heights College, and the Vermont State Colleges shared insights, program components, materials, and research data over the course of two years. During this time we began interviewing incoming and departing students on a systematic basis, interpreting the data through Loevinger's Ego Development scale and the Perry Scheme. Results were published by FIPSE in a booklet entitled *Designing for Development: Four Programs for Adult Undergraduates.*

The second layer found me directing a study to learn how rural adult Vermonters were affected by their return to higher education. A part of FIPSE's National Project IV (reported in Gamson, 1984), we administered a range of developmental measures on a pre/post basis to a sample of sixty entering, continuing, and exiting students over a year-long period. In addition, we conducted detailed preinterviews and postinterviews with twelve students. These were analyzed by trained scorers to determine Perry scores and to isolate the degree and quality of change, the nature of prominent issues, and indications of sig-

nificant developmental components. Chief findings were that
students did develop, generally entering with a good deal of
multiplicity and leaving with a greater degree of contextual
thinking. We described the "modal" adult learner as being in
transition from conformity to awareness of self as a responsible
agent, as increasingly viewing education as an asset to one's
whole life, and as moving away from authoritarian views of
"truth." Prominent themes included development as a journey,
the mentor as guide, "breathing again" as a metaphor of wom-
en's rediscovery of self, and shifting friendship patterns as a
context of development. Details are contained in the report
*When the Thunder Comes: A Developmental Study of Adult
Learners in Vermont* (Daloz, 1981).

Having begun to see some patterns, I applied for and received a Mina Shaughnessy fellowship from FIPSE to look more
closely at how rural Vermonters were affected by their return
to higher education, especially at the role mentors played in development. To do that, I interviewed six mentor-student pairs
on a pre/post basis over the course of a year, following them in-
formally throughout that time. In addition, I tape-recorded conversations with my own students. Most of the vignettes in the
book are based on these interviews and conversations. With one
exception, the names and some of the circumstances have been
changed. As I hope the book makes clear, the results of the
study were often mixed (not everyone changed the way I thought
they ought to) and always fascinating. Out of the experience I
have learned and relearned two things: listening and being heard
are extraordinarily powerful and tragically rare events in most
of our lives, and people are wonderfully, endlessly complex.
Not bad for a federal grant.

Index